HOW TO
INSPIRE
OUTSTANDING
IDEAS

To Prof. Anderson,

With Best Wishes!

4/10/2018

HOW TO
INSPIRE

OUTSTANDING

IDEAS

All You Need to Know to
Create Amazing Solutions

TJ XIA

With Ron Jennings and Amy Xia

ARCHWAY
PUBLISHING

Archway Publishing books may be ordered through booksellers or by contacting:

Archway Publishing
1663 Liberty Drive
Bloomington, IN 47403
www.archwaypublishing.com
1 (888) 242-5904

Because of the dynamic nature of the Internet, any web addresses or links contained in this book may have changed since publication and may no longer be valid. The views expressed in this work are solely those of the author and do not necessarily reflect the views of the publisher, and the publisher hereby disclaims any responsibility for them.

Any people depicted in stock imagery provided by Thinkstock are models, and such images are being used for illustrative purposes only.
Certain stock imagery © Thinkstock.

This book is a work of non-fiction. Unless otherwise noted, the author and the publisher make no explicit guarantees as to the accuracy of the information contained in this book and in some cases, names of people and places have been altered to protect their privacy.

ISBN: 978-1-4808-5177-1 (sc)
ISBN: 978-1-4808-5176-4 (hc)
ISBN: 978-1-4808-5178-8 (e)

Library of Congress Control Number: 2017915440

Print information available on the last page.

Archway Publishing rev. date: 01/03/2018

In memory of my parents Shifang and Yuru.

Contents

Preface

Have you ever wondered where great ideas come from? Have you ever wished you could come up with remarkable new solutions to use in your work and personal life? If so, this book is for you.

Everybody loves great ideas, especially ones that are practically useful and vividly unique. To improve something, create something brand new, or deal with something challenging, people look for brilliant ideas to help them achieve their goals. These ideas can take the form of insightful innovation, shrewd business decisions, or solutions to tough problems we encounter every day. Quite often, a person faces a problem for which either an existing solution isn't good enough or there just isn't any solution available. Obviously, finding your great idea is the crucial first step to get the job done in these situations (even though creating the idea may be a very small portion of the whole process of reaching a goal). Without the idea, you can't even begin the process of solving your problem.

Needless to say, producing wonderful ideas has never been an easy task, otherwise people wouldn't still be talking about Archimedes' story of Eureka that happened more than two thousand years ago. The story focuses on a question posed by King Heiron regarding whether a goldsmith had stolen his gold by substituting silver for gold while making his royal wreath. Faced with the challenging problem given by the king, Archimedes thought about it deeply and eventually got an idea while taking a bath. His ingenious idea was to compare how the water level increased when the wreath and a piece of gold of the same weight were placed separately into a container of water. He reasoned that since gold was denser and heavier than silver, if the wreath contained silver it would be slightly bigger and displace more water for the same weight. This story illustrates a brilliant yet simple idea and has been an inspiration to others for many generations.

The enduring appeal of the story over the ages shows people's fascination with exceptional ideas.

Let's assume there's an effective method for making the job of generating good ideas much simpler. If that were true, everyone would be eager to use it, right? If that's the case, where can we find such an efficient method?

Over the past several years, I have given presentations to local community and professional groups on the topic of promoting innovative thinking because I firmly believe that when more people are able to think innovatively our society will greatly benefit. I must emphasize that innovative thinking is not only useful for invention, research, or product development. Instead, it can broadly help everyone achieve more to lead a better life for themselves, their families, and the society. My presentations describe a four-step method that cultivates inspiration for good ideas. The four-step method is a core process for *anyone* searching for an effective method to make generating new ideas much easier. These four steps are:

Step 1: *Study examples involving outstanding ideas.* What does an example of an outstanding idea look like? It's fairly simple to identify one, as the idea usually is unique and produces clearly positive results. If, after experiencing an event or situation, you can't help but exclaim "That's a great idea!" then it probably satisfies the definition. Develop the ability to pay more attention to noticing examples that you encounter in daily activities and think about how the associated good ideas were brought into being. Unfortunately, much of the time there is little or no indication of how exactly an excellent idea was created. Therefore, studying these examples usually includes a lot of analysis and guesswork.

Step 2: *Extract generalized idea-inspiring approaches.* The purpose of studying an excellent example isn't to just repeat it precisely, but rather to uncover a general approach hidden within the example that identifies how the specific idea was generated. Only generalized approaches can be applied outside the specific circumstances that created them and are much more effective in helping people produce their own ideas in other circumstances.

Step 3: *Make a checklist of the generalized approaches.* Accumulate effective generalized approaches into a checklist. When looking for new ideas, use the checklist as a handy idea generating "toolbox." It contains a bunch of different tools—the generalized approaches—immediately ready for use on a problem.

Step 4: *Inspect how your needs apply to the checklist.* With your goal in mind, check each approach in the checklist to see if it provides insights that could potentially lead to a solution. The process of comparing each of the approaches in the checklist to the desired goal will itself stimulate a lot of high-quality thinking, becoming a hotbed for new ideas. Using the checklist provides a powerful way to discover new ideas a lot faster and produces many more ideas than you'd find without it. The more ideas you produce, the higher the probability of you generating outstanding new ideas. Used frequently, this method will result in achieving the "holy grail" technique for inspiring great ideas with high efficiency.

The four-step method is called the "SEMI method" after the first letter of each step: *Study, Extract, Make* and *Inspect.* As I've presented the SEMI method to audiences over the years, I have received very positive feedback about it. People have told me that they were able to apply the method in their work and personal lives almost immediately.

People who have made extraordinary contributions to our society usually exhibit traits that produce outstanding ideas. However, they are not the only ones capable of great thinking. Ordinary people can develop extraordinary creativity and innovation, too.

The first step of the SEMI method tells us to identify and pay more attention to cases involving exceptional ideas. Our daily experiences frequently expose us to useful cases that happen all around us. Analysis of these cases can help pinpoint the general thinking approaches within them. The following are just a few short examples from this book where ordinary people have created brilliant ideas:

- In 2008, a judge in Florida used an innovative punishment when he sentenced two misbehaved teenagers. The teens had bullied a young female cashier at a fast food restaurant and videotaped the incident. Not only that, the teens had also posted the video on YouTube to show off and humiliate the innocent girl. The judge's sentence required that the teenagers to post an apology video on YouTube that had to include a clear segment showing them handcuffed by the police. The punishment was cheered as being brilliant yet a perfectly fair application of justice (Chapter 11).

- A product designer for a global communications company got a cool idea in 2007 for a unique user interface. His idea was to make individual pixels of a touch screen elevate under computer control. This would give users tactile feedback when pushing buttons on an otherwise flat screen. It was the first 3D touch screen concept ever introduced and at the time was considered a major interface advance in the computer industry (Chapter 3).
- In 2012, the manager of a car company's social media department had an exceptional idea after he read a negative comment about the company's product by an influential blogger on Twitter. The tweet jokingly claimed that the company's car body was mechanically weak and could easily be totaled by a bird dropping. The manager decided to treat the tweet as if it were a serious statement. Using results from careful calculations based on real data, the company officially responded to the blogger's Twitter post and proved clearly that the car was strong enough to millions of bird droppings. Only a few people paid attention to the blogger's original tweet, but the company's response attracted a lot of social media attention. The company's response turned an unfavorable situation into a perfect marketing opportunity for promoting its product (Chapter 9).
- In 2009 a group of MIT students had a bright idea on how to take pictures that would capture the curvature of the Earth with minimal expense. Up until then, this type of sophisticated photography was produced with very expensive NASA instruments. The students used a simple camera attached to a high-altitude weather balloon to take the desired photos. The total cost for the project was only $150! Their impressive achievement was reported on national news media (Chapter 24).

These cases and many others will be analyzed in detail throughout this book. Presenting these examples here only demonstrates that unique and useful ideas can be originated by almost anyone.

The checklist of generalized idea-inspiring approaches (GIIA) is an important part of the SEMI method. The more comprehensive the checklist is, the more powerful the checklist becomes in inspiring thoughts. Checklists built independently by different people in isolation may miss some important concepts. However, if a comprehensive, universal checklist is available to everyone, anyone can benefit from it to produce new ideas. The complete list then becomes a highly efficient tool for use with the fourth step in the SEMI method. The question, then, is where to find the complete checklist.

This topic has fascinated me for a long time. I have conducted a study in my spare time for decades to discover whether there is a finite number of such generalized approaches for inspiring wonderful ideas and, if so, to identify them. I have collected several thousand example cases containing inconspicuous, yet amazing, ideas and solutions for the study. The cases touch on almost every aspect of human activity. The people who created the ideas and solutions found in these cases represent almost every social role that has ever appeared in human history. After a detailed analysis of these cases, I have discovered some interesting basic insights.

An idea is usually deemed great when the creator first expresses the idea and others immediately understand its impact, although none of them thought of it themselves. They highly value the idea and the effort put into it by the creator. However, that doesn't mean that the idea creator is necessarily smarter than everyone else. It could just be that the idea creator happened to have thought about something and discover his idea in those particular circumstances, and it's very possible that a different person in the same group could generate a new great idea in other circumstances.

Because humans are social beings and typically spend time in groups that think similarly, often there are two major barriers preventing us from creating great ideas: (1) inadvertently overlooking aspects of situations that we should have considered, and (2) knowingly avoiding certain aspects of situations that we could have considered. These two barriers are so prevalent, it's no wonder that most people view creation of a great idea as a huge accomplishment. In reality though, generating a great idea is just the simple result of thinking about the aspects of a situation which are easily overlooked or that are intentionally avoided by others.

After having thoroughly studied thousands of cases, I discovered that the number of fundamental techniques used during the processes of generating great ideas is limited, and they stem from finding easily overlooked and/or intentionally avoided aspects of the situation. So far, the study has identified a total of thirty such techniques that encompass all the thinking processes contained in the entire collection of cases, and each case can be clearly explained using one or more of the approaches. The thirty generalized, idea-inspiring approaches are built from the two fundamental discoveries that form the foundation of this book.

The thirty approaches can be broken down into six major categories: *Expand the Footprint, Be Alert for Relationships, Examine Its Evolution, Keep a Balance in Mind, Check Other Easily Overlooked Aspects, and Include Areas People May Try to Avoid.* The first five categories present techniques to uncover easily overlooked aspects of a situation, and the last category addresses how to identify any otherwise intentionally excluded aspects.

This book is organized to be easily understood. Each of the six parts contains between four and seven chapters presenting one generalized idea-inspiring approach per chapter. The chapters examine multiple aspects of the general approach through examples and analysis. A chapter summary with the key points and various aspects of the approach concludes each chapter. Reference source materials are arranged by chapter at the end of the book.

A condensation of all these approaches and their various aspects are presented in a concise summary, The Grand Checklist of Generalized Idea-Inspiring Approaches, at the end of the book. The Grand Checklist is an easy-to-use toolbox for users and you may use it for any type of brainstorming sessions. After reading this book, if you want to create a brilliant idea, you may want to jump directly to the fourth step of the SEMI method and simply match your goal with the appropriate approaches in the Grand Checklist. With the Grand Checklist at hand, you can avoid overlooking any important aspect of a situation when pursuing great ideas or solutions.

People aspire to conceive wonderful new ideas, but often ask: "How do I actually discover a great new idea?" The focus of this book is to primarily answer this long-standing question of "How?" and to present highly effective methods that directly enable you to produce your own amazing ideas. The book is not intended to answer questions of how to build an idea-friendly environment or how to turn an idea into reality—these areas have been addressed by many other books on idea creation. Instead, this book is firmly focused on giving anyone a complete set of practical techniques for incubating outstanding ideas. Equipped with the approaches provided in this book, readers will be able to immediately start generating amazing new ideas.

This book makes the thirty idea-inspiring approaches easy to understand by including nearly two hundred fascinating examples. These examples are intended to help you readily grasp the concepts behind the techniques and reinforce your thinking process when applying the techniques to real-world situations. Innovative thinking can be applied to almost any field of endeavor and, consequently, this book also reflects a broad spectrum of areas where the techniques can be used.

I sincerely believe that this book will provide a major boost in your ability to improve what may already exist, create something completely new, or resolve challenging problems—no matter who you are or what you want to accomplish.

Tiejun J. (TJ) Xia, PhD
Email: tjxia@yahoo.com

Acknowledgements

Many people helped contribute to this book. I would like to thank my friend Ron and my daughter Amy, for their dedicated efforts toward bringing this book to life. Without their assistance, you would probably not be reading this today. I also want to thank my professional editor, Amber Helt, for her expert help with the final version of the manuscript.

I appreciate Glenn Wellbrock's help in providing me with opportunities to practice some of the inspirational approaches presented in the book in real-world technology and business settings at Verizon. Thanks to Jack Wimmer and Chi-hao Cheng for reading the full manuscript and giving me valuable feedback. Thanks also to Danny Peterson for his frequent help with English usage. Thanks to the following people for reviewing sample chapters and/or giving me valuable comments: Eric VanStryland, David Hagan, Shoa-kai Liu, Alan Willner, Christine Tremblay, Mohammed Islam, Stephen Liu, Bobby Xiao, Winston Way, David Chen, Herve Fevrier, Stefan Spaelter, Maura Schreier-Fleming, Robert Ferguson, Ting Wang, Frank Chang, Milorad Cvijetic, Fred Heismann, Mansoor Sheik-Bahae, Mike Hasselbeck, Liz Rogan, Nan Luo, Gary Weiner, Anna Han, Brandon Collings, Eve Griliches, Steve Plote, Tom Depaolantonio, and Mike Bitting.

Last but not the least, I want to express my gratitude to my wife, Sophie. She was the first to read each chapter and provided invaluable insights to my work in progress. Since this book was completed in my spare time at home, she gave up a lot of her free time to support me in this project.

Expand the Footprint

1

Go Beyond Traditional Ranges

We're about to embark on a journey to explore various approaches to encourage open minds and out-of-the-box thinking. To start, let's examine one of the easiest methods where we address a situation involving a known range of numbers. If you can count, then this approach will be easy to learn.

When a specified numerical range is associated with a situation, it's usually easy to identify the largest and smallest values of that range. Even in cases where the end points of a range are not known, there will probably be some sense of the natural upper and lower limits of the range. Once you establish the limits of the numerical range, the first approach to generating exceptional ideas requires you to go outside this range.

Adjust Values That Determine a Range

When there is a clear upper or lower limit of a range, finding a way to extend the range can be quite easy since the values outside the range are defined by the clear limits of the range.

Today, many schools offer a free lunch program for students from low-income families that are unable to provide meals to their kids. The programs are valuable not only in showing compassion for the needy, but also for providing essential nutrition that helps a child's ability to learn. Qualified students receive a nutritious lunch each school day; however, there are at most only five school days in a seven-day week. What about lunches for these children on the other two days of the week? Most people have not likely considered the child's lunches for non-school days.

Fortunately, teachers and social workers noticed this problem and worked together to solve the issue of inadequate nourishment for low-income students over weekends. According to an article published in *USA Today* in 2007, schools and food banks initiated a program called BackPack, specifically targeting this need by having volunteers fill school backpacks with donated food.[1] On Friday afternoons, a needy student can take home a backpack filled with healthy foods such as bread, milk, juice, fruit, and so on. The food keeps the students and even their families from going hungry on weekends. It's been reported that over a hundred food banks have joined the effort, and the program has benefited students from over a thousand schools. The benefits of the program are remarkable. The students who took the food backpacks home paid more attention in class, their absenteeism dropped, and their overall behavior improved. This program was highly welcomed by the students' families as well since they witnessed the progress in their kids with the help of the program.

Initially, because free lunch programs were explicitly associated with school meals, it was assumed that these meals only covered school lunches and therefore the maximum number of free meals was five per week. This is the upper limit of the "normal" range for which free meals were provided. A student's stomach doesn't know if it's a weekday or the weekend; the student will be hungry if he or she doesn't get enough daily food. The creators of this "food backpack" program went beyond the established normal range by thinking outside the box, thus expanding the number five to seven and providing much-needed benefits to the children, their families, and society.

Much like how the food backpack program redefined the upper limit of their given range, the lower limit of a normal range can be redefined as well to provide benefits.

In 1976, Bangladeshi social entrepreneur Muhammad Yunus discovered that small loans could make a huge difference in poor people's lives.[2] While visiting a poor area near the university where he was a faculty member, he noticed that local village women relied on costly private loans to maintain their family bamboo furniture businesses. They used the loans to buy bamboo stock, then paid back the high-interest loan after selling their finished products. The high-interest rates only allowed them to sustain their businesses, not grow them. After noticing this, Yunus wondered why local banks couldn't offer small loans to the poor with reasonable interest rates. At the time, banks weren't interested because they were afraid many of these loans had a high risk of default.

Yunus believed, however, that small amounts of money would substantially help the poor. He believed that they would indeed repay the loan because lower interest rates would enable them to improve their businesses, and therefore their families' situations, rather than just maintain them. After overcoming a lot of bureaucratic and political difficulties, Yunus founded Grameen Bank in 1983. One of Grameen Bank's main goals was to make small loans to economically disadvantaged people who normally couldn't get loans from other banks. The bank developed various unheard-of loan products. For example, it had a loan specially designed for beggars. The amount of a loan could be as tiny as $1.50. The success of Grameen Bank's business model stimulated similar efforts in many developing countries.

Now small loans have changed millions of lives all over the world. To honor his great efforts on social and economic development, Yunus was awarded the 2006 Nobel Peace Prize along with Grameen Bank for pioneering the concepts of microcredit and microfinance. Yunus was also listed as one of the "Top 100 Global Thinkers" by *Foreign Policy* magazine in 2009.[3]

It's hard to imagine a bank loaning an amount as small as $1.50. To meet the needs of the poor people in Bangladesh, Yunus and his bank redefined the range of bank loans, thus greatly extending the lower limit of their market's range. A simple lower limit extension of bank loans has made a huge impact on the economic and social development of poor communities around the world. Think about how you can extend both the high and low limits of your given range.

Possibilities Far Above the Ordinary Range

When thinking beyond a normal numerical range, consider not only the values slightly above or below the extremes of a normal range, but also the values that extend far beyond the original range's parameters. A Dutch artist created a great example of this concept.

In 2007, the Dutch artist Florentijn Hofman created a giant, yellow rubber duck for the world to see, according to Wikipedia.[4] Rubber ducks are a common bathtub toy for young children. To help people affectionately remember their childhood, Hofman decided to create a large yellow rubber duck of unprecedented size: over one hundred feet long! His rubber duck was constructed of PVC material with a fan inside to keep the inflatable duck rigid while floating on the water. Hofman then took his giant duck to various cities across the world. When seen floating in a harbor, the duck's bright yellow color and huge size attracted curious onlookers. People enjoyed seeing this yellow duck that evoked happy childhood memories from the distant past. Hofman's rubber duck, as a work of art, served common people's interest very well.[5]

Hofman expanded the duck's size from a few inches to more than a hundred feet, over several hundred times the concept's original range. This example indicates that there is almost no limit to how far beyond the normal range you can go to provide astounding results.

Possibilities Far Below the Ordinary Range

When thinking about going beyond normal ranges, consider the much smaller values too. Here's a widely circulated brain teaser that tests people's ability to think smaller.

A large glass jar contains black and white beans. A woman lifts the jar and pours all the beans onto a kitchen table. Suddenly, she finds that the beans have completely separated themselves according to colors: the black on one side of the table and white on the other. How can this happen?

The answer is initially puzzling, because the beans have no intelligence at all. How can they self-separate according to colors automatically? Actually, the answer is quite simple: There are only *two* beans in the large glass jar. One is black and the other is white.

The key step to solving this riddle is to not forget the possibility that the number of beans could be much smaller than that in a common situation. Most people immediately assume that there must be at least hundreds, if not thousands, of beans in the jar. "Hundreds to thousands" is probably the normal range of beans in a large glass container, but when you use your out-of-the-box approach and "consider values far below the normal range," it isn't too difficult to find the answer.

This approach steers a thinker to contemplate whether the number of beans could extend far beyond the "normal" range. What if the number of beans in the jar was much more than thousands, which may be the practical upper limit of the normal range? What if the number was much less than hundreds, which seems to be the assumed lower limit of the normal range? If you use the principles in this approach, you can quickly see that the "much smaller" direction is correct. As the bean count is decreased and the number of beans finally drops to two, the two colors will separate naturally when the beans are poured onto the table! Practice thinking about possible situations where using a value much smaller than the values in a normal range.

Possibilities That Approach Infinity

When considering extreme values outside a normal range, don't forget the values that stretch toward infinity. In the following famous case, approaching infinity was an excellent choice when examining the possibilities far beyond a normal numerical range.

More than two thousand years ago, Archimedes coined the famous saying, "Give me a place to stand and I will move the Earth."[6] It's said that he uttered these words when he was trying to explain the mathematics of a lever to King Heiron II of Syracuse in Sicily. The principle of the lever says that multiplying the weight of an object, such as a person, on one end of the lever by its distance from where the lever rests (the fulcrum) must equal the distance of the object to be moved on the other end of the lever from the fulcrum multiplied by its weight. Another way to say it is that in order for a person to lift an object with only their own weight, the ratio of the distance from the person to the fulcrum and the distance from the object to the fulcrum must be inversely proportional to the ratio of the person's weight and the weight of the object. The larger the ratio of the distances, the heavier an object a person is able to lift.

This principle applies to any two objects no matter their weights! Archimedes wanted to make the point as clear as possible to the king, so he decided to use the earth as an extreme example of the object to be moved in his famous quote. As heavy as the earth is, Archimedes claimed that he could lift it using the principle as long as he had a long enough rod to use as a lever. Archimedes' explanation was much more understandable and memorable because he used this extreme case.

Archimedes probably began his explanation using a five- or

ten-foot-long rod of normal length and an object of manageable weight to show how a lever worked. Apparently, this approach did not convince the king, so Archimedes decided to use a much, much longer rod in a mind experiment to demonstrate the principle. To make an indelible impact of the principle on the king, he chose the Earth as a massive weight and used a much, much smaller human body weight to lift it.

According to *Encyclopedia Britannica*, the weight of the Earth is about 6 billion trillion tons.[7] Using the formula, if we assume Archimedes weighed about 100 kilograms and the distance from the Earth to the fulcrum is equal to the radius of the Earth, 4,000 miles, then the rod at least should be 240 trillion-trillion miles long for Archimedes to lift the Earth. Even though a rod that long is impossible, the thought experiment was able to get the point across to King Heiron II. To solve his teaching problem, Archimedes didn't limit himself to thinking about the length of the rod within its normal range but rather the extreme that approached almost infinity! Archimedes' innovative teaching approach was successful, even to this day. After more than two thousand years, people are still talking about his intelligence and imagination. We can't help but ask, what made Archimedes imagine the rod that long? Maybe we'll never know, but we do know that he used the method of thinking outside normal bounds to find solutions. Try this technique and follow in Archimedes footsteps!

Possibilities Near Zero

When considering very small values outside the normal numerical range, keep in mind that "much smaller" also includes the smallest possible natural number value—zero. Let's examine the scenario in which the desired value drops all the way to zero.

Stock trading is a challenging occupation. It's not easy to reliably predict stock price changes, and these fluctuations can happen in a split second. It's human nature for people to enjoy making money by buying and selling stocks, but they hate to fail and lose money. To gain a better investment return, people look for help from knowledgeable stock traders. The profession of stockbroker was created to fill that need. Stockbrokers, theoretically, have much more stock-trading knowledge and experience than ordinary people, since it is their job to buy and sell their clients' stocks at "the right time." However, a long-standing question remains: Do stockbrokers really help clients get better returns? Some people believe brokers are important in making the right decisions and others feel that brokers are not effective. The central issue is whether a broker's knowledge about stock trading has a positive impact in increasing return on investment.

To try to discover the truth, an interesting experiment was conducted, according to an article published in *Daily Mail*.[8] In the experiment a "special" stockbroker was invited to manage a virtual stock fund in competition with a number of experienced stockbrokers. The special broker was not a stock-fund guru from Wall Street, but rather a chimpanzee named Lusha from a Russian circus! Obviously, the chimpanzee knew nothing about stocks; it only cared about bananas. The chimpanzee just randomly created its portfolio by picking colored cubes, which represented different companies. Amazingly, at the end of the experiment the "chimpanzee portfolio" beat most of the portfolios picked by the professional stockbrokers. This result seemed to indicate that brokers' knowledge is not that important, especially if a chimpanzee can outperform them. Of course, this is just a single experiment, far from enough to obtain a definitive conclusion. This chimpanzee probably just got lucky.

The idea to include a chimpanzee in the experiment gives us an example how to think in a unique way. The question as to whether or not a stockbroker positively influences investment results focuses on the effect of a broker's knowledge about stocks. To provide a baseline for the experiment, a chimpanzee was cleverly chosen to compete with experienced stockbrokers. Anyone would readily agree that a chimpanzee has no financial knowledge at all. By including an element with a stock market knowledge level of absolutely zero, no matter which competitor was most successful, the results became much more compelling. This example tells us that sometimes choosing a value of zero is useful when using the method of considering a "much smaller value" than the values in a normal range.

Ranges Related to Time or Space

Ranges can be seen in all aspects of daily life. Time and space are two facets of daily life that are commonly described by ranges of numbers. We often use minutes, hours, or days when we refer to particular time period, and inches, feet, or miles when describing various size ranges. When considering time or spatial measurements, purposely going beyond the normally accepted range provides an opportunity to think outside the box.

There are many unexploded landmines left in countries that still bear the scars of past wars. A lot of information about these mines has been lost over the passage of time. Many of these mines are unknown both in location and to the extent of danger they pose. If a person accidentally steps on a hidden landmine, they may lose limbs or even their life. Beyond safety, the existence of these mines hurt agriculture as well, since people have to avoid plowing and planting in large regions suspected of harboring buried explosives.

This ongoing problem has prompted all kinds of people to attempt to find solutions to it, including social activists and celebrities. For example, the late Princess Diana used her influence to campaign for awareness of this issue and to help those who suffered from landmine explosions. The first key step to solving this problem is to identify the exact locations of the mines using instruments such as metal detectors. During the detection process, a detector is walked over the ground to scan for mines. The instrument beeps when a metal object is detected under the soil. Then the suspected mine is isolated, identified, and eventually destroyed in a safe manner. This method is inefficient, dangerous, and unable to detect plastic mines.

About ten years ago, a Danish biotechnology company reported it had developed a new, more efficient method of mine detection.[9] The researchers at the company had inserted a genetically modified gene into the weed thale cress. When the modified weed grows in a suspected minefield, its leaves turn brown if there is a mine nearby. A tiny amount of nitrogen dioxide leaks from mines that then interfere with the growth of the weed and causes its leaves to change color. This approach is much more efficient than traditional landmine detection methods for large areas. With this new method, airplanes can sow thale cress over suspected areas and, after the weed has grown to a certain level, aerial photography can check the color distribution on the fields. Wherever leaf color shifts from green to brown points to the possibility of a hidden mine. This improved landmine detection scheme is safe, efficient, and can detect nonmetal landmines as well. However, this new method takes several weeks to grow the weed enough to detect any mines.

Traditional landmine detection methods are quite fast. It takes only a few seconds from starting the detection process to know whether a mine has been detected. The Danish biotechnology researchers clearly did not limit their thinking to the normal detection time period when they were searching for new detection approaches. Instead, they focused on methods which can easily cover large areas of *space*, but accepted longer detection *times* in a very large range. The detection *time* was increased more than a million-fold, from seconds to weeks, but the *space* that could be covered also increased by a huge factor! If the researchers did not go beyond the few-seconds range of traditional landmine detection to gain their large area efficiency needs, their new approach would probably not have been discovered.

Another example is about stretching dimensions in space involving a Chinese poet, Liu Ling.[10] Liu lived almost eighteen hundred years ago. He liked to get drunk, believing that when he was drunk it fueled his creative energy to write great poems. His talents were so renowned that he was nicknamed "The Drunk Master." However, Liu also possessed a strange peculiarity: He took off his clothes and wandered around his house naked every time he got inebriated. He steadfastly refused to stop behaving this way and nobody could persuade him to do otherwise inside his own home. One day, a friend came to visit him. When the friend entered the house, the poet greeted the visitor naked.

His friend wasn't very comfortable upon seeing his idiotic behavior and promptly admonished him, saying, "We are all civilized people, right? It's a shame that you do not wear your clothes. This is not appropriate."

The poet listened to his friend, but was unmoved to dress himself. Strangely, not only did he refuse to put on his clothes, but he also began berating his friend shamelessly. The friend was neatly dressed, so how could he be at fault? Here's how the poet responded to his friend: "I believe the sky is my blanket," the poet said. "The earth represents my bed, and my house represents my trousers. That means it is not I who am naked, but rather *you have walked into my underwear*. It is *you* who should be ashamed, not me."

His friend was dumbfounded and speechless.

The poet's argument is quite interesting, as well as curious. Most people have a rough idea of the size of their clothes, which generally matches the size of their bodies. In the case of the poet, he expanded the size of his "clothes" immensely to the size of a house. That increase went way beyond the normal size range of any conventional clothing. Different from his friend, the poet's creativity set him completely free from the restrictions of the normal size range. Plainly, if the house could be considered as the poet's trousers, then the one who should feel embarrassed was not the poet, but his friend. Although intoxicated and a bit bizarre, we can see a point in the poet's thinking.

Summary
When a normal numerical range is defined, out-of-the-box thinking is a relatively easy task to accomplish: just look at the values outside of the normal range as long as it's practical to do so—and be open-minded as to what constitutes as "practical". See the related aspects in the following:

- ☐ Look for values incrementally larger or smaller than the values in the normal range.
- ☐ Think about values much larger than the largest value or much smaller than the smallest value in the normal range.
- ☐ Examine extremely large values up to infinity or extremely small values near or equal to zero.
- ☐ Consider expanding the range in various dimensions such as time, space, weight, quantity, grade, percentage, and so on.

2

Consider More Than "One"

The number *one* is very special. Primitive counting by early humans resulted in the sequence "one and a heap," ignoring any concept of zero or unique numbers above one. This limited their ability to think about "two-or-more" scenarios, only "one and many."

One doesn't represent the absence of anything as zero does, and it doesn't represent more than one as larger whole numbers do. It often represents the concept of the words *unique* or *only*. For objects directly related to the number one, people easily form an instinct that those things are only related to a single form, not multiple forms. People get used to thinking about only a single quantity as an isolated situation and overlook the possibility of multiple relationships. This is a common and unnecessary limitation we put on our thoughts. Phenomena which are usually closely related with a single instance may actually be able to build relationships at a higher level. Proactively examining the family of unitary relationships for multiple relationships may give insight into new perspectives.

"One" Is Not the Only Possibility
It's easy to fall into a so-called "singularity" trap when considering things habitually related to a solitary instantiation. If this trap isn't avoided, possibilities related to new expanded scenarios will likely be missed, which leads to overlooking potentially large areas of opportunity. Therefore, no matter whether a situation is clearly related to a multiplicity or not, don't exclude considering

multiple instances when dealing with topics involving numbers of options. This way, the chance of omitting valuable possibilities will be smaller.

According to a 2006 report in *BusinessWeek*, an executive at Accenture presented a proposal to the leaders of local Indian tribes in the Umatilla Indian Reservation to outsource some of Accenture's work to them, including call centers, document preparation, and software programming services.[1] Since the Indian reservation was in the United States, government-related work could also be shifted to the Reservation with fewer security issues. The cost of living in the area was low, along with lower wages and real estate costs. Native American businesses don't pay corporate taxes, so outsourcing to the area could provide a 10-30 percent cost savings for Accenture. The outsourcing would bring significant benefits to the Indian tribes as well. The collaboration between Accenture and the local Indian tribes would decrease high unemployment rates and grow the tribes' gaming- and government-dependent economy.

When people think about outsourcing jobs, the potential locations that usually come to mind are developing countries such as Mexico, India, and China. It seems that developing nations are the only choice, but Accenture didn't get stuck in this thinking trap. While considering developing countries as one area for outsourcing, they also considered selected areas in developed countries. Even though the executive's proposal looks natural and reasonable today, it was a new thought at the time. As a government-industry analyst at Forrester Research Inc. commented on Accenture's endeavor, "I'm surprised nobody else has looked at this yet." The analyst's revelation was understandable because Accenture was the first major global technical services firm that worked with Indian tribes to create a low-cost domestic outsourcing base. This example demonstrates that when most people believe there's only one choice, they may actually have more—and probably better—options than initially thought. Therefore, try to avoid falling into the "singularity" trap by seeing if the goal may have more than one solution.

More Than One Item

A lot of things may seem only related to one form, i.e., only have a connection to *one*. But nothing limits us from trying connections to larger numbers. Imagine conditions that connect to the number two or three or more. If the original number was not one, but two, three, or four, what would happen? Surely new ideas can be created. Thinking this way provides another method to broaden an open mind.

In World War II, on the European battle fields, one soldier's cap insignia was different from the other soldiers. Military insignias are standardized and are not allowed to be customized. In this example, the difference wasn't the insignia itself, but rather the number of insignia on his cap. It was required that each soldier should have *one* insignia on his cap, but British Field Marshal Bernard Montgomery's black beret had two: one was the emblem of the Royal Tank Regiment and the other was the British General Officer's emblem. Wearing two insignias on his cap was his own idea, and because of this Montgomery became very recognizable. Since he dropped in on the troops frequently, he wanted his soldiers to recognize him immediately when he was there and to feel that their commander cared about them by being visible during battles. Monty's two-insignia approach was simple yet unique.[2]

A military uniform's cap has one insignia, seemingly a rigid rule. No British soldier had ever had more than one insignia on his cap. But Marshal Montgomery was a creative thinker. He broke the convention of "one insignia for one cap." Wanting to stand out to his men, he might have thought, "Why not wear two insignias so my men will recognize me immediately?" And the men would've said, "Hey, the guy wearing two badges is visiting our unit again. He must be Marshal Montgomery!"

Since this story is still being told today, we know General Montgomery's idea worked very well. What we don't know is whether the idea came from his high rank itself or from a creative mind that gave him the ability to climb to that rank in the first place. Here, even only for the sake of being unique, changing the singular number (one) to a higher number (two) demonstrates a simple and elegant solution.

More Than One Function

Expanding functionality beyond something's usual single instance has wide applications to improve creativity. Guided by this chapter's principles of trying to add more functions to something that typically has only one function, can be a valuable exercise.

Several years ago, a radical new design for women's shoes from

CAMiLEON Heels attracted people's attention.[3] In contrast to conventional shoe designs, the heel height of the new design was not fixed but instead was configurable, allowing the wearer to easily change the heel height as desired. Women wanted to have high heels for the evening or at the office. Alternatively, women preferred low heels for outdoor activities so their feet were more comfortable and were less prone to injury. The design constructs each heel from two components. When high heels are needed, the two pieces align vertically so the height of the heel was the total height of the two pieces. When low heels are needed, one piece folds under the other piece, creating a low heel. Thus, the newly designed shoes satisfy women's desire to wear different heel heights for different occasions without needing to buy two pairs!

It's likely that most people have never thought about a pair of shoes that could have more than one heel height since everyone wears shoes with a single, fixed heel. Because single-heel-height shoes are the norm, people are unlikely to think about whether one pair of shoes could have multiple heel heights. Otherwise, why haven't shoes with adjustable heels appeared until recently? The multilevel heel design didn't need advanced technology, nor have women only recently needed for shoes with different heel heights. Look at how people have disregarded the fact that women own multiple pairs of shoes when one cleverly designed pair would meet their needs. With this in mind, how many similar inconveniences today need creative thinking to provide practical solutions?

Think Beyond a Single Arrangement

Admittedly, there are many things in the world that are unique and can only be associated with a single form, and no alternative forms are possible. For example, there is only one moon in the earth's sky, or everyone has only one birthday each year. For these things, breaking the limit of one doesn't seem to work. However, nothing is absolute in the eyes of a creative mind. Sometimes there are still opportunities to expand unique things to higher numbers. The simplest way to discover these new opportunities is to ignore for a moment that the thing in question is uniquely associated with a single form and instead imagine the consequences of a reality in which the thing can be connected to multiple quantities.

In 2003, a new website appeared on the Internet called "Second Life."

It was a three-dimensional, virtual world. In this world, a person could live a completely different life from his or her life in the real world. In this virtual world, a person could create a large house on a huge estate with a magnificent ocean view, for example. A person's appearance could change, allowing them to be a handsome man or a beautiful woman of whatever gender they desired. They could endow themselves with extraordinary abilities, becoming a super rock star, a successful business man, or a mighty tribal chief. They could fly in the sky, swim under water, never get sick, never die, and communicate with people without any language problem. All in all, a citizen of Second Life had almost no limits to doing anything, even things impossible in the real world. This virtual world attracted almost a million registered users in three years, according to Fox News.[4]

Short of science-fiction-like theories, it makes sense that humans can live their lives only once, or, that a person's life can only be related to the number one in this respect. The advent of the Internet provided a new opportunity for breaking the limit of one. How? Things in the real world can have mirror images in a virtual world. Now a person can have two lives, one in the real world and the other in the virtual world. The inventors of Second Life may have been inspired by the power of the Internet to create a second form of existence for people. So, when something seems to only be tightly associated with one instance, try to imagine how it could be expanded beyond that restriction. There's no harm in trying, and the potential benefits of cultivating a creative mind through this technique are substantial.

More Than One Interpretation

Multiplicity is a common phenomenon. A phrase can have multiple meanings, or an action can have multiple interpretations. Multiplicity provides flexibility and abundant choices in the expression and understanding of something. Those with open minds are aware of the existence of multiplicity and skillfully utilize it at the appropriate time to create new ideas.

A professor once told an interesting experience he had had in the days when the Soviet Union was still a powerful empire. At the time, he was an assistant professor who had just joined the physics department at a renowned university. It was very common then for the department to hold "study meetings" to instill the political ideology of the ruling party into its faculty members. During the meetings, the participants were required to study political articles and share their thoughts about them. The articles were full of material glorifying the party and demanding that citizens willingly obey the government.

One day, the professor was compelled to go to one of these meetings. After reading several articles during the session from the government newspaper, the meeting chairwoman began to ask the participants questions like, "What are your thoughts after studying the papers?" Even though most of those present held feelings of contempt for the thoughts in the articles, they couldn't admit to their true feelings. The attendees would usually say something that echoed the thoughts of the chairwoman to avoid trouble.

The professor was an honorable man and didn't want to lose his integrity by repeating the mantra like the others, yet he didn't want to jeopardize his job, either. What could he do? Eventually he found a way to solve this dilemma. When it was his turn to answer the chairwoman's question, he replied, "After our discussion, I have gained a deeper understanding about the ruling party's philosophy, which guides the direction of our country." The woman paused after hearing this, not quite sure how to take it. This was the first time she had heard a response like this. She knew the answer was a bit odd, but couldn't put her finger on how it was different because the answer was politically acceptable. She decided the answer was satisfactory by assuming that the professor meant he had gained a better understanding on the greatness of the ruling party from the meeting. In the following study meetings, the professor's answers were basically the same—that he possessed a deeper understanding than before about the topics presented by the meeting's chairperson.

The professor was caught between a rock and a hard place. On the one hand, he wanted to maintain his integrity by not saying something that would be dishonest. On the other hand, he did not want to cause trouble either by openly criticizing the powerful political doctrines. His clever solution was to stand on the borderline by using a statement with multiple meanings. "Having a deeper understanding" only expressed the level of understanding, but didn't reveal his feelings toward it. This answer could be interpreted either that the professor had a deeper understanding on the glorious ideology or, alternatively, as ridicule of the ruling party's ideals.

The single statement's multiple interpretations preserved the professor's integrity as well as protected his job.

Look for multiplicity potential in everything and take advantage of the flexibility it can provide.

Thinking More Than One Creates New Solutions

For things normally associated with "one," people subconsciously consider only single solutions, not multiple solutions. Learning how to break the limit of one will encourage discovery of different solutions, even if something seems only connected to a singular solution.

Keeping belongings safe and secure when traveling has been a recurring issue for travelers all over the world. They face a dilemma when deciding whether to lock their luggage or not when they check in at airport ticket counters. If the luggage is not locked, they fear their belongings may get stolen. If they lock their luggage, a problem occurs when government TSA agents decide to search the luggage, potentially destroying the lock. John Vermilye, a former TSA consultant and the founder of Travel Sentry saw the problem and came up with a solution. His company created a special type of lock that can be opened by both the traveler and inspectors at the airport, but not by anyone else. The lock has one key for the traveler while the TSA inspectors are able to open the same lock with tool kits provided by Travel Sentry. This lock with a red diamond insignia has become so popular that it's now being used in over four hundred airports in the United States.[5]

People regard ordinary locks as being able to be opened by just one key. Different keys are for different locks. In solving the issue of whether passengers should lock their baggage or not, Vermilye broke the confines of each common lock having only one key to create a single travel lock that can be opened by two different keys. Travelers are confident using the new lock to secure their luggage because they know their luggage is safe from thieves while TSA agents are able to inspect the luggage as necessary. It's amazing that a successful corporation has been built on such a small idea.

"Thinking beyond 'one'" can help in almost any aspect in our daily life. President Reagan was a master of telling funny jokes. One of his best jokes concerned how poor the efficiency of a communist economy could be. One day, a citizen of the Soviet Union went to a car lot to buy a car.

The salesman accepted his down payment and told the man to come back on the same day in ten years to pick up his car. Waiting for so long to get his car wasn't unusual, because people were used to waiting in long lines to get many things in the communist society due to terrible manufacturing efficiency. Before leaving the car lot, the man asked, "Should I come back in the morning or afternoon?" The salesman was a little irritated by the man's question, and replied, "Will it really matter?" The car buyer answered, "Well, my plumbing appointment is that morning."[6] Obviously, one appointment so far in the future isn't that funny, but two such conflicting appointments made the situation comical. Listeners were surprised that President Reagan went beyond using just one future appointment as an example!

Reversed Scenarios: Focus Only on One

As described above, breaking the limit of one may introduce new opportunities for solutions. However, the opposite situation shouldn't be ignored, either. When multiple solutions are considered perfectly acceptable by most people, deliberately picking only one solution may lead to a new perspective.

Southwest Airlines is one of the largest airlines in the United States. However, its business model is quite different from that of other large airlines. Typically, a large airline keeps a diverse fleet to fulfill the needs of its various provided services. For example, a major American airline's mainline fleet is comprised of large numbers of aircraft, including Airbus 320, 330, 350; Boeing 737, 757, 767, 777; and the newly available Boeing 787.[7] Southwest, however, uses just one type of airplane: the Boeing 737, according to *The Economist* magazine.[8] This limits Southwest's aircraft diversity when compared to its competitors, yet this uniqueness yields extraordinary results. Using only one type of airplane brings huge efficiency and cost savings to Southwest. Training the flight and ground crews is much less complicated, as operations are more convenient. The issues involved with shifting airplanes, crews, or boarding gates are minimized because all the airplanes have similar cockpits and configurations. Southwest has been successful using this approach for many years and has won widespread praise in the airline industry. Economists continue to study its business model to understand its secret.

While maintaining a fleet's diversity is a must for most large airlines, Southwest upset the status quo and focused on only one type of airplane, which has played an essential role in Southwest's success. Therefore, in situations where normally multiple different resources are involved, also think about the advantages of reducing the multiplicity to one.

Summary

The number *one* has always been a special and unique number. Any phenomena normally related to a single occurrence seems to imply that these items are only associated within a single form. Thus, when people think about the situation, they tend to only consider a single instance and ignore the less obvious events happening at the same time. This approach expands one's thinking by turning things with single associations into things with additional associations. The following are a few areas you may consider:

☐ When thinking about something normally associated with a singular instance, see if multiple instances are possible.

☐ Try letting something that normally happens in one location happen in more locations, or something that normally happens once to happen multiple times.

☐ Think about how to change something with only one function into something with multiple functions, or something that only serves one objective into something that serves multiple objectives.

☐ See if something tightly bound to a singular form can be related to multiple forms.

☐ Pay attention to multiplicity, such as multiple meanings of a phrase, multiple expressions of an idea, or multiple interpretations of an action.

☐ Don't forget to try reversed scenarios. For a situation normally associated with multiple instances, see if there are potential benefits by reducing the number of instances to one.

Look at More Dimensions

A simple definition of a dimension refers to an independent direction in space. For instance, a straight line is an example of one dimension, a plane is an example of two dimensions, and a box is an example of three dimensions. The concept of dimensions is not limited to just the spatial world, it can also be extended to other characteristics, even though spatial directions are used as the most basic manifestations of dimensions.

One way to cultivate a creative mind is to consider extraneous dimensions that aren't normally considered. For instance, if an object is normally considered one-dimensional, think about trying to add another dimension to make it two-dimensional. For another example, listening to a radio is normally thought of as a one-dimensional activity with only the sense of hearing involved. Television was created by extending the sensory dimensions from just sound to include vision as well. To develop an innovative mind in this respect, it's useful not only to think about the common dimensions but rather explore dimensions that aren't normally considered.

More Spatial Dimensions

To begin the quest for new dimensions, it is easiest to start by expanding simple spatial dimensions. For example, for things which normally have only one direction, adding a different direction can change its number of dimensions from one to two. That's easy, right?

In 2006, a lounge bed that was able to accommodate two people arrived on the market.[1] The unique feature of this lounge bed was its seatback design. Unlike other lounge beds, which have only one seatback mounted at one end of the bed, this lounge bed has two separate seatbacks. The two seatbacks are not situated next to each other, but instead one seatback is mounted on the head end of the square lounge, while the other is attached on the side of the lounge at a right angle to the first seatback. When two people are sitting on the lounge, each faces a different direction. The advantage of this arrangement is that the two people can face each other by each turning their head only forty-five degrees instead of ninety degrees, as in a conventional side-by-side lounge bed. They can talk to each other much more comfortably. The design of the lounge bed is a simple example of how changing a one-dimensional concept into a two-dimensional concept can be very beneficial.

If an object is typically considered two-dimensional, think about adding another dimension to make it three-dimensional. Here is an example. In 2011, George Higa, a user interface designer at Verizon, was granted a patent for a new design of the touch screen, according to *Scientific American*.[2] It was well known at that time that the surface of a touch screen was always uniformly flat and smooth, no matter where it is touched. The designer's new idea was to modify the touch screen so that the texture of the surface could be controlled by raising various pixels to create a tactile surface. Thus, some portions of the screen can be differentiated by a slight elevation on the surface plane of the screen giving unique tactile feedback to the user. For instance, when someone wants to dial a phone number, the shapes of the number buttons will raise up. That makes the numbers easier to distinguish from each other and will help reduce input mistakes. This patent caught the attention of the IT industry and is considered "the future of computing interfaces" by a professor at Johns Hopkins University. This patent basically changed touch screen design from two dimensions to three dimensions. We don't know exactly what method Higa used to generate his idea, but if any smart phone interface designer simply thought about adding one more dimension to the two-dimensional surface, perhaps he or she would have quickly discovered this innovative idea.

A striking example of using a third dimension to improve a commonly thought-of two-dimensional situation is the historic battle where the Ottoman Turk Mehmed II (1432–1481) conquered Constantinople, the capital of Byzantine Empire.[3] In 1453, Mehmed II was preparing to invade

Constantinople, which had been under Byzantine rule for centuries. The city occupied an area that roughly resembled a triangle. The northwest side was protected by a series of heavily fortified walls. The south side that faced the Marmara Sea had heavy protection as well. The only relatively weak defensive point of the city was on the northeast side that faced the harbor of the Golden Horn. The Byzantines felt no reason to be concerned about the harbor side, for the entrance of the harbor from Bosporus Strait was protected by many warships, in addition to a heavy metal chain which could block any enemy ship from attempting to enter the harbor. The city looked secure and continued receiving supplies from Galata, a Genoese colony located across the harbor. With no other adversary nearby, the Byzantines felt confident when facing Mehmed's hostile ambitions.

Mehmed II was fearless and extremely persistent. In the beginning, he focused his attack on the walls on the northwest side. For weeks, his massive cannon fired on the walls, but that only caused limited damage. Moreover, the damage to the walls was quickly repaired by the Byzantines during the very slow reloading of Mehmed's cannon. It seemed the tenacious warrior was in a stalemate, but he wasn't ready to give up. Mehmed analyzed the situation and conceived an idea to defeat the Byzantines. He bribed the Genoese in Galata to allow his troops to build an overland road from Bosporus Strait to the Golden Horn. The road was built with logs, and grease was used on the logs to make them slippery. Then he ordered his soldiers to haul eighty light-weight warships from Bosporus to the Golden Horn over this highway. When Mehmed's fleet suddenly appeared in the harbor, the Byzantine defenders were astounded. They couldn't figure out where the ships had come from and how Mohmed did this. Mehmed's ships successfully blocked the Byzantines' supplies from Galata and forced the Byzantines to stretch the city defenders over a much longer borderline. This effectively demoralized the city defenders and weakened the city's ability to protect itself. Eventually, the five-hundred-year-old Constantinople fell, following only two months of siege. After taking over the famous city, Mehmed II moved the Ottoman capital to this newly occupied city, which is called Istanbul today.

Mehmed's idea changed the entire outcome of the battle. Warships usually move only on relatively flat water. Smooth water is a two-dimensional medium for ship movement. When confined to these two-dimensions, Mehmed's ships were blocked from getting into the harbor of the Golden

Horn. By thinking about how to allow the ships to be able to move vertically *up* onto and over the rough land, not just how to move on a two-dimensional smooth surface, he solved his problem! He extended the familiar two dimensions of the ship's movement to include one more dimension: *height*. It's no exaggeration to say that this method of considering additional dimensions literally changed history.

The above stories are examples of considering more spatial dimensions for one-dimensional or two-dimensional things. However, the thinking technique of expanding dimensions can even be applied to things without dimensions. What's something without dimensions? A point, such as a dot on paper, is conceptually a zero-dimensional object.

Barcodes that are used everywhere today were invented in the 1940s by Norman Woodland and a friend.[4] The process of how they invented it is amazing. One day, Woodland's friend overheard that a grocery store manager was looking for solutions to capture product information during checkout. When Woodland heard this, he became very interested in finding a solution to this need. He wanted to use a code to capture the product data. Unfortunately, the only code he knew about at that time was Morse code, which he had learned during his Boy Scouts days. On paper, Morse code is composed of dots and dashes, and machines in those days were not able to read small dots accurately without expensive focusing optics.

One day, Woodland sat on a beach and used his fingers to draw Morse code characters in the sand, thinking about how to improve the Morse code to make it machine readable. Inadvertently, he left his fingers in the sand and pulled his hand toward himself. Suddenly he saw parallel lines. It was his Eureka moment! Seeing the parallel lines, Woodland came up with the idea to modify the original Morse code to represent product information. The dots and dashes could be represented by parallel lines, the dots by thin lines and the dashes by thickened lines called bars! A machine could read these lines much more easily than reading small dots and dashes, and could do it without the need for the expensive reading instrument. With this idea, the dots and dashes of Morse code became a line-bar barcode. In 1952, Woodland and his friend applied for, and were later granted, a patent on this idea. Even with this new barcode design, it took a while to develop a dependable bar code reader. Today, about five billion barcodes are scanned every day throughout the world!

The inspiration Woodland had at the beach was a matter of changing dots of zero dimensions to one-dimensional lines, and one-dimensional dashes into two-dimensional bars. If he had not accidentally dragged his fingers through the sand at the beach, he probably would never have had this important inspiration. If others had known the method of considering extra dimensions, they may have been able discover how to change Morse code into lines and bars without depending on accidents.

The examples above indicate that spatial dimensions can be explored for opportunities to improve our daily lives. Get into the habit of paying attention to possible new dimensions. After reading this section, turning a table top into a box is child's play, right?

More Generalized Dimensions

The concept of dimensions can be generalized beyond spatial elements. Other characteristics of an object can be viewed as different dimensions as well. For example, an apple has attributes of color, weight, ripeness, sweetness, and so on. These properties can be treated as different "dimensions." Thinking about expanded dimensions outside commonly accepted models allows us to access more opportunities to find novel ways to solve problems and create new ideas.

There are many examples of inventors considering more dimensions in the designs and functions of smart phones. Force Touch, developed by Apple Inc., is a technology to make the touch screen able to distinguish different levels of force being applied to the surface of the screen.[5] Here the level of force can be considered as a new dimension for touching the screen. With this technology, a smart phone can execute different functions based on how much pressure is applied to the touch screen. One application of the technology can be a better way to watch videos on a mobile device. A user can control the speed of fast forwarding or rewinding by exerting appropriate pressure on the touch screen of the device.

There is a well-known classic puzzle about controlling three lightbulbs. In a room, there are three lightbulbs and the door into the room is closed. There are three switches on the outside wall of the room, each of which controls a single lightbulb. The question is that if a person is only allowed to enter the room once, how does he figure out which switch controls which bulb? If there are only two bulbs and two switches, then it is obviously easy.

The person can turn on one switch and leave the other off. When he enters the room, the lighted bulb is controlled by the switch he has just turned on, thus the other switch controls the dark bulb. The more difficult problem appears when there are three bulbs in the puzzle. The answer to this puzzle is actually quite simple. The person turns on the first switch and leaves it on; then he turns on the second switch for a little while, and then turns it off; he does not touch the third switch. Then he enters the room and sees the lighted bulb that obviously corresponds to the first switch. To identify the two dark bulbs, he touches each one to determine their temperature. The one warmer than room temperature must correspond to the second switch, since after a lightbulb is turned off it stays warm for a while. The other dark bulb clearly must then be controlled by the switch that was never turned on.

In solving this puzzle, the key step is to realize that the characteristics of a lightbulb include not only the brightness but also the temperature, even though brightness is the one people generally think about when they see a lightbulb. If brightness is considered the only dimension, the solution to the problem may be impossible. But when the dimension of temperature is included in solving this puzzle, a solution becomes much easier to grasp.

The number of bulbs in the puzzle can be increased past three to extend multi-dimensional thinking. If there are four bulbs and four switches, can it be determined which switch controls which bulb under the same conditions as stated in the original puzzle? Yes! The first switch is turned on and the last switch is left off, while the second switch is turned on for five seconds then turned off, and the third switch turned on for one minute then turned off. After entering the room, the lit bulb has to correspond to the first switch. To identify the three remaining dark bulbs, each is touched to determine its temperature. The room temperature bulb is controlled by the last switch, the warm bulb is controlled by the second switch, and the hot bulb is controlled by the third switch. In this case, the time period for which a switch is on has become a new dimension. The longer the time in which the bulb is turned on, the hotter the bulb. By adding the dimension of time, the bulbs can be distinguished by the temperatures caused by the different periods of time that they are turned on. Therefore, analyzing problems with the approach to add more dimensions can help you quickly discover answers. For practice using this technique, expand this puzzle to involve five, six, seven, or even more lightbulbs.

These examples show us how more dimensions can be identified by exploring the various properties of things. There are many more useful dimensions associated with situations beyond commonly seen dimensions. Search for more characteristics as different dimensions and then think about how each new dimension might be useful in solving the problem or providing a solution. Practicing doing this will sharpen your open-minded skills, guaranteed.

Relationships Between Dimensions

Another aspect of using the concept of dimensions to generate new ideas is paying attention to the relationships between dimensions. A new dimension may increase the usefulness of another dimension or compensate for a deficiency in another dimension.

David was a volunteer in Beijing who built a special media room in his home during the first decade of this century. This home theater was quite simple, consisting of a DVD player, a TV set, speakers, and many stools for his special guests. These special guests were all blind. He used his theater to entertain them by letting them "watch" movies completely free of charge. How could blind people watch movies? Actually, David's media room made it possible. In the theater, blind guests sit on stools, listening to the movie sound track. In addition to the sound track, David narrated the scenes in the movie. With David's help, the blind people could "see" what was happening in the movie: what people were wearing, what the actors were doing, what was the color of the sky, and so on. Tall buildings, busy streets, flying birds, running animals, green trees, and colorful flowers, were all "seen" by the blind movie viewers through David's vivid descriptions. Every weekend he hosted dozens blind people. Influenced by David's generous services, more people joined him to help the blind. Among them were teachers, lawyers, students, news reporters, and even celebrities. The blind movie goers were grateful to David and other volunteers because they were now able to "see" and participate in the full movie experience.[6]

You need your senses of vision and hearing to enjoy movies. Unfortunately for the blind, the lack of sight keeps them from feeling the full impact of the movie images. David found a way to enhance his audience's movie experience by compensating for blindness in the visual dimension through adding more to the hearing dimension. David's thinking about using the dimension of hearing to compensate for the deficiency of sight in his guests made them able to "watch" movies again.

So, when using this concept to help being open minded, remember to include relationships between dimensions as well as adding new dimensions.

Reversed Scenarios: Reduced Dimensions

Even though considering extra dimensions is a valuable method for generating new ideas, reducing the number of dimensions can be a useful approach as well. For example, think about how to create new two-dimensional objects based on three-dimensional items, or new one-dimensional objects based on two-dimensional items.

Rashad Alakbarov, an artist from Azerbaijan, developed a new painting style, though some have reservations about calling his artwork "paintings" in the traditional sense. Alakbarov's paintings disappear completely when the illumination is switched off because what he creates are shadow paintings. One of his paintings is a giant portrait of a human head projected on a wall. The painting is composed of a series of shadows. The shadows are produced by a light source in the back of the room shining through many water bottles hung from the ceiling between the light and the wall. Another of his works is a sketch of a city with vivid images of buildings and castles. The sketch consists only of shadows, too. The artist uses many everyday items in this work, such as books, CDs, wine bottles, dinner plates, plastic tubes, metal wires, etc. Many people thoroughly enjoy these unique paintings. So far, his artwork has been exhibited in cities such as London, Moscow, Venice, and Berlin.[7]

The objects used by the artist to create the shadows are real three-dimensional items, and the space he uses to arrange the objects is three-dimensional as well. However, his goal is to create two-dimensional paintings on a wall. Using a pile of three-dimensional items to generate a two-dimensional shadow painting demonstrates the idea of shrinking dimensions. Therefore, when you're thinking about creating new ideas, consider not only adding more dimensions but also explore the potential benefits of reducing dimensions, too.

Summary

Space is normally measured in three dimensions (length, width, and height). The basic idea behind the concept of a dimension can be applied to other things. The characteristics and attributes of situations or objects can be considered to be different dimensions as well, such as the five senses, the color, temperature, weight and so on. We find it easy to understand the common dimensions associated with everyday things, but we tend to overlook the less obvious dimensions. Thinking about how to discover and extend dimensions opens your mind. The following are a few areas you may think about in this aspect:

☐ Consider more spatial dimensions. For example, consider adding a third dimension to a two-dimensional object.

☐ Think about transforming abstract characteristics into dimensions associated with various objects or situations. For example, think about a person's hearing when only his sight is normally considered, or think about the temperature of an object when only its color and weight are normally considered. Consider the following:

☐ Pay attention to the relationships and interactions amongst dimensions.

☐ Alternatively, think about how you might shrink the number of dimensions.

4

Add One More Type

Almost everything has many different categories and forms of attributes. For example, there are many different types of coffee beans. Consumers are able to choose light or dark roasted, regular or decaffeinated coffee beans from Colombia or Indonesia or Ethiopia, and so on. Different combinations of the various characteristics of coffee beans form a long list of different coffee products that meet the diverse preferences of consumers, even though they are all technically just "coffee beans." From time to time, coffee bean vendors still introduce new products by adding a new type of coffee bean into its product line. This method of Add One More Type can be applied to almost anything when generating useful new ideas.

This exercise will stimulate your thinking and help you discover new paths to a solution. Searching for only one new type of a thing is much easier than needing to find many new ones. One way to find this new type is to be guided by all the known types that already exist and then develop the new type by searching for attributes that are clearly different from the existing ones. If the new type has unique value, the effort is worth it.

Add One More Type of Content
The principle of Add One More Type can be applied to something's content. For example, a service may contain many different types of subservices that make up the elements of the complete service. Adding new content to something is a common practice when using this method.

At the dawn of the new millennium a new online auction item became available in some areas—a nursing work shift, according to an article in *The New York Times*.[1] Registered nurses have been in short supply for a long time and have caused hospitals and other medical facilities to be perpetually understaffed. In the past, hospitals relied on professional recruiters to fill vacancies, especially the undesirable shifts. In contrast to a normal auction where bids *increase* as the auction progresses, nurses bid for the work shift with their acceptable hourly wage, forcing the bids to *decrease* as the nurses compete for the work shift. At the end of the auction, the lowest bidder wins the shift. A successful auction results in a win-win situation for both the employer and the winning nurse. Health care facilities that have tried this new way to find nursing staff have seen significant cost savings and decreases in unfilled vacancies. From the nurses' viewpoint, they benefit from more flexible work schedules by bidding only on the time slots that fit their personal schedules and meet their wage requirements. They also have the option to potentially make more money by bidding on undesirable shifts that are unpopular.

There have always been many different types of auctions. Typical auction items include cars, houses, artwork, jewelry, etc. However, auctioning nursing work shifts had never been seen before. The inventor of the new auction may have used the method of Add One More Type to come up with the nurse work shift as a new type of auction item.

When applying the Add One More Type method, the contents of a service aren't the only contents that can be considered. Contents of many other things can be examined for opportunities to apply the method as well. For example, in 2002 environmental noise data was added into maps. That year, the Environmental Noise Directive of European Parliament and Council established the definition and standard of noise mapping.[2] With the standard, noise levels of a particular area can be measured and displayed on a geographic map producing a "noise map." The map is particularly useful to indicate the noise levels in different locations in cities. Citizens and visitors are able to use the map to find where and when they can find relatively quiet places in a city. The noise map also helps city planners implement action plans to manage noise, reduce noise levels, and to control environmental noise intensities for the long term with the goal of creating a noise-pollution-free world for future generations.

Everyone is familiar with road maps, weather maps, economic maps, etc. The noise map, however, is a new member in the map family. Perhaps the creator of noise mapping explicitly used the methodology of adding a new element—noise data—into the content of maps when thinking about how to display noise levels in a more useful manner.

Add One More Method

There are usually multiple effective approaches to get something accomplished. To gain new ideas, one method is to try to come up with a new approach that reaches the same goal but is different from all existing approaches. Explicitly trying to discover another approach should stimulate creative thinking and may even spawn a better approach.

In 2007, a team at an MIT lab designed a huge image display device for an expo in Spain. The medium used to generate the display was quite special—it was just water. An array of nozzles was set along the top edge of the rectangular display pointing down. The water flowing from the nozzles forms a "screen" of water droplets. The nozzles were controlled by a computer that regulated the flows of water drops. By accurately controlling the timing and water flows of all the nozzles, words and pictures could be formed as water drops fell into the pool at the bottom of the display. The display screen endlessly scrolled the images from top to bottom. This design was so innovative that it was named one of Best Inventions of 2007 by *Time* magazine.[3]

There are many ways to display images on large display screens, such as using light emitting diodes (LED), liquid crystals (LC), micro-electrical mechanical systems (MEMS), plasma, and so on. The MIT team was probably tasked to design a new way to display images that was radically different from all other display systems in order to attract the attention of visitors to the expo. The Add One More Type method could play its role in this situation nicely. By explicitly avoiding using any existing approaches, the team created an intriguing approach by controlling streams of falling water drops. This may have been the exact process of how this award-winning display device design was born. Think about how the concept can be extended to other materials.

Add One More Function

Another way of applying the Add One More Type method involves functions, such as functions of a device, a system, an organization, etc. Almost everything of interest has functions that already exist, but we can still expand them by adding one or more new functions. By focusing on what functions something lacks, an opportunity of adding another function may appear.

Up to the last decade common washing machines had functions designed to wash clothes made of cotton, wool, and man-made fabrics. Normally, a washing machine wasn't recommended for washing fine fabrics such as silk and other delicates. These fragile materials were normally recommended to be hand washed only. A. A. Barnsley, a graduate student in industrial design at San Jose State University, came up with a new function for washing machines, according to a report in *Chicago Tribune* in 2003.[4] She designed a washing machine especially for fine hand-wash materials that worked similar to a salad spinner, reducing abrasion to a level that would successfully wash fine materials without damaging them. The design attracted attention and won an award at an international housewares exposition.

Obviously, the Add One More Type method played an important role in the birth of the design of a washing machine for fine fabrics, where the designer had observed that a delicate wash function was missing from regular washing machines. Thinking of a new function is actually more important than designing the function itself, because the detailed design wouldn't be possible without the first step—finding a new, worthy function.

Here is another example of adding a function. An artificial intelligence software program developed by the Hebrew University of Jerusalem was able to identify sarcasm in everyday language. The program was listed as one of *Time's* 50 Best Inventions of 2010.[5] The new function permitted robots to interpret subtle meanings in sarcastic statements, not just the literal meaning. This new function definitely enhances robotic capabilities and opens up potential new applications in many areas. For example, online comments about a product or service could be analyzed by the software to suggest to the provider which comments were honest and which ones might be phony.

A lot of artificial intelligence research has been focused on developing software that's able to recognize the meaning of spoken words. The main applications of the resulting programs were voice command interfaces between humans and machines. The research team at Hebrew University, however, added a new type of function to their artificial intelligence software that enhanced its ability to understand the complexity of human languages.

Consider the Add One More Type method when exploring new functions.

Add One More Element

Another area where the Add One More Type method can apply is elements of groups, such as departments within a company or types of online retailers. For example, as there are already many different kinds of online retailers, one may ask oneself, "How can another type of retailer be added?" This type of question can encourage new ideas about adding new elements.

There are many different types of match-making websites online, such as Match.com, eHarmony.com, PlentyofFish.com, and so on, who serve millions of subscribers. Is there opportunity to develop a new website to attract yet another group of clients? The answer is probably Yes.

Reported by *USA Today* in 2006, Jerry Miller saw a need for farmers to find mates online. He launched a match-making website, farmersonly.com, that was designed purely for farmers.[6] The web site didn't explicitly exclude non-farmers from participating, but people who didn't know the difference between combines and tractors and didn't respect the farmer's long work hours clearly wouldn't attract potential mates. So, this website self-selects almost only farmers, raising the hopes of farm people who may have otherwise given up on finding life partners.

Our final example talks about adding a new type of staff to hospitals. According to *USA Today*, the Argentinian government in Buenos Aires passed a new law in 2015 that requires all public hospitals with pediatric services to have clowns on their staff.[7] This law is the first of its kind in the world. It was based on the idea that laughter is good "medicine" for healing. A clown, wearing a white medical coat with a red nose, is able to comfort sick children's suffering by telling jokes and stories, using exaggerated expressions, and playing games with the young patients. The clown's antics reduce the young patient's feelings of physical and emotional distress.

This special staff group provides an excellent complement to the medical professionals in hospitals. At the time the report was published, there were already 150 hospitals which had added clowns to the hospitals' personnel lists. The number has surely blossomed since then.

A hospital normally has doctors, nurses, technicians, administration, security, and support staff among its employees. Adding clowns to the list was a clever idea because it dampens the stressful environment of a medical facility with laughter and fun. The Add One More Type approach clearly played a role in the creation of this idea.

Think about adding one more element to an assembly of elements, such as adding a new website to serve a special group of people or adding a new staff position in a hospital, as discussed above.

Summary

No matter how many different types of things belong to the object at hand, there may be an opportunity to add at least one more type that is distinct from the existing types. Any additional type you find will qualify the thing you're dealing with to be considered new, since you've identified new characteristics. These new types may provide more choices or fulfilling certain unmet needs. Consider this technique when searching for new solutions if your goal is to increase the extent of something:

- ☐ Try to add one more type that is distinct in at least one aspect from the existing types.
- ☐ Think of the Adding One More Type method in terms of content, function, appearance, format, category, platform, usage, effect, concept, a way to do something, as the target of an action, and so on.

PART II

Be Alert for Relationships

5

Explore Relationships

One of the most effective ways to approach problems is to try to examine the connections between the different elements involved with your problem. Some relationships will be obvious while others may be less apparent, though some of these less apparent connections may be quite significant. We need to learn to develop our keen observation skills so we can consciously search for connections that are overlooked otherwise. You can also invent connections between things that appear to have no relationships. This practice is particularly useful for investigating potential relationships that haven't been thought of before in order to create new ideas.

Discover Hidden Connections

Finding *hidden* connections are extremely valuable, as the benefits of this already-existing connection has clearly not been discovered and utilized yet. Focus your attention on looking for nonobvious relationships. When you find a hidden connection, you'll be rewarded for your effort by getting new insight into a successful outcome that stems from the new discovery.

Data mining is a term that means searching through large amounts of data to find new information. There is an often-quoted case study that shows how powerful using data mining can be for finding hidden connections.[1]

Sales data from a supermarket chain showed that every Friday afternoon there was a close relationship between customers who bought baby diapers and those who bought beer. This was a quite unexpected finding. Based on this new information, the chain's marketing department guessed that those customers were most likely young men who were new fathers. The marketing team reasoned that before the men became fathers they enjoyed drinking beer with friends at bars on Friday evenings. After their wives had babies, the men needed to stay at home to help their wives with taking care of their young children, but they didn't want to give up drinking on Friday nights. So, the reasoning went that when the new dads went to the store to buy diapers, they also tended to buy beer on the same store visit. If the marketing department's guess was right, why not move the beer next to the diapers to make it easier to find and see what happens? After the beer was moved beside the diapers, beer sales went up.

Before the marketing team saw the data mining results, superficially it appeared that diapers and beer sales were driven completely independently, but in reality, they had a close connection for the new father demographic which hadn't yet been noticed. If the supermarket manager had opened his mind and paid a little more attention, he might've seen this connection and found this new approach to increase beer sales. This example shows how helpful it can be to focus your attention on finding hidden relationships between different variables.

Another example of finding hidden relationships concerns posted gas prices at gas stations. Normally, gas stations advertise three prices for different grades of gas on their big signs: the price of regular gas, that of plus gas, and that of premium gas. In recent years, though, I have observed that many gas stations have begun to display only the price of regular gas, not plus or premium. This change was reasonable due to the fact that the gas prices are generally linked. In most cases, the price change from one grade to another stays at about twenty cents. The price difference between the grades has been so stable that most drivers assume this relationship based on years of going to gas stations. Since people know that the three prices are linked, an experienced driver can easily estimate the prices of plus or premium gas from that of regular gas. Given this, it would follow that showing all three gas prices is unnecessary. After switching to only advertising one price, gas stations have reduced the amount of work and time needed to modify the gas prices on their signs, resulting in cost, time, and energy savings every day. Thus, searching for hidden relationships facilitates the creation of beneficial and profitable new ideas.

Explore Benefits of Known Connections

While looking for hidden connections to stimulate new ideas, pay close attention to known relationships as well. Using a known connection between things in a new way can create valuable results. Here's an example.

An ad for a sugar-free candy appeared several years ago.[2] In the commercial, a lollipop blocked the route of a line of ants. Encountering the huge road block, the ants actually didn't climb over or otherwise touch the candy. Rather, the ant parade diverted around the candy and then back onto the original path. Everyone knows that ants love sugary food, and the ad effectively used their demonstration of ants avoiding their candy to convince viewers that the candy was indeed sugar-free.

The relationship between ants and sugar is well known; it's not hidden or easily missed. The ad designer capitalized on the well-known fact that ants love sugar to convey that the candy is sugar-free in a clear and memorable fashion.

Connecting to Create One-Way Benefits

After observing the existing relationships between variables in your problem, look for ways to build new connections between two different things that can generate positive, collaborative relationships. For example, certain bonds between two things allow for one of the elements to support the other, resulting in the latter benefiting from the connection in a way that did not exist before the connection was built. This type of connection can be created between things that have similarities or between things that have no associations at all.

A store in New York specializing in security products outsold its competitors by a large margin. But why did this store do so well? A careful look at the store revealed the answer quickly. Stores selling security items usually had product advertisements throughout the store and in the front windows hoping to stimulate business. However, this store chose to instead post unusual "advertisements" on its walls. The owner of the store had gone to the local police station and gathered wanted posters for robbers and thieves and hung them on the walls where product ads would normally be displayed. The wanted posters frequently included phrases such as "multiple time offender," or "specifically targets the elderly and children." These posters communicated a subtle message, intensifying the feeling of vulnerability, fear, and the need for keeping valuables safe, reinforcing a customer's desire to buy a device to protect and secure his valuables at home. In many cases, the customer immediately decided to buy a product because of this stimulation.[3]

This simple but significant connection between potential threats and the store's theft prevention products made this store very successful. The store owner's artistic thinking built a strong connection between the products in his store and the wanted posters, using the posters to help improve sales. Who says an open mind is not worth a lot of money?

Create a Mutually Beneficial Connection

If two things don't seem to have a relationship, or only have a loose connection, you can try to create or strengthen a link between them to mutually provide a new form of support for each other.

Having a cell phone is a necessity these days for most people. New generations of cell phones are constantly being introduced. Now, more advanced models become available not long after you purchase "the latest and greatest," stimulating you, the customer, to upgrade again and again. As a result, many people end up with obsolete mobile phones time and time again. Even though recycling programs are available, many old phones remain at home gathering dust or in landfills adding to toxic waste. What could encourage people to recycle their old phones?

A bank in Scotland introduced a unique recycling program called "Trade for a Tree" to incentivize people to recycle their old phones.[4] Pre-addressed cell phone recycling envelopes with free postage were placed on counters in the bank's branches. A conspicuous label in large print on the envelope read, "Recycle your old phone and name a tree." The simple instructions on the envelope stated, "Put your old cellular phone into the envelope, seal it, then mail it. You not only clean up your desk, but you also help save the environment. As a reward, you can name a tree in the Scotland forests after anyone you choose. You will receive a map and a certificate to show the location and the name of the tree."

The idea of connecting old cell phones to trees in a forest provided a mutual win-win situation. The first win was that more cell phones would be recycled and more materials could be reused. The second win was that it raised people's awareness of Scotland's environmental needs, resulting in protecting more forests. The ability to personally name a tree encouraged people to recycle their old cell phones. The inventor of the idea saw the great mutual benefits of this connection. This example shows how joint gains can be created by linking things in a supportive way. Can you think of an area to apply this principle?

Various Aspects of Building New Relationships

There are many aspects one can think about to build new connections between multiple things. New relationships can be established between things with similar properties, things with opposite properties, or things with no common properties. The focus in building new relations, however, must be on those which produce benefits. The following are a few examples.

Keeping loyal subscribers has been a challenging goal for almost all newspaper executives. In one case, the editor of a national newspaper faced this dilemma with an innovative mind. Many of his newspaper subscribers were due to renew their subscriptions at the end of the year. To convince his readers to continue their subscriptions, the editor decided to place an ad in his own paper. The ad didn't boast about the newspaper's high quality, but rather explained its $89.99 annual subscription price from a new perspective. The ad compared the price to the cost of a Texas steak dinner, a bottle of French red wine, or a portion of Italian prosciutto. Then the ad told readers that the major difference between consuming these luxurious foods and renewing their subscription for the same amount of money was that the food consumption was a one-time pleasure, whereas the newspaper subscription was enjoyable for an entire year. The comparison was striking. After considering the prices of the luxury foods, people were favorably inclined to think that the cost for the annual subscription of the newspaper was a very good deal. It's no surprise that many readers decided to continue their subscription after seeing this unique ad.

The newspaper editor cleverly linked the price of a subscription renewal to the prices of commonly recognized grocery items. Both were personal expenses, and the direct comparison strongly influenced subscribers' decisions. Here, the key step in designing the ad was to build a relationship between the prices of two of well-known purchases. This is a relatively easy way to link similar things when searching for new solutions to your problems.

Linking two things with opposing characteristics is not always easy, as they are often incompatible. However, building a relationship between opposing things is important to consider when exploring new ideas. Let's look at an example using a new relationship to reduce tension between people of different religions.

A mosque in a Virginian town needed more space for religious services because the Muslim population had grown so fast. While the imam and his followers were looking for a place to rent, the local Jewish synagogue heard of the need and offered to help. The two groups reached an agreement allowing the Muslim congregation to rent the synagogue's social hall for regular prayer services. The synagogue's kind offer not only solved the space problem but also made the Muslim worshippers feel accepted. From then on, the townspeople saw an interesting event every Friday. In the afternoons, Muslims would go to the synagogue with the Koran to conduct their main prayer service of the week. They took off their shoes, unrolled their rugs, knelt down and prayed in Arabic. In the evenings, Jewish worshippers went to the same synagogue with the Torah to conduct their service. They lighted candles and prayed in Hebrew. Obviously, it's quite unusual for Jews and Muslims to conduct their own religious activities under the same roof peacefully. Local and national newspapers heard about this and reported on the extraordinary, enviable situation.[5]

The close collaboration between people of different religions was rare yet beneficial to both groups and made the relationship between them comfortable, even harmonious. When a Muslim in the town encountered a Jew on the road, he may greet him with a Hebrew greeting, and the Jews may answer back with an Arabic greeting. The rabbi of the synagogue and the imam of the mosque even planned a trip to the Middle East together to share their story with the people there. Perhaps, when the people in that area hear the story, they'll gain some meaningful inspiration.

The ongoing conflict in the Middle East and the tension between Jews and Muslims inevitably affects people's views on the two religions' relationship. Influenced by this common belief, it was hard to imagine that Jewish religious leaders would invite Muslims to come to their synagogue to pray in Arabic. By the same token, it was also difficult to fathom that Muslims would be willing to worship Allah in a synagogue. But the rabbi, the imam, and the people they led were not bound by the status quo. Both sides extended their hands in friendship to one another and made peace by strengthening their connections and respecting their differences. They were open to compromise, to share and to accept each other. While some people still want to maintain isolation between Muslims and Jews, the rabbi and imam took initiative to build a bridge. This shows that developing new relationships between things with opposite properties is not only possible, but can also be very valuable.

But what about things that happen at different times and locations with no obvious connection? Several years ago, an award-winning photograph appeared online. The piece featured a museum visitor standing in front of a large photo of a 9/11 survivor's face. All we could see of the visitor was the back of his head, blocking the view of the middle and lower part of the survivor's face and leaving only the survivor's dusty cheek and bloodshot eyes to be seen. The work seemed to communicate the feeling that the museum visitor and the 9/11 survivor were talking to each other and searching for the truth behind the tragedy. The photograph's title is *Dialogue*. The piece left a profound impression on many people who saw it. It's not a surprise that the work won a gold award in a major photography competition.[6]

The visitor came to the museum at a completely different time from the moment that the survivor's image was taken on the day of the attack. The two events had no previous connection, but because the photographer took a photo of a museum visitor gazing at the survivor's face, the two events became closely linked. As the title of the work suggested, the "dialogue" between the two men was more of a visual interaction, one that doesn't need words. The resulting effect is definitely more powerful than any words could convey.

If you can't find a relationship between two sides of a problem, consider instead making them match each other to create a new relationship or to improving an existing connection. Here, we're using the word *matching* to mean adjusting one thing to better fit more the other.

At an airport near Houston, Texas, passengers complained about the waiting time required to retrieve their luggage after they arrived at the airport. To respond to this complaint, executives of the airport conducted an investigation. They found that the time a passenger spent walking from the arrival gate to the luggage carousal was much shorter than the amount of time for passengers' luggage to be delivered from the airplane to the carousel. It was inevitable that passengers had to wait to get their luggage. To improve the situation, the executives implemented an unconventional approach. Instead of reducing the time to deliver luggage, the airport increased the time it took for passengers to walk to the carrousel by changing the arrival gate locations. With this change, passengers and their luggage arrived at the carousel almost at the same time. Even though passengers had to walk farther to get to claim their luggage, surprisingly, the complaints significantly decreased.[7]

In this case, the airport executives solved the problem by matching the passenger walking time to the luggage delivery time. It's likely that the airport couldn't reduce the luggage delivery time much more, so it decided to add to the passengers' walking time to remove the difference of the two times.

As discussed above, relationships can be built between things with similar properties or opposite properties, between things happening at different times and locations, or by matching one thing to another. Even more ways can be devised to link things together using creative brainstorming.

Summary
Seeing relationships between things which initially seem unassociated will help you generate new ideas. The same is true with building new connections between things, especially between widely diverse things, to facilitate new solutions. Here are several ways to help search for new ideas using this approach:

- ☐ Search for hidden connections between different things to discover inconspicuous relationships, then think about their added benefits.
- ☐ Create a new connection between things from diverse fields. For example, build a connection between things that have happened at different times and/or locations, things that have similarities, opposite characteristics, or no relationships at all.
- ☐ Find a way to have two originally unrelated things match each other.
- ☐ When building a new relationship, consider having one end support the other, or both ends support each other.

6

Combine Things

The word *combination* means uniting two or more things to create a single entity. This is a common method for generating new solutions. However, an open mind is necessary to use this technique to produce superior and innovative results.

So, what kinds of things are ripe for creating new entities by combinations? Things that are radically different, completely unassociated, have contradictory characteristics, or fit other unconventional combinations are well within the realm of consideration for candidates. Many times, it's helpful to do thought experiments to check whether a particular combination is appropriate for the situation before spending too much time on actually implementing the combination. In this chapter, we'll present several suggestions to help you find clues to discover and create unique and effective new combinations. We hope these suggestions will give you a basis for expanding your ability to explore the world of successfully combining things in new ways.

Combine Things from Different Fields
A *field* typically refers to a specific area of knowledge or expertise. Individual concepts are usually directly associated with their own specific fields. Concepts of different fields normally have loose relationships. Here, we're using *different fields* to have more of a generalized meaning to refer to not only different areas of professional skill sets, but also different time periods or different geographic locations. A combination of concepts from

different fields may exhibit a mixed group of characteristics and have unique attributes which did not exist before. This is where great opportunity lies. By freeing yourself to associate disparate concepts and test them, you may generate a lot of original ideas.

After many years of biological research, human genes are finally starting to give up their secrets. Human genes are represented by long chemical chains commonly referred to as DNA. Although 99.9 percent of humans' DNA sequences are the same, there are enough unique sequences in each person to clearly distinguish one person from another. Today, it is commonplace to use a person's unique DNA sequences to determine a person's true identity. DNA is typically represented by a diagram composed of many short lines, and the color and position of the short lines represent the different sequences. When a person's genes are analyzed, the short lines, which represent the person's *unique* DNA sequences, are highlighted in the diagram. Since each individual has a unique DNA sequence, it then follows that each DNA diagram is unique as well. Just like there are no two people that are exactly the same, there are no two DNA diagrams that are identical.

Several years ago, a company, DNA11, introduced a new product onto the market: DNA artwork.[1] The company transforms personal biochemical DNA diagrams into beautiful, fascinating framed works of art. Since each individual's DNA sequence is different, the personalized DNA art is the equivalent of a person's portrait. After the company launched this new product it received many orders from all over the world. Many of these orders came from famous and important people who preferred to have a less obvious, but still genuine, picture of themselves on their walls. It's easy to obtain such artwork from the company. Anyone who wants to order their own DNA artwork just mails in a small saliva sample taken via a kit sent by the company. The company then sends the sample to a laboratory where the person's unique DNA sequences are identified and converted into a DNA diagram. Then the company transforms the DNA diagram into the final work of art.

Science and art are usually thought of as two completely different fields with little in common. Can biotechnology be married with art to result in something of great value? This may have been a question the founders of the company pondered while thinking about starting the business. Before the company created this extraordinary product, DNA diagrams were merely scientific documentation of experimental results in labs. Clearly, few if any people had ever looked at DNA data diagrams from an artist's perspective because the two fields seemed so far apart. What if someone else was innovative enough to use this chapter's Combine Things technique to put together something in science and something in art?

Combine Things with Big Differences

Things with nothing in common normally have few relationships to each other, as expressed by the law of attraction, "like attracts like." The large and the tiny, the heavy and the light, the classical and the modern—these opposites often do not cooperate well with one another. On the other hand, if we purposely put things with major contrasts together, then these contrasts can stand out. Since truly strong contrasts within something are rare, this kind of combination is quite conspicuous and people find the combination results in something new and fresh. If there is more value in the combination than just novelty, such combinations are worthy of pursuit.

In 2005, French dancer and choreographer Dominique Boivin created the unique dance "Exceptional Transportation," a duet performed with his dance partner.[2] The elegant dancing plus beautiful music made this performance quite popular after its initial debut. Furthermore, the dance was exceptionally unique since Boivin's dance partner was not a beautiful girl, but a large *digging machine* weighing more than five tons! The huge size of Boivin's "partner" required the performance be done at a construction site instead of on a normal stage. During the dance, Boivin seemed to be speaking words of love to his partner, displaying tender feelings towards her and even hugging the machine to show his love. The big machine behaved as if it was a lovely female companion. Boivin and the huge digging machine's seamless performance was cleverly coordinated. The show gave the impression that it was not just a dance, but a beautiful love story. It was met with great success and Boivin and his digging machine were invited to perform all over the world.

The dance was a combination of two partners with huge contrasts: the human male dancer and the mechanic "female" dancer. Among many other starkly different characteristics, the male dancer's body was soft while the female dancer's body was solid, the male comparatively tiny against his gigantic partner. However, Boivin expertly fused the two together into a very special duet. The resulting tremendous differences between the male dancer and female dancer did not hinder the expression of the meaning of the story, but rather led the audience to wonder at the unprecedented beauty that came from the contrast. How Boivin designed his dance is a compelling example for the concept of combining two things with enormous contrasts to become something that's actually quite beautiful and unique.

Combine Unrelated Things

Generally, two things that are completely independent of each other have no relationship. If we forcefully put two irrelevant things together, the combination usually generates something strange, and people aren't normally attracted to strange things. But what if the strange result has an attractive side? In that case, the situation may be different and the strangeness has some real value. Why not pursue these types of curiosities?

Angry Birds is a video game that was first released in 2009.[3] The main characters in the game are a flock of birds and a group of pigs of various colors and sizes. In the game's main storyline, the pigs steal eggs from the birds and hide the eggs in their pig pens, causing the birds to become angry enough to want to destroy the pig pens and kill the pigs so they can retrieve their eggs. To play the game, a player uses a slingshot to launch birds at pigs stationed in or around the pig pens constructed of various materials such as stone, wood, and glass. The goal is to hit the pigs directly or to damage the pig pens so they collapse and crush the pigs. A player needs to estimate how far back the elastic strap must be pulled and at what angle a bird should be launched to get the desired result. For example, if the band is not pulled far enough then the bird may land short of the structure. Or, if the launch angle isn't set correctly, the bird may fly over the pig pen instead of striking it. The motion of the bird obeys the laws of physics. The initial speed, launch angle, and gravity determine the flight trajectory of a bird. The game became very popular after its debut and was praised as one of the great runaway hits of 2010.

The basic architecture of this successful game is a combination of captivating animated birds and boring laws of science. Normally, there is no connection between cartoon characters and people using the laws of physics. Video games belong to modern technology, and the Newton's Laws came into being over five hundred years ago. It was the game's development team that combined the two dissimilar fields together to create the addictive video entertainment. Combining new video game technology with old boring science together for the sake of interactive entertainment shows the development team's open-mindedness. Therefore, strive to combine things which don't have any apparent relationships. You may find an idea for a game or something else that becomes even more successful than Angry Birds!

Combine Opposites

What might happen if you combine two things with opposite properties? Online videos are a common example. Oftentimes, you have to watch an advertisement clip before you can watch a particularly interesting video. In this case the two videos counterbalance each other and result in additional business value. You can form completely new concepts by combining two things with opposite properties together, but this is only effective so long as you don't only consider each part by itself.

About forty years ago, two professors, Frank Barnes and George Codding, at the University of Colorado at Boulder proposed their idea to combine engineering and non-engineering courses into a single master's degree program, according to *IEEE Institute*.[4] The proposal obtained support from the school and soon the concept became reality. This program is open to students with a bachelor's degree in almost any major. Students enrolled in the program take electrical engineering and computer science courses along with courses in business and law. The goal of the program is to prepare future leaders with well-rounded knowledge that's critical for making decisions or forming policies. The program has proven to be very successful and has graduated thousands of students, many of whom have become outstanding contributors in diverse fields according to a report from the Institute of Electrical and Electronics Engineers.

In the early seventies, when the program was first being proposed, engineering and non-engineering disciplines were seen as two independent and opposite categories of study. People had not considered an idea like this before, much less having those specific kinds of programs combined. There was a need for out-of-the-box stimulation to propose the idea. On the other hand, any engineering or business school professor could have proposed the same concept and converted the idea into successful programs. Why had so few faculty members ever thought of it? Besides other reasons, a lack of explicit consideration of combining two opposite elements to create a new entity was probably one of the main reasons.

The example above shows how uniting two elements with opposite traits can create a new and valuable program which may last for decades or centuries. The same method can be applied to making new combinations that may only last a few seconds. Here's a perfect example.

As autonomous vehicles are beginning to gain mainstream acceptance, people have begun to worry about new risks robotic vehicles may create, such as accidentally hitting pedestrians on the road. To deal with this potential safety problem, inventors at tech giant Google came up with a unique solution. They suggested coating a layer of very sticky adhesive to the front part of the car with a thin protection layer covering the adhesive to avoid exposing it. If the car hit a person on the street, the collision's impact would break the protective layer and expose the sticky adhesive. The adhesive layer would hold the victim to the front of the car immediately, just like flypaper holding a fly, thus preventing the victim from falling onto the road or beneath the wheels. Consequently, the victim wouldn't become injured any further from the accident. The invention gained a lot of public attention and several national news media outlets reported on this remarkable solution.[5]

In a car-pedestrian crash, the vehicle and the pedestrian are a pair of counterparts with opposite traits. But the Google inventors combined the two, resulting in one solution for when a self-driving vehicle strikes a pedestrian. This idea is exceptional as it's unusual to think about bonding two opposites together. The idea is also very valuable, because even though the combination may only last for a few seconds, the effect may be the key factor governing the victim's life or death situation. Though the usefulness of this invention has yet to be determined, the thought process used in creating this idea is worthy to study and practice.

Combine Things That Already Have Relationships

Combinations are not limited to things that typically aren't related. If two things already have a well-understood relationship, such as two sequential steps in a process or two items that rely on each other to work, it's still useful to consider whether they can be put together into a single step or a single item. One of the main motivators for this type of combination is to simplify things. Simplification usually is viewed as an improvement.

In the middle of the last decade, many hotels introduced a new service which provided increased convenience to their customers. The hotels installed special communication channels directly to airlines' data centers. With these connections, travelers could quickly check in for their flights and get boarding passes in the hotel lobby rather than hassling with the lines at airport check-in counters. With the new service, travelers were able to go to the security check points directly with boarding passes printed out in hotel lobbies, thus saving time and frustration for travelers. The new service was whole-heartedly accepted by the traveling public.[6]

Previously, checking out of a hotel and checking in for a flight at an airport were two different processes. The two separate activities were linked by the sequence in which they happened—checkout must happen *before* a traveler can check in to board an aircraft. But, since travelers needed to go through each of the two processes anyway, why shouldn't the two processes be put together into a single compressed process? The resulting combination benefited everyone: efficiency and convenience for the traveler, reduced lines at the ticket counters for the airlines, and customer perks for the hotels. Perhaps this was the motivation to try to combine the separate activities in the first place. Thinking this way can be applied to many other processes, too.

Combine Different Attributes

Combining multiple individual things can often build a synergistic result, or, a unique feature. The value of the synergy between the individual things cannot be realized until *after* they are combined. Considering the merits of every individual item at one time can lead to a reason to try the combination.

For example, some performers combined ballet and acrobatics to create an acrobatic ballet. Acrobatics lend superb physical strength and coordination, while ballet contributes grace and sensitivity. Audience members now can enjoy the best of both types of art in the same performance. The individual merits of ballet and acrobatics were known for many years before and it wasn't too difficult to put the two together to generate a new form of dance. However, only the people who actually turned the combination into a performance made the concept a reality.

Chinese sociologist Li Yinhe fondly remembers the early days of her courtship with her late husband Wang Xiaobo, a renowned novelist and essayist, according to *Readers*, a Chinese magazine similar to the American *Reader's Digest*.[7] She especially recalled the love letters that Wang wrote to her when he was only her boyfriend. Surprisingly, his love letters were not written on ordinary paper but on musical staff paper. In one letter he wrote: "Wishing our love is just like a song, a never ending song to sing." Written on music paper, the staff lines added a clear sense of beautiful musicality, and the love letter's words complemented it with a warm expression of intimacy.

Wang had a great idea to combine two beautiful things together to produce an extraordinarily memorable love letter. He must have thought about how he could show his feelings by using two familiar artistic methods to achieve a unique expression of his affection. After receiving such beautiful and expressive love letters, how could Li fail to fall in love with him?

Summary

When you want to further open your mind to look for new ideas, here's another way to help you do so. Combining two or more different things may create something new and beneficial. The following are several areas you can consider:

☐ Combine things from different fields.
☐ Associate two widely contrasting things.
☐ Put totally unassociated things together.
☐ Marry two things with opposite characteristics.
☐ Fuse things with existing relationships.

Think About Differences

Typically, comparing any two things will identify some differences between them, because no two things are exactly the same. In the case when the comparison seemingly doesn't expose any differences, looking even deeper usually reveals differences that weren't initially apparent. Actively looking for subtle differences at a more-detailed level can lead to a more comprehensive perspective that can stimulate new and valuable thinking. The specific traits of an item or the aspects of an action are just two exemplary areas to discover small differences. Pay careful and thorough attention to intricate differences when observing something. By intentionally examining things for inconspicuous differences, more opportunities for progress toward new solutions will appear.

Thinking about differences not only includes finding hidden differences but also incorporates the creation of new differences. One of the most important methods to help promote an innovative mind is differentiation. In practice, differentiation shows original thinking as opposed to mundane thinking. It's common for a company to advertise how it's different from, but better than, its competitors by demonstrating its alternative business practices. Remember creating differences among similar things is a common way to generate new solutions. Brand new product designs or fresh approaches to tough situations may appear while introducing new differences.

Notice Different Perspectives

It's common for activities to include fine differences in aspects, such as who will execute it, how it will be executed, and towards whom it will be directed. Each aspect can be different in different situations. These differences normally lead to different results. Taking advantage of the differences is only possible when the differences are exposed, otherwise they remain unknown. Therefore, investigate various aspects of an activity to find the differences, such as people's different standpoints, different requirements, different intentions, and so on. The more differences you discover, the more information you'll have that can aid you in creating new ideas.

Making posters is a common activity that students do for classes. Normally, blank poster boards have no guidelines printed on them, since a printed grid is distracting after a poster is completed. When students prepare a poster, they like to include attractive pictures, photos, lettering, and other materials, but since there is no grid on the board it's difficult to orient the display materials precisely. One way to solve the problem is to use a ruler and pencil to draw a temporary grid. Then, the lines of the grid must be erased after the student mounts the materials. Obviously, erasing is a tedious process.

In 1994, a mother in Texas was helping her daughter prepare a poster for school and encountered the same mounting orientation problem. She wanted to find a better way to do the job and that night she experienced an "Aha!" moment in a dream. Why not print a faint, fine-lined grid on poster boards? The grid would be so faint, it could only be seen when very close to the board and would be invisible from a greater distance. Students using these faint-grid poster boards can see the grid clearly while preparing their posters because they're quite near the board, but the people who come to view the posters wouldn't be able to see the grid while standing so far away from the board, creating the illusion of a blank background. The idea was patented and the new design became a commercial product. Students loved the poster board with the "invisible grid" so much that the poster board company has become a multimillion-dollar business.[1]

It's likely that the student's mother suddenly realized that although a student and a visitor both see a poster board, the distance from which a student sees a poster and the distance from which a visitor sees the same poster are different. After noticing the difference in distances, she came up with an approach to make a grid that would be visible at shorter distances and invisible at longer distances. Teachers, parents, and students everywhere had confronted this problem many times before without devising a good solution. If someone had paid a little bit more attention to the difference between a student's perspective and a visitor's perspective, this unique poster board idea might have been invented a long time ago. This example shows the importance of noticing differences related to perspectives. Such differences can frequently lead to unexpected benefits.

Differences in Time

Many subtle differences are related to time. If something is done at this time or that time, or is done for short time or a long time, the results will likely be different. Therefore, when observing inconspicuous differences between things, don't forget to take into consideration the factor of time.

About seventeen hundred years ago, a clever young man, Sun Liang, ruled the kingdom Wu in the Orient. One pleasant afternoon, the king was visiting his royal garden that was filled with fruit trees. He noticed the plum trees had ripe fruit, so he ordered his attendant to collect a few for a delicious snack. The attendant promptly picked several of the best and presented them to the king. As the king was about to pop one into his mouth, the attendant suggested that he add some honey from the royal storage room so the snack would be even more splendid. The king thought that was a good idea. The attendant rushed to the storage room and returned with a bowl of honey. When the king dipped a juicy plum into the golden liquid, he noticed a few strange objects in the honey. They resembled rice grains with some black specks on them. He asked the attendant to take a closer look. The attendant examined it and quickly reported that the grains looked like mouse droppings. The king immediately became incensed and requested that the storehouse keeper be brought before him since it obviously looked like the storehouse keeper's fault.

When the trembling storehouse keeper nervously approached the king and heard the story, he emphatically replied, "No, good king! That is not possible! I carefully monitor all of the items every single morning when I come to work and again in the evening before I retire! I am very sorry this unfortunate thing happened and it displeases you so, but it was not done by my hand."

Judging by the innocent look on the poor storehouse keeper's sweating face, the king considered that it might not be his fault after all. The only other possibility was that the droppings somehow got into the honey while the attendant was bringing it from the storehouse. If that was the case, then the attendant should be held accountable. Neither man would admit that they were guilty though. So how could the king resolve this dilemma?

The king thought deeply for a while, then asked the attendant to fetch him a small stick. The king used the stick to pull out one of the mouse droppings from the bowl and laid it on a piece of white cloth. Next, he used his dagger to slice it in half and then summoned everyone to observe the divided sections closely. The outer layer of the dropping was damp, but the core was dry. The king took a step back and looked at the attendant who immediately cowered. He was exposed and had to admit his guilt. The defeated man knelt down and pled for the king's forgiveness. When asked why he would do such a thing to the king, he tearfully told the king it was because he had asked the storehouse keeper for some free honey. But the storehouse keeper had refused him, so the attendant wanted to retaliate. He thought dumping a few mouse droppings in the pot of honey would do the trick and get the storehouse keeper into serious trouble. Little did he know the plan would backfire due to the ingenuity of the wise king.[2]

When the king saw the mouse droppings in the honey, it seemed impossible to determine how the disgusting things got there. The king figured out that the key step to find the truth was discovering the time when the droppings came in contact with the honey. If it was the storehouse keeper's fault, the grain would've been in the honey for a long time, causing the whole grain to be damp. If it was the attendant's fault, the grain must have only recently been dropped into the honey. Consequently, the grain would have a damp outer layer and a dry core. Slicing the grain revealed the truth. By looking at differences resulting from time, the king answered a difficult question. So, seek to improve the ability to see hidden differences with respect to time.

Take Advantage of Observed Differences

Similar to differences related to time, differences related to space or location are important characteristics to observe as well. Cultural and environmental differences between countries are particularly apparent to people who travel often. Each country has differences from other countries that are peculiar to it. The words on advertising signs, the way locals express greetings, and the design of buildings are generally different from those of other countries. The customs' differences reflect unique historical distinctions. Besides these obvious differences observed by almost everyone, tiny differences can only be noticed by the few people who are sensitive to them. People who develop valuable new solutions based on small differences found in different places are even fewer.

In 2002, a young businessman travelled to Shanghai. When he was waiting for the elevator in a shopping mall, he noticed a distinct detail. Compared with elevator waiting times in other modern cities, the waiting time for the Shanghai elevator was much longer. Even when he finished reading the advertisements posted at the side of the elevator door, the elevator had not yet arrived. That is not surprising. Shanghai is a rapidly growing city, with many people pouring into the city to find their fortunes. Consequently, it shouldn't be surprising that the elevators' capacities to accommodate the vast influx of people was overwhelmed and therefore created longer waiting times. This triggered an idea: why not replace the printed media ads with video ads? His instincts told him that people would love video ads to occupy the long time while waiting for elevators. With this inspiration, he quickly moved forward with the idea and formed an advertising company focusing on video ads in China. In several years, his company extended its businesses into nearly one hundred cities. His video screens have been installed in elevators, airports, bars, hospitals, and more. By 2008, the company had attracted many international companies eager to develop businesses in China. The company subsequently issued a successful IPO on the Nasdaq stock exchange.[3]

Even back in 2002, the numbers of businessmen who visited Shanghai and experienced the long waits for elevators were probably in the tens of thousands. Of those thousands, it's likely that only a handful of people noticed the waiting time was particularly long there. Among those few who noticed the extended waits, the young businessman probably was the only one who took advantage of his observation of this difference between Shanghai and other modern cities by building a successful video advertising company. This story illustrates a case where paying attention to differences in location resulted in a highly valuable opportunity. If more people used their powers of observation this way, perhaps they too would go on to create high value assets from their discoveries. Therefore, be more aware of differences in order to help create productive new ideas.

Situational Differences

Many times, something will behave differently when it's exposed to different situations. This seems obvious, but these differences may not always be noticed in real world situations. The following example explains this concept.

There is a story about a cook and his master told by Giovanni Boccaccio in *The Decameron*.[4] One day, the master went hunting and killed a crane to bring home to eat. He asked his cook to make a special dish out of the crane for dinner so he could entertain his friends who were visiting. The cook prepared the crane with savory spices and a wonderful aroma wafted out of the kitchen window. The irresistible smell attracted a woman from the neighborhood to the cook's kitchen. When the woman saw the exquisitely prepared bird ready to eat, she implored the cook to let her taste the crane meat. The cook told her he couldn't give her a taste because he would suffer his master's wrath if he was caught, but the woman was persistent since she knew the cook had a crush on her. She threatened to never see him again if he didn't let her sample the crane dish immediately.

The cook struggled with the dilemma, but eventually chose to follow his heart and not his head. He cut off a leg of the crane and gave it to the woman. Then he quickly took the rest of the crane dish to the master's dinner table. His master noticed right away that one crane leg was missing. The master asked the cook why the leg was missing. Surprisingly, the cook responded to his master in a very calm voice, "Sir, cranes have only one leg, not two."

The master did not expect the cook to answer his question this way. The cook's explanation sounded preposterous because everyone knew that cranes have two legs. But sometimes cranes stand on one leg while the other one is hidden under its body, making it appear to have only one leg. The master was furious, but tried not to lose his composure in front of his guests. He told the cook, "Since that is the case, I will show you how many legs a crane actually has. Tomorrow morning, we will go to the river and observe the cranes. Now you may go." The poor cook was promptly dismissed from the dining room. He feared punishment for his brash statement was unavoidable.

The next morning, at the crack of dawn, the master went with the cook to the river. When they arrived, sure enough they saw a flock of cranes resting peacefully, each one standing on one leg. The cook jumped with joy and wildly exclaimed to the master, "Look sir! Each crane has only one leg! Don't you see it?" The master responded, "I'm going to show you how many legs they really have in a few seconds!" The master quickly rode up to the cranes waving his arms vigorously and yelling at the birds. The cranes immediately stirred, lowered their other legs, and flew away in haste. After the master caught his breath and returned, he asked the cook contemptuously, "Now what do you say?"

Undeterred, the cook replied, "If only you had yelled at the crane last evening, that frightened crane would have shown his second leg as well." Hearing the cook's witty answer, the master laughed and decided not to punish him.

Initially, the cook felt there was no way to escape punishment for his deed. But the cook noticed the subtle difference between the previous evening's scenario and that morning: his master didn't try to agitate the crane at the dinner table, but this morning his master yelled and chased the cranes. The situations *were* different! The cook cleverly used the difference to come up with an excuse to save himself from punishment. The tale inspires us that recognizing differences in situations is not only good for generating excuses, but also useful for producing new solutions.

As indicated above, there are differences in time, location, and situation to be discovered. There are also many other differences we need pay attention to, such as nuances in size, shape, requirements, and so on. In short, spotting overlooked, hidden, or slight differences in important areas will provide soil for growing of new ideas.

There is no doubt that the discovery of overlooked differences is important in finding new solutions, but proactively generating differences between things can also be equally important. Similar to seeing differences, there are many ways of creating new differences. The following is a series of examples that delve deeper into this topic.

Generate Differences in Actions

To generate differences in an action, think about the action before it is executed. First, consider how others act in a similar situation, and then think about how to avoid doing exactly what others do. The idea is to focus on discovering a *new* way to perform an action which leads to *better* results. Analyze the drawbacks of the ordinary implementation of an action and then try to determine how it can be improved by using a different approach.

A famous actress was once an ordinary factory worker. Although she had loved the performing arts since childhood, she had never had an opportunity to show her natural talents. One day, a friend's encouraging words inspired her to pursue her dream of acting in movies. She signed up for an enrollment audition to enter a film school even though the acceptance rate to the film academy was very low. More than two thousand candidates were competing for only a dozen positions. The competition was fierce, and only the very best would be accepted.

Her talents allowed her to pass the two initial tests and won the opportunity to take the third and final test. In this audition, the candidates' live performances would be evaluated. One of the scenarios in the audition was to perform what would happen if the candidate returns home after a severe earthquake to find all their loved ones killed and their home destroyed. Standing in front of the ruins, the candidate was to begin their performance. This scenario was designed to test a candidate's spontaneous performance skills and inner passion.

The young factory worker watched the candidates who performed before her, each performing their own interpretation. These candidates all expressed their enormous grief and sadness at losing loved ones and having their homes destroyed. Many of them screamed agonizingly in pain, and others dug through the ruins desperately.

Then it was her turn.

She walked slowly toward the front of the ruins and slowly sat down. Her anguished expression and posture conveyed grief and profound sadness. Her wide, melancholy eyes stared up towards the sky. Not uttering a word nor making a sound, silent tears trickled down her cheeks. She just sat there, quietly crying with a heart swollen with so much emotion, not moving. Although she said nothing, nor did any sound come from her throat, her vivid performance clearly evoked the atmosphere of desperation and tragedy. Poignantly acting out the touching scene, it appeared as if she was asking, "God, why did this happen? Why inflict so much unspeakable pain upon us? We are good people. Why did you take away everything I've held dear? I am devastated." Her unique performance greatly exceeded the director's expectations and even those of the other seasoned members of the evaluation committee. She received a high score for the audition and, to no one's surprise, was accepted to the film academy. Years later, she became a superstar in the movie industry.[5]

In the scenario of a severe earthquake, most candidates immediately thought about similar disaster scenes where people showed their grief by wailing or sobbing and digging in the rubble to recover valuables. Most candidates had tried to mimic these scenes commonly seen in real earthquake events. She took a different approach. The young worker found a way to make her performance different and better than the others by thinking deeper about the situation than the other candidates did. She knew she had to stand out in the intense competition, and she had to make her performance reach an extraordinary level. The candidate must have thought that a disaster brought by an earthquake did not just spell the loss of lives and demolish buildings, but also could be a devastating blow to one's faith in life itself. Disasters make people feel powerless over their destiny. Based on this profound understanding, a brilliant performance shouldn't just be about mourning the loss of loved ones and property but should also show how people could be traumatized by the earthquake, even enough to question God. Obviously, her performance, built on the foundation of her deep understanding and interpretation of the harm caused by earthquakes, allowed her to be better the other candidates.

Before taking action, think about the situation more intently. Take the opportunity to uniquely differentiate that action to improve it from the ordinary, making it stand out.

Differentiate Using Measurements

Use measurable indicators to differentiate as a means to sense whether the benefits of employing that differentiation are better than typical results. For example, if a task is usually completed in a certain amount of time, will finding a way to shorten the time by 10 or 20 percent make a difference? Or, if a user manual for a product is being written in a technical manner, is there a way to simplify it to improve a customer's learning curve by 30 or 50 percent? Stimulate your original thinking by considering how to make something faster, how to save more time, how to reduce a footprint, or how to simplify a process to make a beneficial difference.

In the early part of the 1980s, a young man became a new employee in the sales department of a company. In the department offices, there was a telephone on each salesman's desk, but all salesmen shared a single telephone number. When a call came in, every phone would ring at the same time. The unspoken rule in the sales department was that whoever picked up a customer's call first got to follow up with that customer. Before the man joined the department, each salesman had similar revenues because the chance of answering an incoming call was about the same for everyone. After this man joined the department, the situation changed.

Other salesmen gradually developed a feeling that the new salesman possessed some kind of secret weapon because he was acquiring more customers than anyone else in the department. At the end of the year, his total revenue was much higher than the second-highest salesman. His achievement puzzled everyone. Even if he wasn't new at the job, an experienced salesman would have had a difficult time racking up these kinds of sales figures. What was his secret? When colleagues asked him this question, he always smiled but revealed nothing. Many years later, during a sales team meeting at his own company, he finally revealed his secret. The trick was extremely easy and simple: whenever he was in his office, he always worked with one hand on the phone so that whenever it rang, he was sure to be the first to answer. It's no wonder he stood out with the most sales![6]

Let's review: He was the new on the job and was aware that his lack of experience could potentially put him at a disadvantage to his peers. He wanted to get an upper hand, so he looked for a way to differentiate himself to be the best salesman in the office. He figured the best way to distinguish himself was to make a difference in the speed of picking up the phone. Since all phones rang at the same time, when his colleagues reached for the phone after they heard it ring he had a big head start on answering the call because his hand was constantly ready on the phone. The difference gave him at least a fraction of a second's advantage in the time it took to pick up the phone. Don't underestimate the valuable effect of small time differences. The fraction of a second was the key for him to win the title as the best salesman.

Differentiate by Standing Out

You can also use unconventional approaches to create differences that achieve better results. People are used to seeing ordinary approaches every day. When they unexpectedly encounter a new, different approach, people typically take note of it and find it appealing. A fresh approach to a situation attracts more attention, even though its effects are yet unknown. Although the increased attention alone isn't a solution itself, it can be a good stepping stone to find one.

A national TV network needed to hire a female hostess while preparing to launch a new program series. One of the candidates was a college senior who was nearing graduation. She loved being in front of the camera and her professors encouraged her to audition for the job. There were many competitors vying for the position, so her odds of winning seemed to be low. The TV network called all the candidates together for an interview. The program's director told them the interview would be quite simple: Each candidate would come onto the stage one by one and introduce herself. The candidates then could talk about anything related to themselves, such as past experiences, friends, family, etc. When the director said "Next," that would mean the candidate's interview was finished.

When the interviews began, the college student watched the other candidates introduce themselves one by one. Most of the candidates' introductions were so similar that she became bored and guessed that the director probably felt the same way. Then it was her turn. After walking onto the stage, she didn't introduce herself, nor did she talk about her experiences. Instead, she decided to take a risk and turn the tables on the director. She asked, "When you are planning to make a hiring decision, what is the real purpose of the position? Are you planning to use the hostess's understanding and intelligence to enrich the program, or are you just looking for someone attractive to act as decoration?"

The director didn't expect a young candidate to ask such penetrating questions, and his interest in her increased immediately. He didn't answer her questions but asked her to continue. She then used the opportunity to explain that a TV hostess shouldn't be merely eye candy, and that there have been many intelligent women throughout history who have added major value to their endeavors when included on the intellectual side of the team, not just the aesthetics. Therefore, no matter who won the competition that day, the winner should have all these traits. Her words impressed the director and made her stand out from the crowd of candidates. The director immediately decided that the college student should enter the next phase of the screening process. She was eventually hired for the position and began a quite successful career in television.[7]

When the director required every candidate to introduce herself, the student thought about how to differentiate herself to catch the director's attention. Taking a risk, she ignored the director's instructions and instead discussed her opinions about the role of a female television personality. One way or the other, she was sure to draw the director's attention with this uncommon way to respond. She could've been eliminated immediately if the director hadn't liked her approach. Luckily, her approach made the director recognize that she had an intelligent, open mind that could provide extraordinary and valuable insights. It's likely that the director hired her just because of these special qualities that were revealed when she refused to follow his directions so rigidly. Using an uncommon approach frequently works to attract attention.

As shown above, new differences can be generated by digging deeper into a meaning, setting a faster pace, adding extra efforts, or refusing to follow an assignment. Differentiation can also be generated by considering possible differences in social attitudes, job efficiency, product quality, design requirements, and more. Think about using different methods to handle the same task in different scenarios or enhancing an existing difference to make it more noticeable.

Reversed Scenarios: Remove Differences

Even though the main focus of this chapter talks about how to stimulate creative minds by observing subtle differences or proactively creating differences, the reverse of this method shouldn't be overlooked either. In some situations, hiding or removing differences between things can be just as powerful.

On October 26, 2015, the police were called in to investigate two groups of teenagers fighting on a street in Washington, D.C. The police broke up the fight and asked the teens to leave the area. A seventeen-year-old girl walked up to an officer and started dancing to the hip-hop song "Nae Nae" playing on her phone. The teens were startled when, instead of being provoked, the female officer accepted the girl's implied challenge and challenged her to a dance contest. The officer said that if the girl won the teens could stay, but if the officer won the teens would have to leave. The girl agreed to the challenge and the two started hip-hop dancing face-to-face.

In just a few minutes, it was clear that the officer was the superior dancer. As agreed, all the teenagers left the area and a potentially violent confrontation was avoided. News about this unique conflict resolution received a flood of positive comments. The D.C. police chief praised the response as a good example of positive police-community interactions. President Obama applauded the police officer on Twitter, saying he didn't know community policing could involve the Nae Nae. Even the teenage girl said that she never expected cops to be that cool. Her statement implied that her negative feelings toward police had been softened by the experience. The news raised hope for continued better relations between police and the communities they serve, according to an article in *Washington Post*.[8]

Most people would agree that teenage hip-hop dancers on the street and police officers have almost nothing in common. The police officer in D.C. decided to remove one big difference to reduce the social distance between the two of them. Perhaps the officer searched for where their differences could be turned positive, thinking, "You can dance, but I can dance, too. This is one area where we don't have differences." When the initial focus on differences was replaced with commonality, communication became easier. In turn, the mutual respect fostered by better communication prevented the situation from escalating. The officer's challenge to a dance competition was an innovative and effective idea. If more police officers would try to get closer to citizens by reducing or eliminating unnecessary differences, our communities would be stronger and safer.

Summary
Inconspicuous differences that are especially subtle may provide a jumping-off point for generating fresh ideas. Try to identify concealed

differences associated with a target of interest, as it can help generate unique and beneficial ideas that are often hidden from others.

Creating differences is another important method to expand your open-minded thinking. Differentiation is one of the major aspects of creating distinctions. When trying to generate differences, look beyond the commonplace to help yourself achieve expanded thinking. The following are several exemplary ways to search for new ideas using differences:

☐ Pay attention to the different results of an activity due to different implementers, different targets, or different processes of the activity.

☐ Note different effects caused by different times or locations.

☐ Recognize favorable differences in circumstances, conditions, situations, requirements, relationships, and so on.

☐ Be particularly careful to look for subtle differences since they are inconspicuous.

☐ Create a difference between two things which were originally the same, or, enhance their existing differences.

☐ Look for a measurable benchmark to create a positive difference. Search for opportunities to make valuable differences in efficiency, quality, performance, etc.

☐ Don't overlook reverse-case scenarios where differences can be reduced or removed for taking advantages.

8

Apply Diverse Concepts

When a concept plays an important role in one area, it may apply similarly in another area where it hasn't been used before. After exhausting possible solutions to a problem in its native field, remember that there are many other fields rich in concepts that may apply to the problem. It is advantageous to convert a foreign concept to be appropriate to solve the problem in the original field.

A good example of this kind of cross-fertilization happened shortly after Apple introduced the iPod. Originally, iPods were mostly used by young people for listening to music. Later, professors and college students found wider applications for this new gadget in education. The iPod allowed one to record and playback lectures, which meant it was no longer an issue for a student to miss a class. In this case, the music field's concept of preserving and reproducing live content on the iPod was borrowed and applied to the field of education.[1]

The definition of an *area* has a generally broad meaning. It may represent a field, a physical object, the subject of an action, a time period, a location, etc. Considering ideas from other areas, in addition to those that are familiar, increases the potential to generate new solutions. It also adds another useful element for building a creative mind.

Apply a Method to a New Target

A method usually has a specific focus and affects objects associated with that focus. But can you borrow a method that's normally focused on something else and apply it to positively affect something associated with your current problem? Can the method provide similar advantages if used on the current object of interest? It's helpful to ask these questions when searching for an effective, applicable method to a current situation. Discovering methods applied to other targets that fit into the immediate problem space can produce amazing results. Therefore, constantly be on the lookout for methods that are usually applied to other objects to see if some of them can be applied to the present target.

In the 1980s, *Star Wars* proposed a laser weapon called the Death Star for their ballistic missile defense program. The laser system would instantly destroy the enemy's missiles or other space targets. Even though *Star Wars* has been significantly changed and absorbed into other programs today, the method of using lasers to destroy enemy forces is still being pursued. Recently, the US military applied this fictional *Star Wars* concept to naval and aircraft targets.

In 2010, ex-Microsoft executive Nathan Myhrvold publicly demonstrated a new mosquito-fighting machine that was developed by his new company.[2] The system looked just like a miniature version of the Death Star. It could accurately detect the position of a flying mosquito and shoot it down in midair with a laser beam. In his demonstration, a mosquito flying in a glass box was detected and killed, resulting in a smoking mosquito falling to the bottom of the box. The system was smart enough to only attack mosquitoes, not butterflies or people. It could even distinguish male from female mosquitoes according to the beat frequency of the mosquito's wings. Since only female mosquitoes bite humans, the machine could spare the male mosquitoes while killing only females. The system was efficient, fast, and deadly, claiming to be able to kill up to one hundred mosquitoes per second. The machine could be installed near a house or on an agricultural field to create an invisible protective fence around the area where mosquitoes would not be able to invade without being destroyed. Mosquitos are the main source of malaria, especially in Africa. The disease kills about one million people each year. Myhrvold hoped his machine could be a new weapon to help people fight the deadly disease.

It's said the idea of using lasers to shoot mosquitoes came from a scientist involved in the *Star Wars* project. Missiles and mosquitoes, even though both can fly, are quite different things. If a laser beam is able to shoot down flying missiles in space, why couldn't it be used to shoot down flying mosquitoes? It's probable that the mosquito killer idea was born when the scientist thought about the *Star Wars* concept. By applying the laser destruction method to a very different target, an innovative new mosquito defense system was developed. Applying a method focused on one target to a new target can be powerful, can't it?

Apply Something to a Different Purpose

Most things are used for specific purposes. For example, a watch is used for telling time, a ring is used for showing marriage status, a badge is used for introducing oneself. Open-minded thinking includes considering new purposes for something beyond how it's normally employed. Can something for entertainment be used for education or healthcare? Can something used in the military be used in civilian activities as well? These types of questions inspire the creation of new ideas.

When people check in their luggage at airports, they frequently wonder if their baggage will arrive undamaged at their destination. Even though airports try their best to carefully handle passengers' luggage during flights, damage does happen. The materials used to manufacture luggage are meant to be durable, but because of rough handling, passengers occasionally find damage on their bags at the carousels. To solve this long-standing problem, the owner of a Taiwan-based baggage manufacturing company, Crown Luggage, got an idea when he saw a security guard wearing a bulletproof vest. From this idea, he created a new development plan for his products. In his new plan, bulletproof materials—not normal suitcase materials—would be used to manufacture briefcases and travel bags. It turned out to be an excellent choice. The new product survived a series of tough tests, including powerful hammer blows and overweight people standing on it. After the product was released, it proved to be quite popular among frequent travelers.[3]

Bulletproof material is mainly used for stopping bullets, just as its name indicates. A vest made from the material is able to protect the person who wears it from being hurt by bullets or shell fragments. But the owner of this luggage company used the military material for quite a different purpose. As a matter of fact, the owner's idea was very sensible. As the material can endure the impact of bullets, luggage made with the material should easily survive a very rough journey during air travel. No wonder the new briefcases were so warmly welcomed after being released to the market. Therefore, ignore all known purposes for an object and search for one or more new ways to use it. A great idea may result from it.

Apply an Approach from Another Situation

A technique has a normal environment where it is usually applied. In this environment, its effects can be easily predicted because they are well known. Moreover, if the technique is applied in a *different* environment, it's entirely possible that similar beneficial effects may be seen as well. Always look for positive results from using a technique in a new environment. In this new environment, the odds are good that positive results will follow.

After the 9/11 attacks, a group of people in Pennsylvania initiated an activity to improve relationships between neighbors. According to a *USA Today* report in 2006, they proposed "Invite a Neighbor to Dinner Day" to encourage people to share dinner with neighbors they didn't know very well.[4] The idea was very popular, and many people adopted it. It was a time for people to open their doors to strengthen their community. The state legislature even passed resolutions endorsing the initiative. Even though we haven't seen information about how many people have actually joined in this activity each year, the initiative seems to be a good approach to improve relationships amongst neighbors.

Having a meal together is a common practice for strengthening business relationships. The first person in the group to propose the initiative in Pennsylvania might have been inspired by the concept of business lunch or dinner meetings, but changed "business people" to "neighbors." It's reasonable to think that, given that a business meal can improve relations between business people who are not well acquainted with one another, neighbors sharing a dinner should also be able to improve relations between those who were not familiar with each other. This then is a relatively easy step in applying the approach from a business environment to a community environment. Therefore, a good approach may find a new home in other environments if we are willing to discover them.

Apply a Concept from One Location to Another

Transferring a concept into a new physical space is another way to expand thinking. A space can be a location, an area, or a region. Think about what happens if a concept is put into a new space. What will the concept look like in the new space? What advantages could emerge after the transformation? There are many examples of this kind of thinking producing fresh ideas.

About a hundred years ago, George Freeth (1883–1919) brought Hawaiian wave surfing to the mainland in a demonstration in front of the Hotel Redondo in Southern California.[5] He probably never imagined that the sport would be transferred from the ocean to the sky by two young Frenchmen about seventy years later. Dominique Jacquet and Jean-Pascal Oron invented a new type of sport "skysurfing" in 1986.[6] In water surfing, a surfer stands on a board and rides the face of a moving ocean wave that carries the surfer towards the shore. Skysurfing also uses a board, but the difference is that this board rides on air waves. Skysurfers need superb skills to control the board and maintain an upright position while free falling to generate forward movement. An experienced skysurfer may even perform more advanced aerobatics such as loops, rolls, or spins. Expanding surfing from the ocean to the sky created a new outdoor activity for people who are looking for an extreme adrenaline rush. This story demonstrates the transfer of a concept from the ocean space to the sky space.

A similar example tells of another concept transfer, but this time from the sky to the ocean. Many people have experienced flying kites when they were young. Can the idea of a kite, which flies in the air, fly in another media? Of course it can! The Swedish company Minesto transferred the concept of kites flying in the air to kites flying in the water and developed an underwater kite. The two kinds of kites are alike. The difference is that one flies in the sky and one flies underwater. One is tethered to the ground, and the other one is tethered to the ocean floor. However, the Swedish underwater kite developed is not a child's toy, but rather a serious high technology product. In the Swedish invention, a turbine is attached to the underwater kite to generate electricity powered by ocean currents. Since seawater is much denser than air, deep ocean turbines are much more efficient than wind turbines in generating electricity. The design of the underwater kite was listed as one of the Best 50 Inventions in 2010 by *Time* magazine.[7]

Therefore, borrowing a good concept from another physical space should be on the list of considerations when searching for new ideas.

Apply a Concept from Another Time

Another way to help develop an innovative mind is to try to reuse a concept originating in the past. Historically, many good ideas and concepts have been forgotten or are considered out of date. But these relics from the past may still have value in modern times. In the least, they may continue to contribute wisdom to today's ideas. Search for valuable concepts from the past to trigger innovative thinking when looking for new solutions.

In 2008, Norway announced a doomsday seed vault located on a remote Norwegian island in the Arctic Ocean. The Svalbard Global Seed Vault was created to save various crop seeds in case of an agricultural disaster, preserving millions of crop seed samples from plants used for thousands of years by farmers around the world. If some crop species were wiped out due to wars, plagues, diseases, or global weather changes, the crops could be reconstituted with the seeds from the vault. The vault could be thought of as a modern Noah's Ark for crops. The vault is built at the end of a long tunnel under a mountain surrounded by permafrost and its low temperature is maintained throughout the year to preserve the seeds. The vault can house up to several millions of samples—or, a couple billion seeds. Its capacity is large enough to include seeds from all of the major crops in the world. The seeds stored in the vault are predicted to be viable for more than a thousand years.[8]

Whoever proposed the idea for the seed vault may have been inspired by the story of Noah's Ark, believed to have been built several thousand years ago. To deal with possible disastrous events facing mankind, the Norwegian government has taken this precaution to preserve the seeds of humanity's critical crop species. In ancient times, there was a need to preserve people and animals to survive the big flood. In modern times, we still need similar "arks" to survive potential disasters. The ancient concept of an ark was used again in the twenty-first century for a new, but similar, purpose.

Apply an Idea from Another Field

One of the benefits of knowing about borrowing concepts from other fields is that it will increase the likelihood of learning valuable things from others. For example, an open mind will pay more attention to learning things from other professions to promote cross-fertilization of ideas. When challenged to find a key to a problem, solutions in other fields may provide an answer ready-made for that problem. Many things can be learned from other fields such as techniques, methods, and formats.

As an illustration, if a wine maker wants to know how much wine is in a cask, he just knocks on the cask gently with his knuckles and listens to the sound. It's said that when a doctor uses percussions (thumps) to examine a patient's chest, the idea originally came from wine makers. In principle, the chest cavity is similar to a cask. When thumping the chest and listening to the sound with a stethoscope, a doctor is able to judge if there is liquid in the chest cavity. This is a good example of doctors in the medical field learning something valuable from the wine industry. When people learn from each other's fields, many solutions like this can be transferred between different professions.

Summary

Another component to creating good ideas is to apply a concept from one area to another or to borrow a concept from another field to the field in which you're working. The following are several aspects to consider when borrowing concepts:

- ☐ Adapt the same approach to a different category, field, or goal.
- ☐ Consider the result of the same action if it were applied to a different target.
- ☐ Think about using different content in the same format.
- ☐ Take the same concept into a different time, location, environment, or situation.
- ☐ Let a different thing assume the same function or capability.

9

Heed Both the Whole and Its Parts

The relationships between a whole and its parts are interesting. What people normally think of as a whole usually consists of many parts, like a car which consists of thousands of parts. When people observe something, generally they pay more attention to its properties as a whole but overlook the properties of its individual parts. One of the characteristics of an open mind is to examine both the whole and its parts *equally*. When observing a whole object, explicitly look for its parts, and when observing a part, remember to look at the whole object, which contains the part, as well. Such balanced observations allow a deeper understanding of the relationships between each of the elements and the whole itself.

A Whole Is the Sum of Its Parts

Some things are usually considered only as a whole. When this happens, people are more likely to overlook the fact that they can actually be divided into parts. After identifying something that is typically regarded only as a whole, try to imagine how it can be divided into pieces. Thinking this way may lead to new insights. These kinds of situations crop up quite often in our daily life. For example, when a goal can't be reached in a single step, we usually adopt a step-by-step approach to divide the whole process to reach the goal in several smaller steps.

To prevent harmful global warming from getting out of control, it's important to limit carbon emissions. The United Nations has repeatedly asked that all countries control their carbon emissions, but countries in different stages of development have different priorities and goals that determine their attitudes toward limiting carbon emissions. Developing countries want developed countries to bear more restrictions since they emit the most carbon and have done so for a longer time, while developed countries want developing countries to limit emissions that are vital to their economic growth.

Because of these conflicts, it's difficult for the UN to implement a uniform set of emissions rules for all countries. This situation resulted in a seemingly unbreakable stalemate. Then, scholars from Princeton University proposed a radically new solution: instead of controlling the whole country's carbon emission levels directly, why not control individual citizen's emission levels?[1] Carbon emission caps could be set for individual citizens rather than a whole country. This is really a smart idea. A citizen's carbon emission level is closely related to the person's economic status and lifestyle. Indeed, in underdeveloped countries there are still people who produce a lot of carbon emissions due to their affluent lifestyles, while in developed countries quite a few people do not generate high carbon emissions because of their disadvantaged economic status. To cap emissions on a per person basis is a very fair approach. The responsibility of emission control can be shifted from governments to individuals and still maintain the same goal for reducing countries' emissions. People with high emission levels, no matter where they live, would bear the responsibility to reduce their emission levels, while less fortunate people could focus on improving their living standards rather than controlling their carbon emission levels. The concept of an individual carbon emission cap stimulated a lot of interest after it was published.

Before the Princeton scholars proposed their solution to the stalemate, almost every proposal had focused on how to set goals of reducing carbon mission levels for each country. That led to countries pointing out how other countries should improve, and arguments between the nations were endless. The scholars cleverly observed that a country is composed of many individuals. Therefore, a carbon emission reduction goal for a whole country could be distributed through establishing individual citizen quotas for the reduction. This perspective allowed the creation of a unique way to solve the global warming problem. This solution was likely conceived through data analysis about individual carbon emission level distributions in both rich and poor countries. This example shows how dividing a problem into parts can stimulate the growth of new ideas.

To improve the ability to notice how different parts make up a whole, the following Yugoslavia humorous story may be helpful.[2] One morning, when a man came to the office, his colleagues immediately noticed something was wrong with his shoes. The two shoes were different colors; one was black and the other was brown. Obviously, he had mixed up two different pairs of shoes at home during his rush to leave the house. Wearing a pair of shoes with mismatched colors was unusual, and his office-mates suggested that he go back home to change. Unexpectedly, he refused to follow their advice. "That won't solve my problem," he said. "The pair of shoes I left at home also has one in black and the other in brown."

Apparently, the man had a very rigid view of how his pairs of shoes were related. He seemed to lack the ability to separate the shoes in each pair and consider each shoe individually. Though this is only a joke, it does remind us to pay attention to the individual parts of a whole.

Different Parts Treated Differently

Remember that something that appears as a whole is made up of distinct parts which are the components of the whole. When the whole is seen as an aggregate of its parts, it's easier to analyze the relation between the whole and its parts. You can then ask questions such as: How do the parts form the whole? What is the internal structure of the whole that is composed of the parts? Which parts are more or less important than other parts? This thought flow will lead to a deeper understanding of the object and new ideas may emerge from the newfound understanding.

Steganography is a technique used to hide secret information in pictures by encoding data within an ordinary digital image.[3] It's a perfect way to store secret information securely without any obvious traces. The basis of steganography can be described relatively simply. When a picture is digitized, the color and brightness of each picture element (pixel) is represented by the digital values (0-255) of three 8-bit digital numbers (bytes), one each for red, green, and blue. Considering all possible combinations of the three colors, there are about seventeen million (256x256x256) different colors that can be generated by combining the three numbers. The importance of a single digital bit (a one or a zero), however, depends on its *position* in the digital number. The first (most important) bit in byte represents a full *half* of the number's value, whereas the last (least important) bit in the byte represents only about *a half of 1 percent* in determining the brightness value of that particular color. Since the color of a pixel is represented by a combination of the values of three bytes, therefore, changing the value of the last bit in only one byte changes the color only a very tiny amount.

The basic idea of steganography is to use the *least important* bits to carry secret information. This way, the encoded variations from the original due to the secret information are tiny and can't be detected without prior knowledge. For example, a light pink pixel can be represented by three bytes: 11110101 for red, 10011110 for green, and 11001111 for blue. If the last two digits ("01") of the red byte are changed to "10" by encoding the secret information, that byte then becomes "11110110." This introduces 0.000012 percent change to the color and brightness of the pixel. No one can detect a pixel change that small, even if one knew the original picture extremely well. If the picture was encoded with secret information by changing the last two bits of only one byte in every pixel to carry secret information, the picture could carry a sizeable document without anyone noticing it.

The inventor of this technology must have thought about the structure of the bytes representing the colors of picture pixels. The inventor didn't look only at a byte as a whole value, but also looked at the distinct parts that make up a byte: the bits. When looking at it this way, the difference of importance between the bits of a byte is easily recognized and can be exploited for various advantages. That may have been the brilliant moment when the idea of steganography was conceived.

The approach of breaking down a whole into parts can be applied to many different cases. After Ashton Carter became the Secretary of Defense in early 2015, he proposed a series of initiatives for the purpose of better preparing troops with skills and knowledge for potential future wars.[4] One of those initiatives is closely related to the topic of this chapter. He suggested allowing soldiers to have mid-career breaks, similar to a sabbatical in the academic community. In his plan, soldiers could take up to a few years' leave from active duty to pursue a degree, acquire skills, or build a family. They would then return to the military and pick up where they left off to continue their military career. It's obvious that a more flexible and richer career path would benefit soldiers, but the initiative also benefits the armed forces because soldiers would bring valuable new skills and knowledge from civilian life back into the military.

Traditionally, an entire military career is basically a continuous sequence of career experiences, all within the military. To most career soldiers, leaving the military means retirement. But Secretary Carter doesn't see it that way. In his view, a soldier's career can be divided into multiple smaller advancements where civilian experience development can be intermixed with military career development. If this initiative becomes a reality, future soldiers' careers will be much improved with the flexibility to optimize their development by taking advantage of both civilian and military opportunities for growth. Expectations are that this change will significantly strengthen overall military effectiveness because soldiers will be better prepared.

This same principle has been used in marketing applications, too. As facial recognition technology becomes more advanced, ads are now able to differentiate between the gender and age of viewers. Intelligent billboards can decide to display an ad specifically targeting children, women, or men by sensing the facial characteristics of the audience members. Here is an example. In February 2012, an interactive advertisement screen was set up at a bus stop on Oxford Street in London, according to BBC.[5] It would play a special video clip if it detected a female standing in front of it. In the video clip, girls from developing countries expressed their desire to eliminate gender discrimination and be treated the same as boys. When the poster sensed a male viewer, it would just show a website link to the children's charity organization that created the ad. The behavior seems somewhat unfair to the male audience, but it was deliberately done to remind men of gender discrimination. This ad's debut indicated that ad designers had begun to divide the audience into groups and designed the ad to show content adapted to the traits of each particular group.

A Part as a Whole or a Whole as a Part

The concepts of "whole" and "part" are not absolute, but relative. A part of a whole can be viewed as an independent whole in different situations. For example, when one lid of a set of four covered bowls is damaged accidentally, the set is usually considered to be incomplete. However, if the other three undamaged lids are purposely discarded, then the remaining four lidless bowls form a new complete set again. Isn't that neat? This example indicates how a "whole" and its "parts" can transform into each other. When opening your mind, pay attention to opportunities for such transformations.

The idea that a "part" and "whole" can be converted between each other may also be very useful in daily life. A classic puzzle can be used to illustrate the concept. A young man was going for a spin in his new car with a friend. During the drive, the car got a flat tire. After stopping the car by the roadside to change the tire, he accidentally dropped all five lug nuts down a sewer grate. He blamed himself for his carelessness, but couldn't think of a way to securely mount the spare tire without the missing lug nuts. His friend saw his predicament and made a suggestion. Do you know what the suggestion was? His friend proposed that he remove one lug nut from each of his good wheels then use the three lug nuts to temporarily secure the spare tire. Three lug nuts were good enough to temporarily hold the spare on the car to allow him drive to the nearest repair shop.

The young man's friend was flexible when he viewed the set of lug nuts versus individual lug nuts. His friend considered that three lug nuts were only parts of larger sets of five lug nuts each. However, three lug nuts for the spare tire could be considered an adequate set for the circumstances. The same thought was applied to the remaining four lug nut sets on each of the three good tires. From this example, flexibility in viewing things as a part of a whole or as a new whole can generate valuable ideas.

As described above, a part can sometimes be viewed as a whole in a different situation. The opposite exists, too. In certain situations, a whole can be viewed as a part of another whole. Whether something is seen as a whole or a part depends on the environment where it exists. For example, something viewed as a whole in one domain can be considered just a part in a larger domain. Paying attention to the relationship between a part and a whole in its environment can stimulate new ideas.

To visualize how to view a whole as a part of another whole, let's look at the example how to create a photographic mosaic. A photographic mosaic is a picture composed of many very small but complete pictures.[6] To create a photographic mosaic, a large picture is divided into many small sections. Then, each section is replaced with a different picture that has color and brightness characteristics that are close to those of the original segment. After all sections are replaced by small pictures, the final large picture still looks just like the original one when seen from a distance, but when viewed up close shows the details of the many small pictures. Excellent examples of photographic mosaics include pictures of famous figures, such as a Marilyn Monroe mosaic composed with 840 different movie posters. A conventional movie poster is a complete picture with a lot of details. However, in the Marilyn Monroe's photographic mosaic, each poster is just a small piece of a much larger image, like a big pixel. The invention of photographic mosaics provided a unique experience for viewing pictures.

This technique of making large pictures out of small ones was invented by Joseph Francis in 1993 when he designed a poster of a face at Bell Labs. We don't know whether his inspiration to create a colorful photographic mosaic came from thinking deeply about the relationship between a part and a whole or not. That's not important anymore, but what *is* important is that now we know that thinking about the relationship between a part and a whole can help us create new innovative ideas.

Merits of Individual Parts

There are even more interesting relationships between a whole and its parts. For instance, when other people examine a particular part of a whole, you may discover that focusing on a different part is a better choice after having studied both. When searching for new solutions, checking the individual parts of the whole for their relative merits is a good practice.

As Christmas approached, an executive, who I had known for years and led an organization of hundreds of employees, was thinking about mailing a Christmas card to each employee's home. He wanted to use the card as a bridge to build good personal relationships with his people. He decided to use a photo of his family on the cover of the card. He and his wife had three kids. One daughter was in college, the other was in high school, and his son was in elementary school. If he used a normal family picture of the five of them for the card, it could be a little awkward because most employees didn't know anything about his family. A normal family picture would be too personal for this purpose. But he really wanted his people to know he had a wonderful family. So, he prepared a special picture for the card. The photo showed his family taking a walk on a beach. All of the family's backs were facing the viewer except the little boy, who had his head turned, displaying a funny face. The picture didn't reveal the faces of his wife or daughters but did show all the members of his family. After receiving the Christmas card, the employees and their families truly appreciated the creativity of the card design.

The executive didn't get stuck in conventional thinking when he selected a picture for his company Christmas card, but instead thought about which side of his family would be the most effective choice. This reasoning made the card very appealing and memorable.

Summary

Another way to help develop a creative mind is to keenly observe the relationship between a whole and its parts and understand the possible transformations between them. This technique can be a powerful tool for creativity. Knowing how parts relate to a whole and each other is an effective method for removing conventional thinking barriers. Here are several ways to think about this technique:

☐ If something is typically only considered a whole, attempt to divide it anyway. Then think of it as an assembly of parts and handle the whole on a parts level.

☐ Treat each part differently and explore the individual parts for their unique merits.

☐ Try to convert a part into a whole.

☐ Attempt to transform a whole into a part of another whole.

☐ Focus on parts with the most benefits.

Rearrange Patterns

T here are various patterns that appear in human lives. The concept of a "pattern" here is quite broad. For example, an arrangement of many items in different places is a pattern, and a sequence of many things happening at different times is also a pattern. Repeated patterns become regular patterns. People get used to regular patterns. When a regular pattern appears again and again, people feel that things should happen in that manner. One approach to overcome status quo thinking is to proactively identify and change some regular patterns. When observing a regular pattern, one may ask, "What if the regular pattern is altered?" or "How about rearranging the familiar pattern?" This kind of questioning will definitely help produce new ideas. The approach of rearranging patterns can be used in many areas.

Rearrange Group Members

One type of pattern is called a *group*. Different groups have different members. A pattern formed by groups is not necessarily fixed. Large groups can be divided into smaller groups, as discussed in Chapter 9, or small groups can form large groups, as discussed in Chapter 6. Groups can also be broken up and members from different groups can form new groups. This is the focus of this section. Here, a popular logic puzzle is used as an example.

A young man was driving his car one stormy night when he passed a bus station and saw three women waiting for the bus. They included an old lady who looked very sick, a nurse who was wearing her uniform, and a young woman who he recognized as his neighbor. He wanted to help all of them, but unfortunately his car only could take one passenger. Which one would he help? The answer is a little out of the box. The guy got out of the car, handed the key to the medical staff lady and asked her to take the old lady to a nearby hospital. He then escorted his neighbor back to her home by bus. It looked to be a perfect solution.

In this case, the people involved can be divided into two groups: the driver group and the passenger group. The two groups formed a pattern in this case. The young man obviously thought that rearranging the groups could be a good solution. The most important lesson of this case is that the man didn't let himself be bound to the driver group. His mental flexibility let him come up with the idea to move himself into the passenger group. It's worthwhile to learn his regrouping tactic.

Rearrange Segments

A *process* is usually an assembly of multiple segments or sections. Each *segment* is executed in its own length of time. The concept of segments can also be associated with other characteristics, not just time. Frequently, the same arrangement of segments in a process appears repeatedly, forming a regular process pattern. However, the execution time for each of the segments is potentially adjustable. A regular process pattern can be changed and improved by optimizing the duration of each segment of the process. A former prisoner's story is appropriate to illustrate the principle of repartitioning segments.

Here is the former inmate's true story. It was a long time ago, in the prison where the inmate was serving his sentence, prisoners' meals were distributed by the jailers. At each meal time, prisoners ladled their food into their plates from the trays offered by the jailers. After a prisoner finished his first plate, he was allowed to have a second plate of food. But the prison's food supply was often running low. By the time a prisoner asked for seconds there was often little, if any, food left. Hence, many prisoners went hungry. This prisoner, however, was pleasingly full after every meal. Can you guess how he accomplished that? When he served himself for his first helping at a meal, he only filled his plate to just over half full. This way, he finished his first plate quickly and when he went for seconds there was always enough food remaining because no one else had asked for seconds yet. On his second trip to get food, he filled his plate to overflowing, after which he sat down and enjoyed his bounteous feast at his leisure. This strategy kept him from being hungry the whole time he served his sentence.[1]

Eating a meal in the prison can be considered a process. The process then can be divided into segments: acquiring and consuming the first plate, acquiring and consuming the second plate, acquiring and consuming the third plate, and so on, given that there was more food available for the prisoners. The time consumed eating the first plate was similar for most prisoners because initially their plates were loaded full. But the open-minded prisoner thought to shorten the time to consume his first serving by only partially loading his plate. That allowed him to win the opportunity to always have a full second plate. It's amazing that the idea of adjusting the duration of the meal segments actually solved the fundamental problem of how to make sure to get enough food while he was in prison. Most readers of this book don't have to worry about how to feed themselves in a prison; nonetheless, this prisoner's experience is valuable to remember in other situations as well.

Rearrange Sequences

As discussed above, the time duration of the segments of a process can be adjusted. Not only that, the sequence of the segments can be altered as well. An early process segment may be moved to the back of the process or vice versa. Rearranging a pattern can be accomplished by repositioning its segments or sections. This is another method that will help when searching for new ideas.

Scholar Charles Speroni once told a story that happened in the Italian city of Camerino during the Renaissance in his book, *Wit and Wisdom of the Italian Renaissance*.[2] One day, a group of people were practicing archery outside the city walls. A new archer's arrow accidentally landed far from the target, slightly wounding a nearby royal prince. People of the group brought the terrified archer before the prince. The crowd began to suggest various punishments that the poor man should suffer. One of them was particularly ruthless. He proposed to have one of the archer's hands cut off so that he wasn't able to indiscriminately shoot arrows ever again. Luckily, the prince didn't agree with this suggestion, saying that the proposed punishment would only be effective if it had been carried out *before* the poor archer shot the arrow. The kindly prince eventually set the man free.

Normally, as in the case above, the sequence unfolded where the clumsy archer made the mistake first, then would have suffered the consequences. But, the prince thought about the situation more deeply. His thinking went this way: if the man who suggested the punishment had really wanted to prevent the accident from happening, the punishment should have been carried out *prior* to the archer releasing his arrow, not afterwards. As this approach was highly impractical, the prince's argument for freeing the man made more sense. Obviously, the prince didn't want to anger the crowd, so he couldn't refuse the proposal outright. Instead, he reversed the normal sequence of mistake, then punishment. Using this logic, the punishment proposal immediately lost its appeal.

Deviate from a Pattern

When a regular pattern is formed, people normally tend to follow it, either consciously aligning their actions with the pattern or imagining how things may evolve from the pattern. In this kind of common situation, it may be beneficial to try deviating from the pattern to discover what may happen if the pattern isn't followed. While others are stuck in patterns, intentionally departing from a pattern is a technique for thinking outside the box.

The popular "three-kick rule" joke fits the topic of this section nicely. A man from a large city was hunting in a distant rural area. He shot a large bird that fell into a farmer's backyard. While the man was climbing the fence to retrieve his bounty, the farmer came out and told the man he wouldn't allow him onto the property without permission. The man explained why he needed to get into the farmer's backyard but the farmer's response was still no. The farmer said, "That's too bad. The bird is on my property, so it belongs to me."

The man didn't give up so easily, though. He threatened to sue the farmer for stealing his bird. The farmer responded, "Have you heard about the three-kick rule? Here we normally use the rule to solve small disputes like this one and have no need to go to court." The guy asked, "What's the three-kick rule?" Then the farmer patiently explained the rule. "Well, first I kick you three times, then you kick me three times, then I kick you three times again, and so on, until one of us gives up." Hearing the farmer's explanation, the city slicker thought for a while and was sure that he was much stronger than the old farmer. If they could kick each other equally, he felt he would easily have the advantage. Therefore, he agreed. So, the farmer wound up for his first blow. He pulled back his boot then fiercely kicked the guy's butt. Even though the farmer was thin and short, the kick was still painful. The man held his breath, enduring this attack and looking forward to returning the favor soon. Then, the farmer kicked the second and third time, and the man almost collapsed. Suffering the intense kicks, the city slicker exclaimed, "Now, it's my turn!" Unexpectedly, the old farmer said, "Wait a second, I give up, you can have your bird now!"

Apparently, the city slicker was stuck in a pattern. He thought the process would continue as the farmer had explained, where the farmer would kick three times and then he would kick three times, and so on. He didn't know that the old farmer possessed a creative mind. The farmer didn't follow the regular pattern and intentionally deviated from it. Even though the city slicker got his butt whipped, he learned a valuable lesson. Now that he had a firsthand demonstration, from then on the city slicker should be able to think more broadly and try out new possibilities that stray outside normal patterns.

Pairs of the Positive and Negative

Positives and negatives naturally coexist. Pairs of the positive and the negative can be viewed as patterns as well. Exploring the advantages of properties of such pairs is another way to seek new ideas. Something negative can be normally compensated for by something positive. Also, positive and negative pairs can be generated from scratch. To do this, first create something negative, and then create something positive to counteract it. After this process of pair generation is complete, the system returns to the original state and may seem as if nothing has happened. However, during the negative-positive creation cycle, some valuable things may have been created. Just like taking pictures, if a photography subject wants to always appear with open eyes in a picture, the best method to use is to first have the subject close his or her eyes, then open them just before the picture is taken. The close-open pair of opposites helps to reach the goal of guaranteed open eyes on pictures. The following is an example of how the two elements in a positive-negative pair can create good values.

At the opening ceremony of the 2010 Vancouver Winter Olympic Games, one of the four giant pillars of the indoor cauldron system didn't rise due to a malfunction, causing Canadian Olympic Champion Le May Doan to be unable to light her section of the cauldron. That was an awkward moment. However, at the closing ceremony, the organizer of the Games decided to reenact the opening ceremony cauldron lighting process. "Workmen" played by comedians pretended to work hard to repair the fourth pillar. After they "solved" the problem successfully, the pillar eventually rose to its correct position and Le May Doan completed her job of lighting the cauldron. The cauldron system was finally shown to the world in its full glory. The embarrassment of the opening ceremony's fiasco was nullified by the successful outcome of the closing ceremony.[3]

The inability of one of the cauldron pillars to rise at such an important event was inarguably a negative incident. But a negative incident can be compensated by a positive event. That's why the organizers of the Games inserted the humorous program that involved the "repair" of the pillar in the closing ceremony. The addition of the new skit left a very positive impression of the Games on the audience and TV viewers around the world. This positive counterbalance more than canceled out the negative effects from the opening ceremony. Therefore, pay attention to patterns of pairing relationships between the positive and the negative, and remember to turn negatives into the positives and obtain a pure gain.

Summary

Delving into the relationships in regular patterns is one way to develop a creative mind. However, just exploring these patterns is not enough. Altering the existing patterns is sometimes helpful in generating positive outcomes. When rearranging patterns consider the following areas:

- ☐ Expose groups and reassemble their elements to form new groups.
- ☐ Adjust the relative size of segments belonging to an assembly or a procedure.
- ☐ Tune the sequence of segments in a process.
- ☐ Deviate from the regular pattern if it's more beneficial that way.
- ☐ Form positive-negative pairs to gain net benefits.

11

Set Reference Points

Most people form opinions about matters they encounter everyday by examining the relative relationships between things. For example, the tallest skyscraper the city where a person lives is typically considered "very tall" when compared to other buildings in that city. The same building can be considered "quite short" when compared with the Burj Khalifa in Dubai, UAE, the world's tallest building.

People's feelings and actions are frequently perceived in the same way. For instance, if someone wants to buy a dozen eggs, that person may be willing to drive a few more miles to save a dollar on the eggs after comparing the egg prices in different supermarkets. If buying a car, the same person may not be willing to visit another car dealer in another location just to save a couple hundred dollars on the car price. Why is the person willing to visit more stores to save a dollar, but isn't willing to visit multiple car lots to save hundreds of dollars? The reason may be because the reference points for the two cases are quite different. For the egg case, the reference point is perhaps five dollars—the cost of the dozen eggs, while for the car case the reference point may be fifty thousand dollars—the list price of the car. Since people's feelings or actions depend on reference points they set either consciously or subconsciously, thinking about how to set proper reference points becomes a worthy approach.

Identifying and setting reference points have many applications. When dealing with market competition, a company may decide how much it needs to improve based on setting its competitor's performance as a reference.

Similarly, when handling a bad situation, an optimist may choose a worse scenario as a reference point to gain a sense of comfort, or when describing the advantages of a product a salesman may choose an inferior product as a reference to show his item as superior. All of these scenarios reflect the usefulness of appropriate reference points.

Select a Reference Point When Searching for Advantages

Advantages and disadvantages are relative. Whether a person or an object has an advantage totally depends on who or what is being used for comparison. In movies, we often see scenes of big bullies showing their dominance at school and threatening their meek schoolmates. But out of school, the same bullies often are complaisant towards vicious street thugs. Why is their behavior so different between school and the outside world? Many times, it's because their superior physical strength gives them an edge over their weaker peers, but their strength is still inferior to the brawn of real-life criminals. By noticing the nature of advantages and disadvantages, people tend to select reference points that show their advantages and hide their disadvantages.

A classic humorous police joke shows the importance of choosing right reference points to maintain an advantage. The policemen at a precinct were assigned to patrol an area that included inspecting bars for drunks and troublemakers. One particular officer chose the same small, slender colleague as his partner every time he was assigned to patrol this area. Over time, the other policemen in the station began to wonder, *Can they really be getting along with each other that well?* One day, another cop finally couldn't contain his curiosity and quietly asked the officer, "Why do you always pick the skinny guy as your partner?" "It's obvious," the officer replied. "Think about it. When we're trying to arrest a drunk, which one of us do you think the guy will chose to hit?"

Most police officers know very well how to use a physical advantage in body size over a smaller person. In this case, even though the officer's build may be just average, when he chooses a much smaller colleague as his reference he always holds an advantage when dealing with physical confrontations. If the officer hadn't considered this up front and carelessly picked any random officer as his partner, and if that partner turned out to be burlier than he was, then he would be the one to suffer. This is just a fictitious story, but it shows how critical it is to choose the right reference point if you want to maintain a certain edge.

The Reference Point Determines the Relative Size

A quantity described as being either more or less depends on where one establishes the reference point. Similar to advantages and disadvantages, if you use a smaller quantity as the reference, the quantity being compared to it will still be considered "greater" relative to the reference quantity, no matter how small it is. Conversely, if using a larger quantity as the reference, no matter how large that quantity is, it will still be considered "smaller" relative to the reference. The chosen reference point is the key to determining what *more* (or *greater*) and *less* (or *smaller*) means.

During the Eastern Han period of China, at the end of a year, the emperor decided to give each scholar in his court a sheep as a reward for their services over the past year. When the scholars were preparing to receive their rewards, they discovered that the sheep were not all the same size. Some of the sheep were slim and some were fat, some were short and some were tall. Distributing the sheep fairly among the scholars became a problem. While most scholars were arguing over the best way to distribute the sheep, Chen Yu, another scholar, suggested that it would be better to let everyone pick the sheep they each preferred. He then indicated that he would be the first one to select his reward. While other scholars were pondering what kind of sheep they were going to pick, Chen chose the skinniest and smallest sheep. Chen's selection caused the other scholars to feel embarrassed. They could no longer argue about the size of the sheep they would receive and each man quickly picked one and left for home.[1]

None of the sheep were the same size, so the question of how they could be fairly distributed among the scholars was a difficult conundrum. The problem seemed to have no solution, Chen Yu, however, easily solved the problem by setting a reference point of quality for the sheep. Since he picked the sheep with the lowest quality, any sheep picked by other scholars thereafter should be considered as "better" quality than his. Conceding this, who then could complain about the quality of his sheep?

Importance Is Relative

In daily life, people pay a lot of attention to what they consider to be important. Most people want to try to achieve their important goals. When facing difficulties reaching an important goal, a person will likely use all means available to overcome the challenges. If a person comes across a more important goal while chasing his original important goal, however, the person may be quickly distracted from the original goal and switch his attention to the new goal. Based on this interesting phenomenon, a person's attention can be refocused by establishing a more important reference point.

During WWII, Britain's MI5 intelligence agency operated its most important double agent, Juan Pujol Garcia. Garcia pretended to be a German agent hiding in the UK who lead a fictitious espionage network for the German government. He fed false secret information to his spymaster in Germany. Before the end of WWII, his most critical task was to trick Hitler into believing that the D-day landing would take place in Pas de Calais, not Normandy. However, according to accounts in *The Telegraph* he got into big trouble.[2]

Because of the sensitive nature of his job, his Spanish wife and children had to stay inside their home most of the time. His wife couldn't interact with other people very often, and it was out of the question for her to travel to her hometown in Spain. The purpose was to minimize the family's mobility to prevent any possible leak of her husband's true identity. After a long time living in these conditions, she became very depressed. She often quarreled with her husband and insisted on going to Spain to see her mother. When all her attempts failed, she threatened to go to the Spanish embassy and expose her husband's secrets. This was a devastating threat to Garcia since his work was critical to the success of the invasion in Normandy. MI5 was determined to stop Garcia's wife from carrying out her crazy plan, but they couldn't do very much to stop her because she was Garcia's wife.

Where was the solution to this tricky problem? It was Garcia's genius that caused him to propose that he and MI5 act out a deception focused on his wife. One day, she was brought to a secret MI5 interrogation center to meet her husband. Garcia was dressed in camp clothing and was unshaved. Garcia told his wife that, because of her behavior, MI5 had arrested him because the agency had started to believe that he might really be a German spy. Terrible consequences were waiting for him, he told her. After hearing his words, she swore that she never really meant to carry out her threat to tell his secrets to the world. She had just become so frustrated and hoped that her actions would lead him to treat her unhappiness more seriously. Then, she swore to the MI5 officer that she would actively help her husband if the agency would release him. Both Garcia and the MI5 officer were relieved that the deception had worked, and shortly afterwards MI5 ordered Garcia to be "released." From that time on, Garcia's wife didn't cause any trouble and the D-day invasion was carried out successfully.

Facing his vexed wife, Garcia's clever move was to set a reference point involving the concept of relative importance. His wife had felt that her reunion with her family in Spain was her top priority. To reach the goal, she was willing to go to extremes, making threats and even declaring to commit suicide. But her husband set a more important goal for her to focus on: saving Garcia. If Garcia was deemed a German spy by MI5, she would lose a lot more than her right to visit her family in Spain. Compared with the new goal of saving her husband, her original most important priority suddenly became insignificant. In the new situation, would she continue to fight for her original goal? Apparently not, because setting the right reference point in the process had solved this difficult problem.

Set a Beneficial Reference Point

The magnitude of an advantage depends on the relationship to its reference. For a given performance, the lower the performance level of its reference, the greater advantage it's perceived to have. Therefore, creating a more favorable reference point may help to strengthen an advantage. Here's a simple example to explain this principle.

Some retail stores utilize a special pricing strategy. Stores sometimes purchase two different qualities of products: standard quality and premium quality. The vast majority of the purchases are standard quality goods. Only very few premium products are acquired, mainly for display purposes. Often, the store's purchase price of a premium quality item is not significantly higher than that of the standard items, for example, only by as much as 30 percent. But when the stores establish retail prices for the two different grade items, they don't use a ratio of prices linked to their

purchase prices. Instead, they set the retail price of a standard item at a
nicely profitable level, but set that of the premium item much higher, for
example, as much as three times that of the standard item. They do this
hoping that consumers will compare the two products and their prices and
find that even though the quality of the premium item is better, the price
of the standard item is disproportionally lower. Consequently, consumers
tend to favor the price of the regular goods and are thus strongly attracted to
them. Stores employ this technique because they want customers to buy a
lot of regular-quality items. They use the prices of the premium items only
as references. When the reference price is set very high, the lower prices of
the standard goods look like a big advantage. Therefore, consumers should
be alert to this gimmick when comparing a nice low price to a similar item
with a very high price.

Things Can Reference Each Other

When a reference is established for something, the second thing then
becomes a reference for the original thing as well. In other words, the
relationship between the two references is mutual, just as in the example
of merchandise prices discussed in the last section. When the price of the
premium item is used as a reference, the price of the standard item is considered to be very low. If this is reversed and the price of the standard item
becomes the reference, the price of the premium item is now considered to
be very high. Even though this reasoning is straightforward, not everyone
may easily realize it. The following example sheds some more light on
this argument.

About a thousand years ago in China's Song Dynasty, Wang Pang was
the young bright son of a duke. One day, a friend gave his father two deer,
one a roe deer and the other a water deer. When the friend heard that the
duke's son was really smart, he proposed doing a test. The friend pointed
to the two deer and asked the five-year-old child, "Do you know which
one is the roe deer and which is the water deer?" Wang had never seen the
animals before and had no idea which was which, but he wasn't daunted by
the question. He replied with confidence, "The one next to the water deer
is the roe deer and the one next to the roe deer is the water deer."[3]

Wang Pang could not answer the gentleman's question directly, he
decided to use an approach where the two animals referenced each other,

which wasn't easy for a five-year-old boy. Unfortunately, Wang wasn't able to accomplish a great deal with his brilliant mind due to a short lifetime. The response to the deer question he gave at five years old, however, led him to be well-known throughout history. Even today, after many generations, people are still telling this amazing story.

Summary

Any comparison is relative. Perceptions are built on observing and understanding the relationships between references. Therefore, setting proper reference points may allow things to be promoted to a more valuable status. The following are a few ways to try to set appropriate reference points:

☐ Choose a proper reference to maintain an advantage.
☐ Adjust a reference point to improve a gain.
☐ Set a fitting reference point to produce a better outcome.
☐ Establish a new reference point to shift focus.
☐ Let things reference each other.

Examine Its Evolution

PART III

Examine Its Evolution

Look Back to the Beginning

In any undertaking, there is always a jumping-off point that determines how we approach what we want to accomplish. However, in most cases our goals are only met when the starting points are clear and understood well enough to guide us to our goal. If the starting point isn't correct, our eventual solution may not solve our problem. Unfortunately, people oftentimes lose sight of their reason for beginning an effort in the first place because they focus so heavily on developing the solution. It's easy to forget the reason why a problem was important, especially when the development of the solution appears to be making great progress. Periodically revisiting the original premise will help identify disconnects between the initial objective and the current stage of working on a solution. This exercise may also lead to unexpected discoveries, and thus stimulate more creative thinking.

A Flawed Plan Invites Flawed Results

A plan is the basis for a series of actions that lead to successfully meeting an objective. When a plan is put into practice, people usually work on the plan step-by-step. Too often, the process focuses only on achieving perfection at each step of the plan in order to give the best chance for success. However, this practice is blind to the value of continually revisiting the overall plan during its execution to assure it is still valid.

What if a plan has hidden flaws? Will the outcome still be successful? Probably not. When surprises turn up during a plan's execution, these flaws often result in a *complete restart* of the effort. Therefore, you should revisit the original content of the plan periodically during its execution so that if you encounter a problem, you already have a valid and well understood basis for modifications in place.

According to a legend, in 1846 an aging Chinese Emperor, Tao-kuang of the Manchurian Ching dynasty, decided it was time to choose the heir to his throne from among his nine sons. Seven of the princes were quickly eliminated for various reasons, leaving the emperor to select from just two sons: fourteen-year-old I-ju and thirteen-year-old I-hsin. Both sons seemed to have reasonable royal attributes, although I-ju was more levelheaded and I-hsin was smarter. The emperor secretly favored I-hsin, but he still had to make a clear case for which of the two he would choose to inherit his throne.

The emperor finally came up with a plan to make the decision. He would proclaim a hunting contest for the entire royal court, thus creating a real-life situation that would let him see which of the two sons possessed the best characteristics needed to be emperor. When they heard about the event, the two princes' reactions were quite different. I-hsin was very excited, but I-ju was worried. Both boys knew very well that their father would be evaluating each of them during the hunt for abilities such as leadership, bravery, and gallantry to support his choice of an heir. I-hsin, an aggressive and skilled hunter, approached this occasion as a wonderful opportunity to show off to his father. I-ju, however, dreaded the upcoming contest since he could not hunt as well as his brother and would certainly lose the competition.

I-ju couldn't think of a way to win the contest, but then his wise personal tutor gave him a surprising idea. The tutor said that he could guarantee that I-ju would leave a winning impression on his father if I-ju would *not* try to beat his brother, instead allowing I-hsin to easily out-hunt him. Without a better idea, I-ju reluctantly agreed to his tutor's seemingly strange thought.

The next morning as the hunt commenced, everyone but I-ju tried their very best to slaughter as many animals as they could. I-ju appeared disinterested in the entire spectacle, only making feeble attempts at hunting.

After a full day of depopulating the forest, the hunters returned to the palace with their trophies. The emperor told the hunters to display their prizes so he could judge who was the best. I-hsin easily had the most trophies, showing the emperor that he clearly had the characteristics needed to be an emperor. When it was I-ju's turn, he walked up to the emperor with empty hands. The emperor was astounded by this shameful show of cowardice. But before the emperor could begin a tirade about his poor showing, I-ju said, "Father, please forgive me for not bringing home any trophies. It was not my hunting ability, but rather, I felt *sorry* for all these animals. It's now springtime and most animals are in their mating season. I felt compassionate towards them and didn't want to harm the animals at this important time of year." After hearing I-ju's explanation, the emperor suddenly realized that the animals should be protected during the spring season and only hunted when necessary. How could he have overlooked that? The emperor was impressed by his son's kindheartedness in place of bloodlust. He immediately thanked I-ju for reminding him of this and told the entire royal court, "Now *that* is the way an emperor should think!" Before long, the emperor announced I-ju as his successor. Later, the second-rate hunter became the next ruler, Emperor Hsien-feng.¹

Originally, I-ju seemed to be in a very poor position to win his father's approval. If I-ju had tried to compete on the same terms with his brother in the hunting event, he would never have triumphed over his brother. His personal tutor's strategy was brilliant because it did not involve I-ju trying to compete using traditional comparisons. Rather, he let I-ju question the starting premise of conducting a hunting event in the first place. The tutor thought beyond the usual criteria for winning by modifying the original premise to achieve the real unspoken goal of the emperor. This way of thinking provided a path for I-ju's tutor to discover the real issue: the emperor should never have planned the hunt during the mating season. Thus, I-ju was able to demonstrate even more important leadership qualities and impress the emperor. By adopting his tutor's advice, I-ju got around his inadequacies and won the recognition that established his position as future emperor. In this case, the tutor's questioning of the hunt changed the course of history!

Understand People's Views from Their Perspective

A person's opinion is closely tied to their understanding of the world. A simple illustration of this happened when Bill, an Arkansan college student, arrived at an Ivy League campus to make a name for himself. Bill bragged loudly that farmers in Arkansas grew the largest watermelons in the world. He made a big deal of this to impress his fellow students.

Not everyone was amazed by this. Upon hearing Bill's boast, one student just smirked at this country boy.[2] The student was probably from a big city and wasn't impressed at all by Bill's Arkansan watermelons. In Bill's hometown, growing huge watermelons was an impressive feat, but in the student from the big city's eyes, it was boring. In this case, the difference in Bill's and the student's perspectives were caused by the difference in their backgrounds.

Duke Mu ruled over the powerful state of Chin in ancient China around 600 BC. One day, he welcomed an envoy named You Yu from the West Rong tribes to his lands. Duke Mu was known far and wide to be wise and virtuous, and so Yu had been sent by the leader of the West Rong to learn all he could from a visit with the Duke. To impress Yu with the stature and power of his country, the Duke lead him on a personal tour of his opulent palace, showing Yu many treasures. However, the envoy was not impressed with the magnificent palace or the countless treasures. In fact, Yu told the Duke that fine palaces and treasures did not prove how strong and prosperous the Duke's country was, but rather it meant Chin was wasting precious resources. The Duke was surprised to hear such a candid statement from an envoy, and in turn he asked Yu, "Then what *is* the real sign that shows a country to be strong and prosperous?"

Yu replied to the most powerful man in Chin, "Treat your countrymen with kindness and sincerity, and in turn they will swear loyalty to you. Governing a country is similar to a person presiding over his body; he can more easily get extraordinary things from it if it is trained to be strong *before* extreme demands are made from it." Duke Mu listened and nodded, appreciating Yu's insightful answer. The Duke was so impressed that he later asked Yu to stay and become his top advisor. With Yu's help, the state of Chin became even more prosperous under Duke Mu.[3]

Duke Mu's original understanding of greatness was limited to the traditional way of measuring it. Before meeting Yu, he thought magnificent palaces and treasures represented the greatness of a country. Yu deeply challenged the Duke's original criteria when he questioned the starting point of the Duke's assumption. Fortunately, the Duke was perceptive enough to realize that his original view that only money can represent wealth and power was wrong. Perhaps if the Duke had critically examined his understanding of the concept *before* Yu made his comment, he would not have focused his tour on only material riches.

The ancient Chinese weren't the only ones who knew that one must examine the basis of a statement: the Spartans knew it too. Around 300 BC, Philip II of Macedon invaded Greece. The Spartan city of Laconia refused to give up even after many neighboring cities had surrendered to the invader. Philip II then sent a threatening message to the Spartans: "If I invade Laconia, you will be destroyed, never to rise again!" The Spartans quickly sent a reply to Philip II. The reply contained only one word, and because of that one word Philip II abandoned his plan to conquer the city. The response was a simple "If."[4] The clever Spartans reminded Philip II to check the basis of his claim. If the basis was not true, how could his threat become a reality?

Improve Starting Points

People often like to begin where others have begun before. Sometimes, they think that those particular starting points have led to success before, so why shouldn't they lead to success again? Other times, people may think that it's easier to start from a known starting point than work to create a unique beginning. Unfortunately, the easiest way usually tends to detract from critical examination of whether the starting point really fits all the requirements, or perhaps whether it is one which can be improved upon. It's always good practice to question the starting point, even if it may already have a lot of support or seem obvious, to increase your ability to discover improvement opportunities.

Uninterruptible power supplies are backup power units which fulfill important roles in places like hospitals, telecommunications facilities, and computer centers. The concept of a backup power unit is quite simple. When the electric grid supplies utility power normally, a backup power unit stores up power to its capacity. When an electrical power outage occurs, the backup power unit automatically switches to its internal power supply and continues to provide electricity to critical equipment until utility power is restored. Almost all backup power units use batteries to store this standby energy. But batteries pose problems—such as short lifetimes—and require the handling and disposal of dangerous chemicals.

Some years ago, the start-up company Active Power decided to *not* use batteries in its new designs for backup power units. Instead, the company engineers used heavy spinning wheels (flywheels) to store standby energy, similar to conventional batteries (chemical) but in a different form (mechanical). During normal operation, electricity from the utility grid maintains high speed rotation of the flywheel inside the unit while providing power for the normal needs of the attached equipment. When the utility power is interrupted, the unit quickly switches to pick up the load by calling on the energy in the flywheel for conversion into electrical power, which in turn supplies electricity to the equipment connected to it. The flywheel-based design of this backup power unit presents no pollution problems and has an indefinite lifetime; it's an innovative and truly "green" product.[5]

Before this innovation appeared, the designers of backup power units might have thought there wasn't a better way to store backup energy because all previous conventional designs used batteries. Even though most backup power unit manufacturers use batteries as the starting point for their product designs, Active Power's engineers didn't just simply follow the status quo. Instead, they rethought the fundamental starting point and worked to improve it.

Avoid False Starts

If you examine the starting point critically, you may also avoid wasting the time and effort that stems from beginning from an *incorrect* starting point. If a starting point has a problem, the efforts following the starting point are likely to be much less productive, or even futile. So, examine your starting points critically to assure they are reasonable before problems arise. This minimizes wasting resources while pursuing a goal with a wrong starting point.

There's a well-known joke that goes something like this: A teacher and a student are discussing a situation where two men fall into a sooty chimney simultaneously. To begin, the teacher asked the student: "Assume that two men fell down through a chimney at the same time. One came out dirty and the other came out clean. Which of them was going to wash up?"

"Let me think about it," replied the student. "It must be the dirty one who was going to wash up."

"Wrong." the teacher said. Then he explained, "Actually, the exact opposite is true. The clean man looked at the dirty man and thought he was also dirty; therefore, he went to wash up. The dirty man on the other hand, looked at the clean man and thought he was also clean, so he didn't need to wash up."

The student thought it over and found his teacher's explanation very clever.

The teacher continued his questioning. "After a while, these two men again fell down the chimney at same time. Just like before, one came out dirty and the other came out clean. Which of these two was going to wash up this time?"

The student had learned his lesson last time, and after pondering for a while he said, "It must be the clean man who was going to wash up since he looked at the dirty man and thought he was also dirty."

"Wrong!" the teacher exclaimed. "Last time, the clean one looked into a mirror and saw that he was actually clean. The one who should wash up was the other guy. Then he told the dirty man his finding. So, this time the dirty man decided to wash up."

Oh, they knew the truth this time, the student thought to himself.

Finally, the teacher said, "Let's try again. Once again, these two men fell through the sooty chimney at the same time. One came out dirty and the other came out clean. Which of them went to wash up?"

This time, the student had absolutely no idea how to respond, but he thought very hard anyway. Eventually, he muttered, "I believe it was the dirty man who went to wash up."

"You are wrong again!" the teacher admonished. "Think about it, do you think it's possible for two men to fall through a chimney at the same time and only one come out dirty while the other comes out clean?!"[6]

The student was trying hard to answer the teacher's questions as they were asked. However, the problem was with the premise of the teacher's questions, i.e., the starting point of the dialogue: "Two men fell through a chimney at same time and one came out dirty and another came out clean." The starting statement was absurd. If the student had critically examined the starting point of the teacher's questions from the beginning, he wouldn't have spent so much time and energy searching for answers that made no sense in any case. Therefore, don't forget to check the starting point.

Summary

Every event in our lives has a starting point. When we focus heavily on a goal's progress, we sometimes forget where that goal originated from. You can often discover if a process has some issues by closely examining its starting point, thereby saving yourself a lot of time and energy. So, when you want to generate valuable new ideas, one approach is to check the starting point of your event early enough to identify potential problems and allow time for improving the process. Here are some things to think about:

- ☐ Reassess your justification of the starting point, even though you seem to be nearing a good solution.
- ☐ Check if the starting point can be improved, even if it seems valid.
- ☐ Verify if the original premise is still suitable with the possible situational changes.
- ☐ Frequently re-examine initial conditions to find opportunities to save time and energy.

Consider Changes

Continuous change is a fact of life regardless of whether we notice the changes or not. A *change* is a situation where something becomes different over time. When thinking about change, people tend to consider what the meaning of the change represents and what influence the change will bring. Clearly observing changes facilitates thinking. Unfortunately, a lot of time people don't notice—or worse, ignore—changes and therefore don't have a chance to generate thoughts based on those changes. To stimulate new thinking, try to be more sensitive to changes and explore opportunities brought on by those changes.

On the other hand, for something that seemingly doesn't change, introducing changes can expose new aspects of it. When something remains constant, over time people get accustomed to it in that state and are less likely to question whether it could be improved or made more dynamic by introducing changes. Because people normally tend to overlook static components in favor of things that are constantly varying, the chances of transforming static components into dynamic ones are even less likely. Proactively trying to introduce changes to things perceived as constant is another characteristic of an open mind.

Be Aware of Changes Occurring in the Process
The very idea of a process implies change because there's no need for a process if nothing changes. When you observe something changing during a process, think about how the change could be used to your advantage. For

example, if a task can't be accomplished at the beginning stage of a process, wait until the process develops into another stage where the situation becomes different than the one at the beginning. Then consider whether you can do the task at this new stage. Open minds always examine the evolution of process stages and remember to examine the potential benefits that may be brought by each of the stage changes.

Clinics and hospitals routinely give shots to patients. Each time a nurse finishes a shot, the used syringe and needle must be disposed into a special recycle bin to avoid needle stick injuries. The needle is usually very sharp. It's a serious matter if someone on the medical staff gets stuck accidentally, because a used needle contains a patient's body fluids. Each year, such incidents happen in many medical facilities, but no one could find a good solution to this problem until Dr. Sakharam D. Mahurkar of Smart Syringe redesigned the traditional syringe by adding a mechanism to prevent a used needle from harming anyone. The newly designed syringe works identically to a traditional syringe at the beginning of the process of giving a shot, where the needle is in front of the plunger to facilitate a normal injection. The difference becomes clear after the injection stage is completed. A mechanism pulls the used needle into the now-empty plunger using a passive spring retractor, which then locks the needle inside the plunger. This way, the sharp tip of the used needle is inside the plunger and isn't exposed to cause an accident. This new syringe design increases the safety of giving shots significantly, dropping the probability of having accidental needle-stick injuries to almost zero. This protects the medical staff from injury or infection and provides a better peace of mind.[1]

Dr. Mahurkar cleverly took advantage of the plunger's content change during the process of giving a shot. Before the shot, the plunger contains the injection solution. After the injection, the plunger is empty. Noticing this change might have provided the opportunity for his invention. He must have thought that if the used needle could be protected somewhere after a shot, no one could be hurt. But what could provide a needle guard? Eureka! Could the empty plunger be a good place to hold the used needle? Yes! After he reached this critical point in his thinking, designing a mechanism to retract a used needle into the plunger was just a matter of simple mechanical engineering. The important lesson here isn't to show how to design a smart mechanism, but rather to provide an example of seeing changes during a process, and using a later process stage to solve problems which can't be solved at an earlier stage.

Search for Hidden Changes

Hidden changes normally happen either in an isolated location or when no one is present to notice them. However, in some situations, careful analysis can uncover hidden changes through logical thought. Since few people discover hidden changes, finding them will likely generate original thoughts that escape other people.

Recently, a Belgian insect expert, Patrick Goossens, became famous for photographing insects, specifically of damselflies and their relatives. He took pictures of the insects only at a very special time of day: shortly before sunrise in spring or fall. At this time, the temperature couldn't be too cold or too hot; the sky could not be too dark or too bright, and the humidity had to be a specific value. He was looking for a special moment when damselflies were still covered in dewdrops condensed on their body after a night of rest. Only under those conditions could he carefully take pictures of the damselflies with natural light without disturbing them. Because the damselflies were covered in many tiny dewdrops, the insects glittered like sparkling jewels. The photographs are astonishingly beautiful. Few people had ever seen these kinds of pictures before. The insect expert might have been the first person who noticed and took pictures of damselflies in these unusual circumstances. It's not easy to catch the perfect moment to take these photographs. Goossens said the best time to take photographs is fifteen minutes before sunrise and that the time window is only a few minutes long, per a *Daily Mail* report.[2] It's not surprising that it was so long before anyone was able to take these pictures. Today, anyone can enjoy seeing the insect expert's never before seen, dew-covered insect pictures online.

There have always been many photographers keen on working with insects. However, before the Belgian entomologist, it looks like no one had ever taken such beautiful, dew-covered insects pictures. Possibly, this happened because few people thought that the external appearance of an insect could have a significant change over a period of twenty-four hours. Near dawn, covered in dewdrops, a damselfly looks quite different from its typical appearance during the day. Because the transformation happens under darkness, when people are sleeping, it's not surprising that people hadn't observed the change. Fortunately, the dewy condition was discovered by Patrick Goossens and recorded in pictures where people now have the opportunity to enjoy the unusual beauty.

So, hidden changes that happen and can't be seen should still be pursued and studied for opportunities. If someone else had thought about what changes a damselfly could go through in less than a day, they might have considered the effect that dew may have on them. If that were the case, people might have enjoyed the new photo series a long time ago.

Adapt to Changes Quickly

Our fast-paced society generates continuous changes stemming from advancing technology and many other influences. An open mind pays attention to these changes and takes advantage of them quickly—if they're beneficial.

A humorous story tells of how a Parisian antique shop owner successfully sold five female sculptures. He originally wanted to sell the five sculptures as a single group, so he assembled them together and put out a sign which read "A Family of Goddesses." However, the first interested customer only wanted to buy the most beautiful one, so the sculptures became a group of four after the first sale. The owner then changed the sign to read "Goddesses of the Seasons," implying that each remaining sculpture represented a season. The next customer bought only the pair of sculptures that represented spring and fall, leaving summer and winter behind. The owner changed the sign again to read "Goddesses of Sun and Moon," one representing day and the other night. The next customer bought only the "Goddess of Sun." At this stage, only one sculpture was left. The owner changed his sign yet again to read "Goddess of Loneliness." The last customer liked the name a lot, perhaps because she was a lonely person as well, and bought the sculpture immediately. The owner had now sold all sculptures of the group by using names befitting each situation.[3]

Other shop owners in the same situation probably would have tried to sell the sculptures by just putting out a sign saying "Goddess Sculptures" in front of the group display. This owner, though, was different. He kept changing the sign to fit the number of sculptures that were still left. Each time the sign was adjusted to appropriately highlight the number of sculptures left. Each newly adapted sign gave customers a feeling that the remaining group was unique. By introducing changes to fit each new situation, the shop owner demonstrated the value of continuously adapting to new conditions to achieve better results.

Add Dynamic Changes

When something normally remains static, consider turning it into something dynamic. In this case, *dynamic* means something that keeps changing over time and thereby may contain more opportunities for improvement, since something that has dynamic content usually offers a variety of opportunities versus something that's static. If those dynamic contents lead to better results, the effort is well worthwhile.

When I first saw a Norelco electric razor in a department store, a drawing on the side of its packaging caught my attention. The drawing was a schematic diagram of a special technology used by the electric razor and clearly showed consumers why this razor gave a very clean shave. The rapidly rotating blades in the razor's head were used to cut hairs close to the skin, but the designers also incorporated a tiny metal component in front of each blade. This metal component contacts a hair just before the blade does, lifting the hair slightly before the blade cuts it off close to the skin. By lifting the hair before cutting it, the cutting blade is closer to the root of the hair. After the hair is cut off, the lifting component and blade move on and the remaining part of the hair retreats *below* the surface of the skin. The effect is that the remaining hair root is almost invisible so the skin looks and feels extra smooth after using this razor.

The best result a conventional razor can produce without the special lifting component is to cut the hair on the same plane of the skin. The lifting design introduced a dynamic property to the hair to cause the hair to be stretched a little bit just before being cut. Looking at the whole cutting process, the height of the hair is no longer a constant. Even though the hair is lifted for a very short period of time, and the lifting height is very small, the temporary change in the height of the hair improves the shaving effect by a lot. The lesson to be learned here is that when you encounter something which normally remains static in a process, try to find a way to make it dynamic in order to reap potential benefits.

Changeless Things Can Change

Many things in the world seem to be constant. A mountain just sits there; nobody expects it to change its position or shape by itself unless there is a major event like an earthquake. However, not everything that seems to be constant is incapable of change. If there could be a benefit in changing something that initially appears to be invariable, it may be possible to introduce changes in it.

The Suite Vollard in Brazil was one of the world's first spinning buildings ever to be built.[4] It has fifteen circular floors in total, of which eleven floors can independently rotate clockwise or counterclockwise. In one hour, each floor can rotate up to 360 degrees. The tenants of the building are able to enjoy landscapes in all directions without stepping out of their apartments. That must have been a completely new experience for the apartment residents. After the building was completed, architects used its unique design as a case study. Its design, construction processes, and tenant experiences are valuable information for future building designs containing dynamic features.

Several years after this building was completed, another architect designed an even more radical dynamic building, The Dynamic Tower of Dubai.[5] This is an eighty-floor, moving skyscraper where each floor can rotate independently. The occupants of the building could also enjoy a 360-degree landscape like the tenants in the Brazilian building. Additionally, the horizontal cross section of the building would not be round, but triangular. Since the external shape of the building is a combination of effects from each triangle-shaped floor, the shape of the building would be determined by what the respective angles of the various floors are at any given moment. When different floors rotate to different positions with various rotational speeds, the shape of the building would constantly change. That means viewers on the street would see a different appearance of the building when they look at it at different times. Few people would ever have seen such a spectacle before. If this building had been built, it would definitely have become a new landmark in Dubai.

Introducing a dynamic element into skyscraper designs has completely changed the convention that buildings are meant to maintain their shape and viewpoints. Prior to dynamic buildings, most people were used to buildings being in static states and few would have thought about transforming them into moving entities. Even most architects probably thought the same. Converting static building designs into dynamic building designs illustrates the inventiveness of the artistic architects of the moving buildings. Like these architects, developing the ability to introduce a dynamic quality into static things will foster creation of intriguing new things.

Usual Circumstances Welcome Positive Changes

Many things people find commonplace continue to exist that way until someone improves them by initiating a change. The person originating the change requires two attributes: one is having an intention to introduce the change, and the other is having an idea to implement the change. Without these aspects, the process for the change cannot even begin.

The 1956 Olympic Games were held in Melbourne, Australia. Since the Cold War was in full swing then, the political struggles between countries inevitably influenced sports and cast a shadow over the Olympic Games. A number of countries boycotted the Olympics as a sign of protest. Some countries, even though they participated in the Olympics, did not allow their athletes to have contact with athletes from other countries. The political conflicts also caused high tensions between the athletes themselves. The water polo match between Russia and Hungary had to be cancelled due to a bloody fight between the players from these two countries. Although the Olympic Games were based on goodwill, peace, and harmony, the animosity and tense atmosphere in 1956 led the members in the Olympic Organizing Committee to worry that these Games might be remembered as a failure.

Near the offices of the Committee lived a seventeen-year-old student named John Wing. When he learned what was happening at the Olympic Games, he became deeply saddened. He wanted to change the situation and make it a successful Olympics, even though he was just a young student. He got an idea and wrote a letter to the Committee with a suggestion. He sent the letter anonymously because he didn't want to be embarrassed in case the Committee thought his idea was ridiculous. He proposed that when the athletes enter the stadium during the closing ceremony, they shouldn't follow the order that was used in the opening ceremony, where the athletes from each country marched into the stadium separately in sequence. He proposed that in the closing ceremony, all athletes, no matter which country they came from, should walk into the stadium intermixed with one another as a big group. Thus, there would be no way to separate the athletes into political groups and athletes could enjoy themselves and wave to the spectators all together at the same time. All athletes would march under only the Olympic Games flag. Conflicts, wars, and politics would be impossible to associate with any specific individuals in that moment.

The Committee read the letter and loved the idea. They modified the closing ceremony plans immediately to follow the student's suggestion and the result was excellent. The unpleasant memories accumulated during the games were appeased by the newly introduced fellowship of the closing ceremony. Over time, the 1956 Olympic Games were remembered as the "Friendly Games." Since then, the same approach has been adopted as the official format for closing ceremonies and is still being used to this day. Thirty years after the Melbourne Games, John Wing announced his name publicly and received an Olympic medal for his historic contribution to the Olympic Games. A street in Sydney was also named in his honor.[6]

Before the 1956 Games, athletes paraded in the same format during the closing ceremonies as they did during the opening ceremonies: each country's athletes marched separately into the stadium in sequence. This was a format people had gotten used to and nobody had ever thought about changing it. The 1956 Games experienced so many disturbances due to political conflicts that it verged on a failure even the Olympic Committee wouldn't have been able to redeem. Amazingly enough it was solved by a seventeen-year-old boy. The idea he proposed was simple, but it was a breakthrough in mindset. Because the change focused the closing ceremony on the Olympic spirit rather than the participating nations, it's not surprising that the Organizing Committee adopted to the change immediately. It's surprising, though, that none of the seasoned Olympic Games officials could come up with an idea as good and as simple as this one. They needed to practice the skill of opening one's mind in order to introduce beneficial changes. So, even when dealing with things that have existed in a steady state for a long time, don't overlook an opportunity for making a helpful change.

Introduce Alternative Approaches

When a common approach does not work, a change to the approach must be introduced. You can take a radically different method to changing an approach (besides doing adjustments and modifications) by substituting the original approach altogether. Here's an example.

According to a 2015 BBC report, very few families in Cuba were allowed to access the Internet since the government had a strict control on public Internet access.[7] In recent years, however, many Cuban families have been equipped with Internet-ready tablets and laptops. The members of the families, especially the young generation, were eager to obtain the latest information from the Internet. The Internet cravings were so great, underground start-up companies emerged to focus on providing Internet-related services. For example, one of the companies secretly downloaded various content weekly from the Internet to large capacity hard drives, downloading things like soap operas, movies, TV shows, and popular apps from websites outside of Cuba. The distributors of the company then visited their service subscribers' homes with the hard drives. A subscriber could copy whatever contents he liked from the hard drive and the company would charge the customer based on how much and what he copied that week. Even though the customers were not able to be online, they were almost on the Internet with the company's service, just with a time delay. The alternative Internet service was so popular in Cuba that advertisement firms had chased the underground Internet-service companies to reach new clients via the magic hard drives.

When accessing the Internet did not work via telecom online services, the founders of the start-up companies must have thought about changing the way people would obtain content from the Internet. They devised a different method to replace the existing-but-forbidden one. As people were not able to download whatever they liked through online connections, why couldn't the Internet contents be moved to a movable media—hard drives—then let people download the contents from them? It seemed the perfect solution to the special Internet problem.

Therefore, when planning to introduce a change to an approach of doing something, in addition to considering modifying the original approach, make sure to include fundamentally different approaches as substitutes.

Chances for Change Are Endless

The types of changes that can be useful are almost boundless, so opportunities to introduce changes are unlimited as well. If there is a desire to introduce a change into a situation, there is a high probability that there is a way to do so.

Here is a story of Zen told by Master Hong Yi (1880-1942), a Chinese artist and Buddhist monk.[8] A long time ago, there was a temple that had a nunnery just across the street. A young monk lived at the temple and a young nun lived at the nunnery. For some reason, these two ended up arguing with each other whenever they would occasionally meet. One morning, the monk was standing at the temple's door and saw the nun leaving the nunnery. The monk asked the nun, "Where are you going?" She replied, "Where my feet are going is where I am going." The monk was stunned at the nun's rude answer. The monk went back into the temple and sought guidance from his master. His master gave him some advice, saying he could instead ask her, "If you did not have feet, where would you be going?" The monk remembered his master's words and couldn't wait to use the retort on the nun.

The next day, the monk was waiting at the temple's door early in the morning. When he saw the nun came out, he quickly asked the same question he had asked yesterday. "Where are you going?" The nun replied, "Where the wind goes is where I am going." The monk did not expect the nun's answer to be different from yesterday's response to his same question. Frustrated, the monk was again speechless. The monk consulted his master once more. The master advised, "No matter what she is following tomorrow, you can always ask, 'If you did not follow something, where are you going?'" Having heard his master's "one response covers all" solution, the monk became very confident about his next encounter. The third morning, the monk was waiting for the nun again. As soon as the nun came out the door, he quickly asked his original question yet again. "Where are you going?" The nun cleverly retorted, "I am not going anywhere today." What? The monk was baffled again, speechless, and disappointed at the failure of all of his previous days' preparations.

The nun's answer to the same question was different each day. The changing responses made all the monk's preparations useless. If the same question had been continued to be asked by the monk, the clever nun's answer would certainly have been different each time. The nun showed that chances to employ a diversity of changes are endless.

Summary

Changes constantly happen around us. No matter how small or large a change is, so long as you observe it, it can stimulate your thinking and form a basis for new actions. So, it's important to develop a keen sensitivity to changes. Introducing changes is another important aspect. The purpose of introducing changes is to add one or more variations to some characteristics which are normally seen as constant or unchangeable and to determine if those changes produce positive results. Remembering this principle will expand your mind and make life more interesting. Check out the following:

- ☐ Pay attention to hidden or unnoticeable changes, large or small, in processes or situations.
- ☐ Don't underestimate the importance of small changes, as they may have significant meaning.
- ☐ Introduce changes proactively if they are beneficial. For example, create and apply changes to quickly adapt to new situations.
- ☐ Alter something which is normally static so it becomes dynamic to produce an improved result.
- ☐ Don't assume that something which seems immutable can't be changed in a positive manner.
- ☐ Make changes by substituting an element in a process or a thing.
- ☐ Recognize the endless ways to introduce changes in life.

14

Take One More Step

When people take on the challenge of solving a problem or creating something new, their thought process will eventually grind to a halt. There are a number of reasons for not continuing. Maybe they think they have reached the answer they are looking for, or perhaps they believe that they've run out of information. Of course, you can't continue to ponder a topic forever. However, as the title of this chapter suggests, there are probably ways to take another step in a thinking process when others ordinarily stop, if you persevere.

If you've ever played chess, you may have heard, "Think three moves ahead." Chess players typically win more often if they plan their next three moves (not just the next move) on each of their turns, including calculating how their rival could respond to each of their moves. Although the advice of thinking three steps ahead is good, you may want to consider thinking *four* steps ahead instead of *three*. That way, you may see what others don't see because you took the extra step. This is an example of applying the Take One More Step concept to play a game. In general, if you take another step on your way to a solution, you may generate more new ideas.

Take Another Step to Open New Frontiers
One of the advantages of thinking one step further is that the approach forces you to not stop deliberating at the point where you would normally give up. You can push yourself to go one step more, asking questions like "What happens next?" or "Then what?" If others are actively working on

something new, you may want to think about the next new thing once the current project is accomplished. Thinking in this way will put you one step ahead of the others, ready to achieve the next goal.

In the past several years, the rise of drone technology has attracted many manufacturing companies to join the rush to develop these unmanned aerial vehicles. Drones have served in many capacities for military and civilian purposes, from attacking terrorists to helping volunteers monitor wild life. Some online retailers have even started to use drones to deliver goods to consumers' back yards. The drone industry is only at its beginning stages and its full potential has yet to come. Not everyone in the industry, however, is working to develop or manufacture drones. According to *Popular Mechanics*, at the 2015 tradeshow of the Defense and Security Equipment Industry in London, the German defense company Rheinmetall Defence Electronics displayed a new drone-related product.[1] It was not a drone, but a drone killer! The company had anticipated that despite drones bringing in a lot of technological advantages, they could also bring negative aspects as well. Drones are small flying objects that are hard to detect. If used by someone with bad intentions, a drone could cause significant damage to a military or civilian target. Therefore, people should have the ability to defend themselves against a drone before it could cause harm. The product developed by the defense company is a laser gun whose strong beams were able to destroy or disable a flying drone almost instantly. A video made by the manufacturer showed the laser gun shooting down a drone in midair several thousands of feet away in an exercise where the drone pretended to invade a massive sport arena. The drone killer drew a lot of interest at the show.

While other manufacturers fiercely competed to develop new drones to capture market share, the German defense company thought one step ahead. The members of its R&D team probably figured out what new demands would need to be addressed when drones became a commodity. After taking the extra critical-thinking step that resulted in their new idea, filing a patent to protect the drone-killer design, forming a development plan, and producing the product were relatively straightforward.

Therefore, when many others are jumping aboard a hot trend, think calmly about what will be new when the current trend becomes just ordinary. In this way, you'll probably discover a new frontier on the horizon.

Add Another Step in a Process

Another advantage of explicitly taking another step beyond what is obvious at the time is that it helps you to see opportunities which may occur in the next stage of a development. Otherwise, you may miss seeing the potential benefits of the extra effort.

Here's a good example of how you can take advantage of thinking one step ahead of the curve. To prevent abuse of online registration processes from spammers, websites added a now widely used special validation capability to the registration process called CAPTCHA. In the validation step, a person who is registering on a website is required to read a distorted image of random text and correctly respond by typing in the corresponding text. The text image is pre-distorted so that automated character recognition software programs are unable to read it, only a human can. This validation approach effectively blocks robotic attempts to register websites.

Built on the concept of CAPTCHA, an evolutionary program called reCAPTCHA was subsequently developed by a team at Carnegie Mellon University to help digitize old books, magazines, newspapers, and other documents. In the Internet era, most written materials are already in digital format, so the material can be stored, shared, and searched online easily. Unfortunately, many of the materials generated in the pre-Internet era exist *only* in printed formats. Converting all these materials into digital formats by hand is nearly impossible. So, optical-character-recognition programs have been developed for computers to scan and convert these documents into digital data. However, no matter how good the recognition software is, inevitably there are many words which cannot be interpreted by software correctly. Thus, documents generated by character recognition programs still contain many mistakes.

The innovation of reCAPTCHA lies in how it uses the words which couldn't be recognized by character recognition software as the images of text used in normal website registration verification processes. Extending the idea of CAPTCHA a step further, reCAPTCHA then uses the human-interpreted results from people who read the CAPTCHA verification images to find the correct meaning of the text images. An originally mistaken word is submitted many times as a verification word by different people, and those human responses to the word are combined and sorted to determine the correct meaning of the word. The corrected result is then fed back into the original converted document to correct the mistake.

It's estimated that there are over a hundred million website registrations every day in the world. Assuming each verification event uses about ten seconds of human attention, those events then represent a total of a quarter-million hours of intelligence work each day. The website registrations become a "free" gigantic and powerful collective-intelligence workforce. The results of the invention are impressive. By 2013, just for *The New York Times*, more than ten million articles were digitized with the help of this invention![2]

The Take One More Step principle is illustrated quite well in reCAPT-CHA's innovation. Its inventors obviously weren't content with the success of just using distorted word images to verify website registrations. Many people would conclude this great success was sufficient and that no further improvement was needed. That may be true, but why not get even more value by extending the CAPTCHA program and using it as a basis for solving other problems? When the CAPTCHA concept was approached this way, you can easily recognize the benefit of tapping the power that the correct validation answers provided from the mass of online registrations using relatively little additional effort. In this case, it capitalized on the existing human interpretations to solve the limitations of character recognition software.

We should continually think about extending an existing solution *one more step* to provide other valuable innovations.

Think One More Step to Identify Consequences

Many times, thinking another step ahead helps you to see possible negative consequences of the approach as it develops. Some unacceptable consequences may not be obvious and are either unseen or ignored. However, when bad consequences are identified ahead of time, you have the opportunity to decide what actions need to be taken. Those resulting actions are a direct benefit of "thinking one step further." Actually, people understand this relationship quite well after they see the consequence. We often hear people say, "I should have had thought of that before." Most people would agree that that statement recognizes the obvious *after* it is pointed out; that they should have taken the one more step *before*.

About twenty-six hundred years ago, it was the Spring and Autumn period of ancient China. The country was divided into many states. The largest one was the State of Chu and its head was King Zhuang. The king initiated a series of wars with other states because he wanted to gain control of the entire country. One day, after he was victorious in a major battle, he hosted a huge celebration banquet to reward his generals and soldiers. In the banquet, the king and his soldiers thoroughly reveled in their hard-earned victory. When dusk fell, the king wished to continue their jovial merrymaking. He ordered several large candles to be lit and had his two most favorite concubines raise a toast to the soldiers.

Suddenly, there was a gust of wind and the candles were blown out. In the dark, a soldier groped one of the concubines. She tried to stop his crass behavior but the soldier continued fondling her. During her struggle, she pulled off the ribbon on the man's hat. When the candles were lit again the offending soldier left quickly. The concubine reported the incident to the king and asked the king to find the soldier without a ribbon on his hat and punish him for his misdeed. The king listened to his concubine's tale, thought it over for a while, and then gave the following order. He told all the men to take off their hats so that they could drink more easily. Following the king's order, the men all took their hats off. Without hats, no one could identify the man whose hat didn't have a ribbon.

Years later during a brutal battle, the king got into a perilous situation. A courageous general led the army and fought fiercely, eventually defeating the enemy and rescuing the king. Afterwards, the king wanted to express his profound gratitude to the general, but the general replied, "No, it is I who should thank you, your majesty!" He then confessed to the king that he was the man who had inappropriately touched the king's concubine at the celebration banquet. He was sincerely grateful to the king because the king had decided not to punish him by ordering that all the soldiers take off their hats.[3]

King Zhuang had a long-term vision. When his concubine wanted him to seek out the guilty man based on his ribbonless hat, the king thought one step further. If he had done what his concubine wanted him to do, identify the ill-behaved man and carry out a just punishment, what would its consequence have been? The generals and soldiers might have resented the king for executing a general just because his concubine had been touched. Such a punishment was normal at that time for such an offense, but it would have caused discontent among the king's followers. The king really needed the generals and soldiers to be cohesive to help him realize his goal of conquest. That's why he decided to overlook the offense and let the offender go. The result proved that the king had made a very smart decision that ultimately saved his life.

We can see from the above example that thinking an extra step ahead will help us to see possible serious consequences and take necessary actions to avoid such events. In turn, if we don't think far enough ahead when considering how a situation will turn out, negative results may occur without warning. If such unintended consequences happen due to lack of a desire to think further, most people will blame themselves, thinking, "Why didn't I think of that?" However, by then it is likely too late.

Here is another example. Since ancient times, human beings have wondered, "Are we the only intelligent creatures in the universe? Is Earth the only place with living things? If there is extraterrestrial life, what do they look like and are they smarter than we are?" Until recently, people did not expect answers to those questions in their lifetimes, though they were still curious. However, the dawn of space travel has stimulated our burning curiosity to search for extraterrestrial life and to communicate with aliens. Now human beings are able to launch spacecraft which can travel within and beyond our solar system. Theoretically, these spacecraft can search for life on other planets belonging to other solar systems and even contact them.

In 1972, NASA launched Pioneer 10 to chase this dream of discovery.[4] Pioneer's mission was to eventually leave our solar system and go into deep space. People hoped that someday during its journey it would encounter other forms of life, particularly intelligent life from another solar system. For this purpose, the spacecraft carries a plaque, an aluminum plate anodized with gold. The plaque contains basic information about the Earth and humans. The mission designers hoped extraterrestrial intelligent life would discover the plaque and understand its meaning, and thus be able to figure out where the Earth is in the universe, and perhaps visit us. Along with other information, the plaque also contains engraved images of a man and a woman, the shape of our solar system, and the position of our solar system in space. By overlapping the human bodies and the silhouette of the Pioneer spacecraft, an intelligent life form may be able to understand the size of the human body.

NASA did not stop the effort to discover extraterrestrials using only one spacecraft. NASA launched Pioneer 12 in 1973, and Voyager 1 and Voyager 2 in 1977.[5] The Voyager spacecraft carry even more information about us. They each carry a golden record, which is a large disk like phonograph record. The record contains sound and picture information about humanity's life on Earth. It contains greetings in fifty-five different languages, music from different nations at different times, sounds from nature such as wind, thunder, and bird's chirping. The designers of the record hoped that someday an intelligent alien species will find the record and decode its content so they will know they have neighbors with good wishes in the vast lonely universe. On September 12, 2013, NASA announced that Voyager 1 had left our solar system and officially entered interstellar space, heading towards its next destination: another star similar to the Sun.

Many people want these spacecraft to bring exciting news of discovery, but renowned physicist Stephen Hawking poured cold water on people's hopes in a 2010 series broadcast on the Discovery Channel, according to The Telegraph.[6] He warned the world in the interview that it is better not to contact extraterrestrial life, since we don't really know whether contact with extraterrestrial intelligent life would be a blessing or a curse. He thinks that it's very likely an extraterrestrial civilization may view the Earth as a resource they can exploit, and may view human beings purely as intelligent labor they can enslave. If that is true, are not all of humanity's efforts in trying to contact extraterrestrial life essentially asking for big trouble?

It's surprising that the spacecraft's plaque and record designers apparently did not consider how critical the information is that was intended to be understood by alien life. Why did no one think more thoroughly about the consequences of what could happen in the next step? It would be fine if the aliens were benevolent, but what if they're more intelligent and have reasons to harm us? If that is the case, our efforts to communicate information about the Earth to other civilizations in turn may have put our beautiful planet in danger! Are we prepared for the potentially dire consequences of the mission planners' not thinking about the next step? Steven Hawking thought one more step ahead.

Be Prepared by Thinking Ahead

Imagining potential future evolution paths of something can help you predict its possible outcomes. Ask yourself these questions: If this happens, what will happen because of it? If an opportunity evolves, what should I do to capitalize on it? If a bad situation evolves, what should I do now to minimize it? If you make a habit of looking at possible future consequences of actions, you will be better prepared to deal with various outcomes.

Here's a legend about an eminent Japanese businessman who was the founder of a large consumer electronics company. One day the businessman, accompanied by several of his executives, went to dinner at a famous steak house. When they finished their main course, the businessman told the executive sitting next to him in a low voice to call in the master chef of the restaurant. The executive glanced at the businessman's plate and saw that half of the steak was left uneaten. He wondered whether the chef would be upset since it appeared the customer may not have found the meal to be satisfactory.

The chef quickly came to their table. He was apprehensive, since he knew these guests were very influential. Surprisingly, the businessman told the chef that he had nothing to worry about. The businessman said the steak was great. The reason he called in the chef was to let the chef know he could only eat half of the delicious steak since he was of advanced age and his appetite wasn't as good as it used to be. The businessman's simple explanation kept the chef from feeling bad when he would see the uneaten portion sent back to the kitchen. After the businessman's explanation, the chef was able to breathe a sigh of relief and was grateful for the old man's kindness.[7]

The businessman was an expert in thinking one step ahead. He not only thought about the leftover steak being wasted, but he also thought further about the chef's feelings upon seeing a half-eaten steak being thrown away. No chef would be happy to see his customer throw away a fine dish that he had worked on so carefully. The businessman used his outstanding thinking skills to show his kindness and generosity of spirit.

Summary

Any thought process will stop at a certain step because either it has obtained a satisfactory result or it lacks the information required to go further. The Take One More Step principle encourages you to resist the desire to end your thought process and instead try to think of what will happen after the point where others normally stop. The following are a few tips in using this technique:

- ☐ Think about what the next stage could be to explore new opportunities while most people continue to focus on the current stage.
- ☐ Contemplate what new benefits might arise during a concept's evolution.
- ☐ Identify future benefits or problems ahead by examining more stages down the road and take action to secure or prevent them.
- ☐ Consider additional steps to gain a more complete picture of your situation.

Notice What's New

New resources are constantly appearing throughout our lives. There's so much new information about stuff that's available from a wide variety of familiar outlets like TV, newspapers, and websites whose sole purpose is to expose you to current news. The word *news* can be traced back to Middle English in the fourteenth century as a plural for the adjective *new* or *new thing*. News items include new products, new data, new phenomena, new perspectives, new ideas, and so on. The appearance of new things enriches people's knowledge and introduces them to fresh information, expanding their scope of thinking and providing additional triggers for generating unprecedented new solutions. This chapter focuses on how to improve creativity by paying more attention to new things and exploiting their potential advantages.

Connecting to Something New

Actively connecting something that has newly emerged with something that already exists can provide opportunities for improvement of the pre-existing item. There are always aspects of situations that can be improved, such as efficiency, performance, convenience, appeal, and so on. It is not trivial, though, to build relationships between what exists and something new, which can lead to an improvement.

To show how to improve something by connecting it to newly available resources, let's look at a story about online commerce giant Alibaba. According to *Business Insider*, in 1995, Jack Ma, a young English interpreter from Hangzhou, China, traveled to the US to help a company with a financial transaction.[1] During his trip, he visited a friend at his home in Seattle, Washington. It was there that Ma, who had never touched a keyboard before in his life, discovered the Internet. At that time, people in the US and other western countries were learning how to use search engines for finding merchandise on the Internet. As a test, Ma entered the word "beer" into the search window. He was surprised that the only results were brand names of beers, which were well known in the US, but no Chinese beers were listed. He immediately became excited by the Internet and its potential to be extended into other geographies. He realized that the Internet could help companies in China improve the way they were doing business by opening doors to expose themselves to an almost unlimited number of businesses and potential customers, especially for medium or small-sized companies. When he returned to China, Ma built an online service company that provided a platform to support businesses that wanted to take advantage of these vast new opportunities. After experimenting with the concept, he founded Alibaba with his friends in 1999. The company grew very rapidly, and currently it has a majority share of online sales in China. On September 19, 2014, Alibaba became the largest IPO in the history of the New York Stock Exchange. Alibaba's success dramatically improved how many Chinese companies did business.

The terms *online* and *Internet* were no doubt unfamiliar to most people back in 1995. To young Jack Ma, the terms were not only unfamiliar, but they also represented brand-new concepts. He reacted by thinking about how those new concepts could be employed to bring about improvements. That's why, when he discovered the Internet, he immediately realized its colossal importance and came up with an idea that could improve Chinese companies' traditional ways of conducting business. He got the idea by *actively* noticing and then acting upon the improvements that could be gained from this new capability. Imagine what would have happened if Ma had surfed the Internet in his friend's home just for fun and hadn't deliberately thought about how this new platform could be used to benefit Chinese companies. If he had not pondered the possibilities, the largest e-commerce company in China today would certainly have a different name.

The name "Alibaba" has its origins in the Arabian story of "Ali Baba and the Forty Thieves," where a poor woodcutter named Ali Baba discovered and opened a cave full of treasure with the password "open sesame." In modern times, Jack Ma opened his door by enabling traditional commerce to use the power of the Internet to turn it into the treasure of electronic commerce. Two lessons can be learned from this story. It is advantageous to notice when new information is exposed, and to *actively* think about how it can benefit existing things.

Solve Problems or Fulfill Wishes with Something New

Sometimes problems occur in life where there are no apparent solutions, and sometimes people's wishes or desires are unable to be fulfilled. That doesn't mean, however, that the problems have no solutions at all, or that there is no way to fulfill a wish in the future. New resources often shed new light on solutions to old problems or how to grant unfulfilled wishes. When encountering these situations, think about things that have come to light recently and examine them to see if the new resources can be brought to bear on the problems or help grant wishes.

Car crashes are a serious problem that doesn't have an adequate solution to eliminate them. According to Wikipedia, there are roughly 1.2 million deaths and 50 million people are injured in road accidents each year worldwide.[2] Car crashes cost the US $300 billion annually. With short distance wireless communication technology becoming more advanced, this problem may soon be solved. According to the US Department of Transportation's initiative of vehicle-to-vehicle communications for safety, in the near future cars on the highway will talk to each other via short range communication signals.[3] Each car will exchange critical information (such as location, speed, and direction of travel) with its neighboring vehicles so all vehicles can be aware of each other in real time. Some scenarios include: cars that discover a dangerous situation will immediately inform other cars of it, cars that change speed suddenly will send a message to other nearby cars so they can act on the information, and cars that plan to turn or leave the highway will warn the cars around them before they make the maneuver. This new communication system between cars will significantly reduce car crashes and improve their occupants' safety. The problem of car crashes, if not completely solved, will be greatly reduced when these systems are deployed widely in automobiles.

New things can also help to realize people's unfulfilled wishes. Here's an example just for that. Long distance physical contact has been a wish for many generations. Since ancient times, it has been an unrealistic dream to have two people who are great distances apart be able to feel physical touch from one another. This desire has been possible only in the realm of science fiction, and perhaps in dreams—until recently. One of the Best Inventions of 2006 selected by *Time* magazine has changed the situation.[4] CuteCircuit developed a "smart" shirt that allows two people who may be thousands of miles apart feel an embrace between them. The shirt has embedded sensors and actuators that detect the touches, temperature, and heartbeats of the person who wears it. The sensor's outputs of each shirt are then transmitted to the remote wearer's shirt by using short range wireless communication between the shirt and a nearby mobile phone that, in turn, connects to the long-range wireless cellular network that links to the remote mobile phone and its shirt. After a shirt receives the data from its counterpart shirt, it then recreates the associated gesture, body warmth, and heartbeats with its embedded actuators. With both shirts communicating between each other in real time, the two people wearing the shirts can feel physical hugs with each other.

This "smart" shirt invention only became possible when (1) cellular mobile networks were widespread enough to simultaneously cover the locations of both participants, (2) short distance wireless technology became developed enough to reliably transmit data between complex devices and mobile phones, and (3) sensor/actuator technology became sophisticated enough to detect and provide realistic sensations. Obviously, the designers of the shirt must have focused on the newly available technologies to accomplish one of humanity's longtime dreams. Something to be learned from this example is that when examining something new, try to detect what new capabilities or methods it provides. After that is done, think about how it might be applied to solve problems or fulfill wishes. This last step may result in a satisfying "ah-ha!" discovery moment.

Create Something New from New Resources

Knowing about something new can not only help in providing solutions to old problems or unrealized hopes, but it can also provide a catalyst to generate something else completely new. Since all newly discovered resources have some properties that were unknown before (otherwise they wouldn't be new), these properties may be used to help stimulate the creation of totally new things, such as new designs. Without the stimulus of recently discovered resources, new things stemming from them may never be discovered.

Years ago, a number guessing game called *Limbo Unique* became available online.[5] The multi-player Internet game supported an almost limitless number of players. Here's how the game worked. After the game started, each player was allowed to enter a guess at a natural number one at a time into a dialog box on the screen. Players could enter numbers multiple times if they desired. The game software remembered all the numbers entered by all the players. At the end of the game, the player who had guessed the smallest unique number (meaning only that particular player had submitted that number) won. This challenge of number guessing made the game quite interesting. The number a player guessed could not be too small, otherwise it would easily overlap with numbers guessed by other players. The number could not be too large either, otherwise it would likely not meet the "smallest unique number" condition. This was a game in which each player's behavior strongly depended on behaviors of all other players. During a game, each time a player entered a number the web page would show the relative position of the player's number in the mass of all entered numbers from all players. For instance, when a player entered the number 315, the screen might show that 315 was unique but there currently were 9 unique numbers from other players that were smaller than 315. When a player didn't know details of the numbers entered by other players, guessing what number should be entered to win the game was a big challenge.

After the Internet became popular, many traditional games like chess, poker, and even mahjong were turned into online versions. Friends thousands of miles apart could play against each other just as if they were sitting next to each other. The origin of this smallest unique number guessing game described above, however, was very different from the new versions of traditional games. It was a completely new game that only could have been spawned by the Internet. Without the capabilities of the Internet, it is hard to imagine how such a game could have been possible. The game required many people to play the game simultaneously, but no player knew the numbers entered by other players who were competing. The developers of the game must have seen the huge possibilities for new ways of human interaction brought on by the Internet. The Internet allowed many online users to be connected to the same platform but still be relatively independent of each other's online behaviors, and this became the core enabler of the game. So, when examining a newly discovered resource, don't forget to think about what other totally new things might be created because of it.

New Opportunities from New Situations

New things may bring secondary opportunities to light, like creating a big market or lowering costs. Taking advantage of such opportunities is another way to help open your mind.

After the transcontinental railroad was completed in the 1870s, a lot of heavy-labor jobs (like lumberjacking) were created along the exploding railroad lines. The laborers' jobs were very hard on clothing and the worker's pants deteriorated quickly from the constant wear and tear. This created a pressing need for more durable work pants. Jacob W. Davis saw this unmet need, so he and Levi Strauss developed a new type of pants for the workers. The pants were made from heavy duty cotton duck or rugged denim cloth. In addition, the weak points in the seams and pockets were reinforced with copper rivets. These pants were the ancestor of today's popular jeans that are worn throughout the world. It could be said that the opportunity to create jeans was generated by the new situation that the transcontinental railroad provided.[6, 7, 8]

Another example shows how new things can provide opportunities to reduce costs. The arrival of email has brought great convenience for written communication. With email, we no longer need to buy stamps to send letters and wait days for delivery. We can send messages of almost any length to as many people as we want, virtually free. In addition, emails reach their destinations almost instantaneously no matter where the destinations happen to be. Compared with traditional postal service mail, the cost to send a letter and the time to deliver it has been greatly reduced. Of course, these electronic improvements also give the same advantages to junk mail generators. By transferring junk mail from post offices to email systems, the junk mail people save a huge chunk of money. That's probably the reason why we receive so many junk emails everyday now. Whether it is considered good or bad, the birth of email provides nearly cost-free written communication for almost everyone.

So, pay more attention to the opportunities made available by new resources. It's a waste to ignore these opportunities. The inventors of jeans didn't waste the opportunity of creating rugged pants to satisfy the needs of building the transcontinental railroad, and junk mail generators don't waste the opportunity to decrease their cost of sending written communication due to the emergence of email systems. Take a lesson from these inventive people who took advantage of the stimulus brought on by new things and did not waste their opportunities.

Advantages from New Phenomena or Conditions

New things sometimes may represent new phenomena or new conditions. The new phenomena or conditions can be used as fertile soil to grow new ideas as well.

In the 1990s, several companies started developing passive radar systems, which are quite different from the traditional active radar systems, according to a 2003 report of *BusinessWeek*.[9] An active radar system is composed of a transmitter that sends radio waves toward an object and a receiver that detects the echo of the wave reflected from the object. Based on the time delay and strength of the echo signal, the radar is able to determine the distance and size of an object. In a passive radar system, there is no transmitter but, instead, passive radar uses existing radio waves generated by countless devices in wireless communication networks that exist almost everywhere today. The receiver detects the changes in the ocean of radio waves continuously generated by wireless communication networks. If an object is moving in the radio wave "ocean," it will disturb the wave, just like a navigating ship causes ripples in water. Passive radars can detect this disturbance and analyze it with sophisticated software, then determine the position and size of the object. The passive radar system can be used by police to monitor traffic flow and congestion. The military can use the system to spot invading aircraft. Using passive radar for air defense has a unique advantage over traditional radar, since almost all anti-radar missiles attack radar by detecting the position of the transmitter in a radar system. The passive radar system does not have a transmitter, so an anti-radar missile is ineffective.

Along with the advantages of personal untethered communication, ubiquitous wireless networks brought with it a new phenomenon: the radio ocean. Since wireless towers and mobile phones are everywhere, the radio signals emitted by the towers and mobile phones form a radio wave "ocean." Any moving objects that reflect radio waves, such as cars or airplanes, aren't able to escape being in the ocean and thus must move through it, enabling them to be detected. This new phenomenon must have provided inspiration to the designers of passive radar systems. They may have thought: why not use the recently created radio wave ocean of wireless devices to detect moving objects and eliminate the transmitter? Think of this example for inspiration to pay more attention to new phenomena and find innovative uses for them.

Notice What's New in Time

In our daily lives, new things are constantly happening. These newly available resources can be taken advantage of in time. Much of our time is spent updating our knowledge of recent news. Frequently, it is smart to take advantage of newly available resources as soon as they appear. Product designers and talk show hosts use this concept very skillfully, don't they?

Here is a classic soldier joke about an event that happened in a military camp. Sunday was a day free from duty for the soldiers stationed in the camp. One Sunday, a group of soldiers decided to go into town by train to have some fun. Their sergeant told them they had to be back to the camp before dusk. By nightfall, none of the soldiers had returned to camp and the sergeant was upset. Finally, one soldier appeared at the gate of the camp the next morning. The sergeant, who was waiting at the gate, demanded that the soldier explain why he was late. The soldier explained that his watch had stopped the previous day's afternoon and he consequently missed the train back to camp. He then got a cab, but the cab broke down along the way. After that, he went to a nearby village and borrowed a horse, but the horse died before he could get back to camp. He then decided to walk the rest of the way. That was what had made him late.

The sergeant thought the soldier's explanation made some sense, so he didn't reprimand him immediately. The second soldier returned soon thereafter. When the sergeant asked him his reason for being late, the explanation was almost exactly the same as the first soldier's story—watch stopped, missed train, cab broke down, horse died, and walked back. The sergeant was annoyed and then became flabbergasted when more soldiers came back, one after another, all with explanations that were the same as the previous soldiers. Now the sergeant was really angry since the soldiers were obviously lying. When the last soldier showed up at the gate and started to say, "My watch stopped and missed the train, so I got a cab . . ." the sergeant lost his temper and interrupted him. "Are you going to tell me that then the cab broke down along the way, you went to a village and borrowed a horse, the horse died . . . right?"

Surprisingly, the soldier said, "No, my cab didn't break down."

"Then why were you so late?" questioned the sergeant. The soldier grumbled, "There were so many broken down cabs and dead horses on the road, how could the cab drive me back to our camp on time?"

Obviously, the last soldier had paid close attention to the immediate situation. He thought quickly and used the explanations given by his fellow soldiers only moments before for his own defense. He cleverly updated his strategy based on the most current information available. This tale shows the value that can be gained from knowing the most current information and using it to your advantage quickly.

Summary

Paying more attention to newly available resources nourishes your thinking capacity. For perpetual problems, the solution may hide in something that was only just discovered. For unfulfilled wishes, a recently discovered development may provide opportunities for hope. New resources may bring opportunities not only to improve something that already exists, but also to create brand new things not yet seen. New things are emerging endlessly, so continually strive to improve your powers of observation to constantly refresh newly available resources. Work to transform these new assets into valuable new ideas. Here are several areas you may want to consider:

- ☐ Be sensitive to things that are fresh and new. Frequently check up on what has become available recently.
- ☐ Investigate whether something new may present an opportunity to improve what exists.

☐ Find out if a newly discovered item may be the key to solving a longstanding, unresolved problem.

☐ Try to create completely new things that no one has ever thought of before with newly feasible resources.

☐ Pay attention to new concepts, new methods, new platforms, new trends, new products, new technologies, new situations, new theories, new viewpoints, and so on.

☐ Be timely in how you take advantage of new resources.

Keep a Balance in Mind

16

Think Symmetrically

Many things have counterparts which are direct opposites. For example, for *Yin*, there is *Yang*; for *positive*, there is *negative*; for *up*, there is *down*. By generalizing this concept, we can find more pairs of opposite counterparts, such as *father* versus *son*, *forward* versus *backward*, *my opinion about you* versus *your opinion about me*, and so on. Thinking symmetrically means that when you're thinking about something, you remember to think about its opposite counterpart, too. Many people use this without knowing it. For example, when people hear about a free lunch, they not only think about its positive benefits, but also its potential negative effects. That is a type of symmetrical thinking! However, it is uncommon for people in a lot of situations to explicitly think about a situation in a balanced way. Concentrating on thinking more symmetrically will help you identify the possible, and sometimes hidden, opposite counterparts of the subject and provide more opportunities to develop your open mind.

If Not Me, Then You

One area where you can apply symmetry is the implementation of an action. When someone plans to execute an action, think about whether the action implementer's opposite counterpart is able to take the action instead to improve the outcome.

After 9/11, tighter airport security caused a lot of stress and frustration for many travelers. Everyone, regardless of race, age, or gender, was required to follow strict security screening procedures to ensure maximum safety on airplanes. All passengers had to empty everything from their pockets, take their belts and shoes off, pull out their laptop computers and other electronic devices from their bags, and put their coats and luggage in plastic bins to be X-rayed. Travelers needed to arrive at the airport quite early and wait in long lines for security checks. It was all very inconvenient. Passengers wished the government would find a better way to handle the airport screening without compromising security. One option was for the government to implement a new program where travelers were pre-screened and special boarding passes were issued to let them pass the checkpoint without detailed screening. However, this kind of selective screening would raise obvious discrimination concerns, such as profiling, so it didn't seem feasible to implement the program.

In 2005, however, the Transportation Security Administration (TSA) began the trial program Registered Traveler to improve a traveler's airport security experience.[1] In this program, the *passenger* would voluntarily initiate a security pre-screening process that would include a thorough background check. When TSA approved the traveler as low risk, the traveler would then be issued a Registered Traveler card. With this card, a traveler didn't need to go through the lengthy security process at airports; instead, they could access a special security lane and were able to pass the security checkpoint much faster than other travelers.

The key point of the Registered Traveler program was that the background investigation would be initiated by the traveler, *not* the government. This way, the program would avoid the drawback of presumed government bias. In the context of thinking symmetrically, the government and the traveler were a pair of opposite counterparts within an action: initiating traveler background investigations. In this case, it was ill-advised for the government to initiate a selective investigation of travelers because of potential discrimination issues, so could the traveler (the opposite counterpart of the government) initiate the same investigation? Yes, of course. It's unwise for the government to select travelers for pre-screening unless the selection would be random, but the *traveler* could self-select and make the request to be pre-screened, avoiding the problem of discrimination. Remember, when an action is performed by an implementer, think about how the implementer's symmetrical counterpart may be able to accomplish the same action with even more benefits.

Behave Contrarily

Most people get used to how others preform certain tasks or operate in certain situations. We even learn to anticipate these behavioral actions. Under such circumstances, try to see if you can think of an action opposite to the action everyone else is taking and find benefits of this opposite action.

In April 2014, a YouTube video was posted about a policeman who stopped a car on a local road.[2] In the video, a cruiser with its lights on followed a car and orders it to stop. The driver, a young woman, stopped at the road side and the police car parked behind her. The policeman walked to the driver's side window and saw that the woman was bewildered.

"I didn't violate any traffic laws. Why did you pull me over?" the lady asked with a puzzled look. The policeman explained to her that he had followed her car for a while and that, at the last stop sign, he observed that she had come to a full stop before continuing across the intersection. The policeman really appreciated that she had followed the traffic law so conscientiously. To show the police department's appreciation, the policeman pulled out a hundred-dollar bill and handed it to the woman, telling her she could keep it.

"Is this for me? Really?" The woman was astonished, but happily accepted the money. She was totally unprepared for this windfall. The interesting video clip received millions of hits in just a few days!

It's common to see police stopping cars, and no one thinks much about it unless they're the one pulled over. Stopping a car not for a violation but to reward the driver, however, is unheard of. In this situation, the police department showed an impressive ability to think symmetrically. When they invented this tactic, they must have thought, "We always give tickets for violations of traffic laws, why can't we also reward drivers when they carefully follow the rules?" Therefore, for any particular action, think about its symmetric action that may produce benefits.

Is Turnabout Fair Play?

When an action is applicable to an object, reflect on whether the action may be applicable to the object's opposite counterpart as well. Try it to discover if there are benefits by doing so. People are naturally biased toward one counterpart or the other, primarily because they don't realize that the other exists or haven't thought about symmetry. In many cases, there's no reason why an action can't be applied to both sides of a pair of symmetrical counterparts.

In 2008, there was a case involving a group of badly behaved teenagers in Florida. According to a report on *USA Today*, two of the teenage boys played a prank on an unsuspecting girl at a fast food drive-through. The sixteen-year-old driver ordered drinks from the girl at the window. After the girl handed over the drinks, she reached out to give the driver the change and was met with a whole cup of icy cold soda thrown all over her from the car. The boys roared with laughter. Before the girl could react to their cruel attack, the car swiftly accelerated out of the driveway, leaving the unfortunate girl dripping and flabbergasted at the window. This cruel prank was recorded by the fifteen-year-old boy in the car and was soon uploaded to YouTube. The brazen pranksters proudly flaunted their practical joke for the world to see, humiliating an innocent young girl who was just doing her job. However, the teenagers didn't know that the girl was a very tough cookie. She persevered in chasing down the teenagers, and from the YouTube clip she tracked down their names and home phone numbers, eventually leading the police to arrest the suspects. The case was tried in court and the boys were found guilty. When the court decided what kind of punishment should be applied to the boys, the judge's decision was somewhat surprising. The judge ruled that the teens should create an "apology video," which contained not only their apologies to the girl, but also showed a picture of their arrest when they were handcuffed facedown over the hood of a car. The judge ordered the teens to put the video on YouTube for anyone to see. Posting the video clip was an apology to the victim, but it was also a deterrent to other kids who may have had any similar intentions.[3]

The judge's ruling was unique. The teenagers thought it was cool to put the video on YouTube for people to see their mischief and how the poor fast-food girl was humiliated. If we view the teens and the girl as a pair of opposite counterparts, the act of exposing an embarrassing video on YouTube can be applied to both of them. Since the teens had put the video on YouTube to embarrass the girl, it was perfectly logical that the teens could post another video on YouTube to show *their* embarrassing moments as well. It was a totally symmetric way to design a punishment for the teens' previous actions. This ruling was so innovative, it was covered by the media. What we can learn from this example is that when an action is applicable to one object, think about whether or not it can be applied to its opposite counterpart, too.

A Good Thing Might Be Bad

One of the results of thinking symmetrically is that when there is a clearly attractive positive property, there may be a co-existing negative property that is unattractive. Even though advantages are clearly preferred, an advantage and a disadvantage are still a set of twins. A lot of time, the more advantageous something is, the more disadvantageous it is as well. Thinking symmetrically reinforces the notion of explicitly remembering to think of the potential disadvantages that correspond to the more obvious advantages. Thus, when others only see an advantage, symmetrical thinkers will find both parts and expose their differentiation. If you only identify the benefit, and the opposite counterpart of the benefit is not considered, problems may loom ahead for your idea.

Here's the famous Battle of Red Cliffs.[4] At the beginning of the third century, the Han Dynasty, which had ruled China for almost four centuries, was coming to an end. During this tumultuous period of instability, various warlords controlled their separate territories. After numerous battles among the warlords, General Cao Cao emerged as the most powerful. By 207 AD, General Cao had gained total control of the land north of Yangtze River. The east side of China faces the Pacific Ocean, and the west side of China is a high plateau. The Yangtze River, flowing primarily from west to east, divides northern and southern China. At that time, the southern area of Yangtze River was controlled by a joint force of two warlords, General Sun and General Liu. The Sun-Liu army used the Yangtze River as a natural line of defense. However, General Cao wanted to fulfill his dream of controlling all of China. To reach that goal, he had to cross the river and defeat the Sun-Liu army.

In 208 AD, General Cao gathered a huge army at Red Cliff, a town on the western shore of the river. (In that particular section of Yangtze River, the river is oriented south-to-north.) General Cao ordered his soldiers on the west side to be trained to use boats so they could cross the river to fight with the Sun-Liu army on the east side. The Yangtze River is often windy and has high tides. General Cao's soldiers came from the highlands in the northern region and were not used to the training involved with naval warfare. Many soldiers became seasick. Then, someone on General Cao's staff made a suggestion that aroused his interest. The idea was to increase the stability of the boats by interlocking the boats with iron chains. If many boats were interlocked into single "giant boats," its huge mass would minimize the rocking. General Cao liked the idea a lot and immediately ordered his troops to link the boats together. After the boats were connected, sure enough, the soldiers were able to walk on the boats just as if they were walking on land. It was very stable indeed, and the seasickness problem was solved.

At the same time, the generals of the Sun-Liu army observed General Cao's interlocked boats and came up with a brilliant idea to defeat him. A few days later, a messenger from an old general in the Sun-Liu army, General Huang, arrived at General Cao's camp in secret. The messenger told General Cao that due to unfair treatment in the Sun-Liu army and fear of General Cao's military power, General Huang had decided to defect to General Cao's side with his men. General Cao was pleased to hear this message and set a time for General Huang to surrender.

On the promised night of surrender, General Cao's soldiers, now used to living on the "giant boats," saw a fleet of boats quietly crossing the river from the other side. Each of the moving ships was covered with a tarp. It appeared from a distance that the surrendering troops were under the tarps. General Cao was standing on his flagship, ready to happily welcome General Huang. When the quickly approaching fleet crossed over the middle of the river, a loud bang suddenly came from one of General Huang's boats. It was a signal! On this signal, General Huang's fleet began belching smoke and soon burst into flames. Hidden under the tarps were not surrendering soldiers, but highly flammable materials covered with oil and grease. The few soldiers who had started the fires on each of General Huang's ships jumped into smaller escape boats, which were towed behind the flaming fleet.

General Huang's soldiers cut the tow ropes and rowed the small boats back to the Sun-Liu camp. With the help of a heavy east wind, the unmanned flaming fleet quickly floated toward General Cao's connected ships like giant fiery arrows. On impact, General Cao's ships caught fire and the resulting inferno rapidly spread. General Cao's soldiers were not prepared for this at all. Although they tried their best to disconnect their ships so they could escape, the fire spread too fast. They had no time to save the boats and their lives. The intense fire lighted the sky high above the river. As a result, General Cao's soldiers burned to death or drowned. General Cao luckily escaped, but most of his army did not. General Cao's ambitious war plan was utterly thwarted by General Huang's ingenious ruse.

When the idea was proposed to General Cao to interlock the boats in his fleet, why didn't he think about the idea symmetrically to see both the advantages and disadvantages of the concept? Interlocking the vessels together solved the seasickness problem, but in case of fire the ships could not independently maneuver, so how would they escape? In the absence of such symmetrical thinking, General Cao's troops were almost annihilated entirely. Perhaps, if General Cao had used a little symmetrical thinking, maybe the outcome of the battle at Red Cliff would have been very different and changed the course of history. Unfortunately, history accepts only facts, not "what ifs," but it does provide lessons for later generations.

They're Thinking the Same Thing

Symmetrical thinking can be used in almost all aspects of our lives. For example, putting oneself in someone else's shoes is a manifestation of symmetrical thinking. In order to fully understand a circumstance, we should not just see something from our own point of view, but also tackle it from our opposite counterpart's viewpoint. If a person blindly considers a situation only from a single perspective, it would be difficult to understand all of the different aspects. Even though the following story is fictitious, it illustrates the basics of this argument.

A businessman read of new discovery by explorers concerning a small, isolated island in the ocean. The island was unique in that the people living on the island had two horns on their heads, like buffalos. In short, they looked freakish and bizarre. The businessman began to think about the potential business opportunities of the discovery. He figured that if he could secretly capture one of the islanders, take the creature back to civilization, open a live show, and put the captured creature on display, it would bring him riches. Everyone would want to see the strange two-horned man. Who would want to miss seeing it? Ticket sales would go through the roof.

Having made up his mind, the businessman rented a yacht with the necessary equipment and quietly went to the island alone. The result of his journey, however, surprised everyone, including the businessman.

Two weeks later, a large tent appeared in the island's market square. Outside the tent's door, a wooden plate was plastered with an announcement written in the unique island language. The announcement read: "I have captured a strange alien, who has *no* horns! You have never seen such a creature before. If you want a peek at this creature, get your tickets here now! The ticket price is one island dollar for adults and half price for children." The islanders rushed into the tent to see the so-called "alien." Inside the tent, the businessman was locked in a cage, naked and chained with hollow eyes, looking completely different from his usual civilized appearance. Visiting islanders pointed fingers at him and exclaimed loudly in their language, which the poor businessman could not understand. As a result, the lucky islander that captured the businessman made a lot of money at the unfortunate businessman's expense.

Why was the outcome of the businessman's plan completely out of his expectations? The big mistake the businessman made was that he did not evaluate his plan with symmetrical thinking before he sailed to the island. Yes, it was true that a captured two-horned islander was the businessman's opportunity for fortune, but why didn't the businessman represent a business opportunity for a two-horned islander as well? In this case, an otherwise well thought-out business plan backfired on the businessman due to his lack of symmetrical thinking.

Summary

Typically, things have symmetrical counterparts, e.g. *advantage* versus *disadvantage*, *leaving* versus *arriving*, *government* versus *people*. If you want to cultivate a creative mind, remember to think symmetrically and try to avoid the natural human tendency to only think about one side of an issue, forgetting the other side. When thinking about something, you should not only look at the things obviously related to your object but also consider its symmetrical counterparts. This can help you identify counterparts which are easily overlooked and grasp a more complete picture. Here are some situations where thinking symmetrically can be helpful:

☐ If someone performs an activity, see if his opposite counterpart that is able to perform the same action.

☐ When most people perform the same action, examine whether a symmetrical action may be carried out as well.

☐ An action is normally done relative to someone or something, so think about whether the action may be done relative to a symmetric counterpart.

☐ If something happens in a particular situation, imagine what would happen if it were in a symmetrical situation.

☐ If A takes an action toward B, consider what would happen if B took the same action toward A.

☐ Develop the habit of putting yourself in your counterpart's shoes.

Recognize Complementary Parts

In most cases, what we notice about something is usually just a part of the whole picture. The rest of the picture can be considered as its complementary part. Most of the time people pay more attention to one part and pay little or no attention to its complementary part. For example, when people read a story about a businessman's accomplishments, they may not think about the failures that led to his success. These failures represent the complementary part of his success story. Therefore, one approach to expanding your mind's creativity is to proactively look for complementary parts of things, especially unusual ones. New ideas can be discovered by exploring the unnoticed complementary parts.

Don't Overlook Complementary Parts

Sometimes people confuse a complementary part with a whole. They think one of the complementary pair is the whole and miss the other, that leads to an incomplete picture.

A head librarian must be quite knowledgeable. When a library patron has a question that cannot be answered by the other librarians, the head librarian should have an answer, right? The famous French librarian Duval, working for King Francis I, did not think so.[1] When visitors to his library had questions, many times Duval would simply answer, "I don't know." He did not make excuses just because he was the king's librarian.

One day, a visitor became upset by Duval's repeated response of "I don't know." The visitor asked him, "Does the king pay your salary for you to answer visitors' questions this way?" Duval wasn't angry when he heard the visitor's insulting question, but instead he replied modestly, "The king only pays me for what I do know, not the part I do *not* know. If he wants to pay me for what I do not know, I am afraid all the treasure he has would not be enough!"

Clearly, the visitor didn't realize that "the knowledge the librarian possessed" and "the knowledge the librarian didn't possess" were a pair of complementary elements. When the answer to a visitor's question was within Duval's knowledge, he would supply an answer. If the question wasn't among the knowledge Duval possessed, then the question had to be in its complementary part—the knowledge he did *not* possess. In such cases, the librarian's answer should of course be "I don't know." Duval saw the whole picture, while the visitor confused himself by seeing only the one part and believing that it was the entirety of the realm of knowledge.

Kofi Annan, the seventh Secretary-General of the United Nations, once told a story about how an English teacher taught him a good way to observe complementary parts.[2] At the time, he lived in Ghana, where he and his friends would learn English in their teacher's office. One day, the teacher pulled out a large piece of white paper and put it on the wall. On a corner of the paper was a black dot. The teacher asked the boys to identify what they saw. The boys answered the teacher's question quickly, "A black dot." It seemed to be the perfect response. But the teacher was disappointed because none of the boys said, "A large piece of paper with a black dot." The teacher's purpose behind performing this "black dot" experiment was to broaden the boys' view of the world. The test left a deep mark on young Kofi. Since then, wherever he went, he always tried to understand the whole picture when observing something and avoided jumping to conclusions by only seeing one part of it. After he became the Secretary-General of the United Nations, he often reminded people to not only notice the terrible things that were being done in the world, but also see the many beautiful things happening every day to improve human lives.

The black dot was just one part of what the teacher put on the wall. Unfortunately, the boys only saw the black dot and overlooked its complementary part, the large piece of white paper. We don't know if this "black dot" experiment left a lifelong lesson to each of the boys that day, but we do know that the teacher's effort continued to benefit the former Secretary-General of the United Nations for the rest of his life.

Complete the Picture by Finding the Complementary Part

Complementary parts exist in many areas. People are often naturally biased when looking at a complementary pair. Creating a deliberate process to find a complementary viewpoint will help you remember that there are complements to most things. Only when both complementary parts are known will a clear picture of the whole be complete.

Many years ago, I was teaching physics at a university. To encourage my students to understand the contents of textbooks more completely, I gave them a quiz. I asked the students to tell me what was said between page seven and page eight of their textbook. The students tried to answer the question by quickly turning to the indicated pages. They immediately realized that this was a strange question, since page seven and page eight were opposite sides of the same physical page, so how could there be information *between* those pages? The students thought the answer should be "nothing," but they knew the answer couldn't be that simple, so they waited for an explanation.

I suggested that perhaps the information that was *between* the two pages was the content the author knew but didn't write down. The real goal of the quiz was to tell the students to think beyond the information explicitly described in the textbook and to read *between* the lines. I wanted the students to know that there were many things the author didn't say in the book, and that, when reading a book, they should not only understand what had been said in the book but also consider what was *not* said in the book. A student will grasp the information and concepts more completely in a book by reading in this way. The quiz obviously had some impact on the students; maybe because they had never thought of that approach before.

A textbook can't contain everything about a subject. The contents are just a part of the knowledge the author chooses to write about. Information that is controversial, inconclusive, or too difficult for readers to digest will probably not be included. The information the author chooses to reveal and the information the author ignores can be thought of as a pair of complementary parts. By observing this, and paying attention to both the stated contents and the contents not spelled out in the book, readers can get a deeper understanding than others who merely read only what the author says in the book. This approach can be used in many situations. Try to determine *both* complementary parts of something. This way, you won't miss seeing the whole picture.

A Part Changes with Its Complementary Part

The boundary between the two parts of a complementary pair may not be rigid. There may be interactions, adjustments, and compensations between the two parts. You can adjust a boundary to manipulate the complements into producing favorable results. Here is an examples illustrating this principle.

Once, when I gave a presentation promoting innovation to a group in Dallas, Texas, I noticed that the projector I was using had a unique feature. The projector had a high-power lamp so that the image projected on the large screen was very bright. When I completed the presentation and turned off the lamp, I heard its fan speed increase a lot almost immediately. The high-speed air flow quickly cooled down the lamp and the projector's power could then be turned off safely in less than thirty seconds. This feature contrasts with other projectors that normally need several minutes of cool-down time. It's interesting to analyze this feature with respect to the topic of this chapter. The total electrical power consumed by a projector is limited to a maximum based on its power supply design. Basically, we can consider the power consumed by the lamp and that by the fan as a pair of complementary parts. During a presentation, the energized lamp consumes most of the total power available and the fan uses only a small fraction of it. After the presentation is over and the lamp is turned off, the fan can then draw much more power, giving the fan an opportunity to increase its speed to reduce the cool down time.

This is an innovative example of increased efficiency. A similar adjustment between the two parts of a complementary pair can have applications in many other areas, too.

Choose the Part That Yields a Better Result

When something is divided into a pair of complementary parts, the two parts may not be equal in size or other traits. If the entirety of something is known, then when one complementary part is known, the other part will be known automatically. Why? Because the unknown part is equal to the remainder when subtracting the known part from the whole. Why not compare the two parts and select the one that has the same effect but causes a better result?

The February 2016 issue of *Business Insider* published an interview with Paul Krugman, who received the 2008 Nobel Prize for economics.[3] The interviewer asked him about his views regarding global economics and politics. One interview question was about who he would support in the 2016 presidential election. He didn't admit who he would endorse, but he did indicate who he wouldn't support. He was quite critical of Bernie Sanders, and he stated that he didn't like any of the Republican candidates. He never directly said who his favorite candidate was, but after his unique response, was there any lingering doubt as to whom he'd actually support?

In the early stages of the 2016 presidential election campaigns, hopeful candidates included a crowd of Republicans and two Democrats. Paul Krugman didn't say who he favored. Instead, he declared who he wouldn't support: any of the Republican candidates and Bernie Sanders. This put all of the Republican candidates and Bernie Sanders into one category, and the only remaining viable Democratic candidate as the category's complement. Did he then really need to say the name of the person he would support? The result was that even though he didn't utter the alternative candidate's name at all, Paul Krugman let the world know who he favored!

The story shows that calling attention to one part of a situation can be a useful communication tool to call attention to its complementary part. Study this example and think about how to apply this principle to areas you are interested in.

Summary

When thinking about something, don't forget to pay attention to its complementary part as well. Two complementary elements usually accompany each other to completely characterize something. Complementary factors are frequently overlooked when observing something. Noticing complementary aspects can provide opportunities for new insights. Among the methods for thinking about complementary parts are the following:

☐ Explicitly think about identifying the complementary parts of everyday things.
☐ Choose the complementary part that delivers a better result.
☐ If using one aspect doesn't work, try its complementary part.
☐ Try adjusting the ratio between a complementary pair to favor the more advantageous one.
☐ Take the opportunity to improve the performance of an element when its complementary part changes.

18

Find Favorable in the Unfavorable

Unfavorable situations happen all the time in the form of defects, failures, trouble, delays, setbacks, futility, hardship, bad luck, obsolescence, lack of resources, market declines, and misjudgments, amongst others. It's human nature to try to avoid these situations, eliminate them, or limit their adverse effects. A benefit to having an open mind is that when confronted with an adverse situation, you will not only consider how to minimize its negative effects, but go one step further and look for opportunities to generate positive results from it, potentially replacing the unfavorable situation with a favorable one. Wouldn't that be wonderful? On the other hand, when a favorable situation is encountered, don't forget to look for possible adverse factors as well. Developing a habit of always looking at both favorable and unfavorable properties will cultivate your creative mind.

Change the Perspective
One approach to dealing with an unfavorable situation is to investigate whether there is any way that it can be viewed favorably. If so, this method may generate highly desirable results. It's often just a matter of perspective to transform it into a blessing in disguise. When viewed from a new perspective, the same situation may reveal completely different results.

Skyscrapers adorn the downtown area of many large metropolitan cities. However, the crowded buildings give GPS positioning systems a big challenge. Since their tall frames often block GPS signals from satellites, it is unfortunately quite common for someone driving in a large city to be unable to use their GPS location services. According to Polaris Wireless's website, a new idea to overcome this problem was proposed some years ago. Cities now are filled with all kinds of radio waves, including those from satellites, wireless towers, and other radio devices. All of these radio waves are blocked and deflected by buildings differently, based on their unique combinations of specific propagation characteristics of the radio waves at a particular location. These characteristics act like the "radio fin-gerprints" of the city. If the city's location-dependent radio fingerprints are mapped and recorded in a database, the geographic position of a specific location can then be determined by measuring the properties of the radio waves at a location and matching it to the database using a look-up table. This system is a great complement to the GPS system that faces challenges in large cities.[1]

It's a fact that concentrations of large buildings block GPS signals and is a clearly unfavorable situation for GPS location services. But, if the perspective on this situation is changed to look at the interference in a positive manner, we observe the unique radio wave signatures and deter-mine location by matching the characteristics of the signatures. Then the interference produced by the buildings is no longer considered unfavorable and becomes favorable. In other words, the approach proposed by the idea wouldn't work without the previously viewed unfavorable interference from the buildings. This example shows that changing a perspective may lead to transforming an unfavorable situation into a favorable one.

Turn Unfavorable Factors into Favorable Factors

An unfavorable situation is caused by one or more unfavorable factors. Another way to deal with an unfavorable situation is to find ways to convert the unfavorable factors into favorable ones that will improve the situation. Explicitly identifying and working to change these unfavorable properties is a preferred action.

There are many homeless people all over the world living at the bottom tier of society unfortunately. They often sleep on the streets, wander aim-lessly around cities, and frequently lack adequate food. More fortunate and kind-hearted people try to help them by supporting shelters and donating food. A gentleman living in Scotland, Mel Young, found a special way to help homeless people around the world. He proposed the idea of encouraging homeless people to play soccer. He wanted to rebuild homeless people's self-confidence enough to return to society by playing various positions on soccer teams. In 2001, Mel Young and Herald Schmied co-founded the Homeless World Cup. The first tournament was held in Austria with eighteen international teams attending in 2003.

Since then, the Homeless World Cup has been held in a different city every year. The homeless in many cities have even formed their own soccer teams. During the Homeless World Cup season, teams from different countries come together to compete. For example, the 2014 tournament was held in Santiago, Chile. Sixty-three teams from forty-nine countries joined the competition. It was reported that out of the participants in the tournaments, the vast majority said that their experiences with the Homeless World Cup initiative had a positive impact on them and made significant changes in their lives.

Through the Cup, many homeless people have made strong friendships, become self-confident through establishing a can-do attitude in their lives, and now feel they haven't been totally abandoned by society. Many of them have returned to the better days of their lives when things weren't as bleak. Many have reunited with their families, brought joy back to their loved ones, and embarked on new lives. Through these positive changes, they have regained respect from their communities and ordinary people have shown increased compassion for homeless people after learning about the Homeless World Cup. Perhaps the world has become better because of a soccer ball.[2, 3]

Few would deny that homelessness is a distasteful aspect of society. Encouraging the homeless to participate in soccer is likely to have a positive long-term impact for them to change their lives than the short-term effects gained by just providing food and shelter. Participating in soccer assists the homeless in changing their views about the world and their attitudes towards life, helping them to reintegrate into society. Young's cleverness shows that he didn't just help homeless people with their basic needs, but also raised their self-esteem. Turning a negative situation around by changing its unfavorable factors is a good means to employ when trying to approach a problem at a new angle.

Transform a Challenge into an Opportunity

When an unfavorable situation presents itself, the most common reaction is to overcome it as quickly as possible. The ability to create a favorable situation during the process of overcoming an unfavorable one is uncommon, but it's far more superior to concentrating on conquering the unfavorable situation alone.

A legendary story is told about a well-known restaurant in an eastern European country.[4] In the early twentieth century, the restaurant was very successful under the leadership of its owner and was considered an elegant example of a fine restaurant specializing in local cuisine. Many famous public figures were regular customers. The owner's children also worked at the establishment and were of great assistance to the owner. As the owner grew old, he began to consider which of his children would be the best choice to succeed him. The owner had pondered long and hard on this issue, no less than that of a king when choosing a successor.

One day, an important banquet was held at the restaurant. Everything was going smoothly until, suddenly, all the lights went out unexpectedly. The guests put down their eating utensils and wondered if it was an electricity outage. The next moment, the owner's oldest son, who was helping his father cater the banquet, calmly led a team of waiters into the hall, each holding a tray with brightly flickering candles. The waiters then carefully set down several candles on each table. The son and his staff didn't show the slightest hint of panic and acted like this was all part of the plan. People began to whisper, "Could this be a surprise event orchestrated by the owner to entertain us and not a power outage after all?" Indeed, after all the tables received candles, more candles were also lit around the hall. Then the son greeted all the guests in a strong voice and asked them to enjoy their meals in the cozy atmosphere of a candlelit dinner. Then the guests looked at the flickering candlelight that made the banquet room appear to be both elegant and mysterious, as if all the guests were floating in the dreamy merriment of a wonderland. The guests enjoyed themselves in the unexpected yet pleasantly surprising candlelit dinner. In reality, an electrical outage did occur. The owner's oldest son, who kept his composure and used his quick-thinking skills, had changed an awkward situation into a pleasant atmosphere of sophistication that appeared to be all pre-planned. His ability to handle such a crisis so well enabled him to quickly go to the top of his father's list for becoming the rightful heir to the business. Later, under the son's leadership, the restaurant experienced even greater success.

It was unfortunate that a sudden power outage happened during an important banquet at the restaurant. To cope with such an incident, many restaurants would have reacted by sending waiters and waitresses rushing to light candles on guests' tables so the guests could continue to dine. This restaurant owner's son didn't just think about how he could provide enough light for the guests to continue eating, but also thought of how he could turn the unfortunate incident into a positive opportunity for guests to enjoy the charming experience of a candlelit dinner. A seemingly pre-planned formal lighting ceremony would explain why he and the waiters set candles on the tables gracefully, and also explained why decorative candles were also lit around the room. His objective was to create a lovely atmosphere to let his guests feel that the outcome was even better than if the darkness from the power outage hadn't happened. This was the difference between the son and other restaurant managers. Therefore, when facing an unfavorable situation, don't just think about how to eliminate it quickly, but also think about how to use the situation to create a favorable situation. This demonstrates a way to extend thinking.

Focus on Positives

Every aspect of an unfavorable situation is not necessarily negative. On the contrary, there are often many positive aspects, although the negatives may be more prominent. Consequently, another way to treat an unfavorable situation is to focus exclusively on its positive features and ignore the negative aspects. Focusing on the positive attributes of a situation can reduce a generally negative disposition. Rebalancing the two opposing aspects by increasing the impact of the positives can influence more favorable results.

A TV advertisement for diamond rings, which I watched in a hotel room when I was traveling to Asia several years ago, was quite impressive. The ad was not for rings with large diamonds, but rather for rings encrusted with many small diamonds. Rings with small diamonds are generally graded as inferior to rings with large diamonds and, consequently, it must not have been easy to design an effective marketing approach to attract buyers to the rings. But this ad was designed to be especially compelling.

The ad described the rings by saying, "We are introducing a type of ring which abounds with a myriad of dazzling facets that surpasses all other types of diamond rings! Wearing this beautiful diamond ring will turn heads with its shimmering elegance!" The ad's statement was very appealing without twisting the truth. The number of small diamonds in these rings was significantly greater than that of rings with larger diamonds. Each tiny diamond in these rings was cut in similar way and polished just as the larger diamonds. So, there were many more light-reflecting facets in the small diamond rings than in the rings with the large, higher-grade diamonds. This advertising approach must be very effective in attracting customers.

Most people traditionally favor rings with large diamonds. That predisposition makes it difficult to create an enticing story for rings with small diamonds. Customers feel that this type of ring has little appeal other than being cheaper. In this case, the marketers astutely identified a unique aspect of the small diamond rings that could strongly compete with large diamond rings and could even put the large diamond rings at a disadvantage. This ad must be successful because it helped alleviate traditional perceptions, allowing prospective customers to see the bright side of the lower-grade diamond rings.

There's a classic joke that takes the principle of "focus on the favorable aspects of an unfavorable situation" to the extreme. An employee in a company was especially lazy. He had accomplished almost nothing in the course of an entire year. At the end of the year, his boss called him into his office, intending to lay him off. The manager asked him, "You have done nothing this year and have made almost zero contribution to our company's business. Give me a reason why I shouldn't fire you." Unexpectedly, the employee rolled his eyes and calmly replied, "Okay. When I go on vacation, you don't need to find a replacement to cover my job!"

The lazy employee's words were entirely true. He didn't do anything anyway, so whether he was on the job or not didn't really matter. So, if he went on vacation, of course the boss would have no need to find someone to cover his absence. Even though the lazy employee apparently had little value to the company, his way of thinking showed that he had a better ability to tackle challenges from a unique perspective than most of his colleagues.

A Negative Situation May Be Positive in Other Circumstances

Viewing a situation as favorable or unfavorable usually depends on its circumstances. A situation that is seen as unfavorable in one circumstance isn't necessarily unfavorable in another circumstance, or may even be perceived as favorable in yet another circumstance. Given this, it is prudent to examine the circumstances of a situation that is considered unfavorable, and then look for circumstances where the same situation can be considered as favorable.

Around the year 1907, the Scott Paper Company of Philadelphia had a whole railroad car of paper delivered for the company's production of soft, thin toilet paper. Because of a manufacturing problem, however, the delivered paper was too thick and couldn't be used to make toilet paper. Facing this situation, the head of the company, Arthur Scott, had to make a difficult decision. It would be simple to just send the paper back, but it would cost someone a lot of money to replace. Then, Scott remembered a story in the local newspaper where a school teacher had developed a novel way to limit the spread of germs. She had given soft paper to students with runny noses so they didn't need to go to the bathroom to use toilet paper to wipe their noses. Thinking about this article, Scott got an idea to use the rejected soft—but too thick—paper to make paper towels. The railroad car of paper was made into towel-sized sheets and marketed as sanitary paper towels. The paper towels were disposable and very hygienic because they were only used once, helping to prevent the spread of germs. The paper towels were quite successful after being introduced to the market. Today, it's hard to imagine a kitchen without paper towels![5, 6]

The situation had started off as clearly unfavorable. The whole railroad car of paper was considered unusable because it was too thick. Ordinarily, when a paper shipment didn't meet the requirements, it would be returned to the manufacturer. Arthur Scott thought beyond that simple reaction. He figured that since the paper wouldn't make good toilet paper, it might be good for some other purposes. That thinking, along with associating his materials with the article about the teacher, stimulated him to conceive the thick and soft paper towel. Keep this in mind when facing an unfavorable situation, and don't be discouraged.

Think about whether unfavorable situations can turn favorable for you in different circumstances, just like the situation of the railroad car full of rejected paper.

Reversed Scenarios: See Negative Aspects of a Positive Situation

Common sense says that pros and cons are involved with almost everything. In the above sections, we considered cases where finding favorable factors in unfavorable conditions is the main focus. The same notion is applicable to the opposite situation. When presented with a favorable situation, examining its potential unfavorable aspects is necessary, too. This way, it's possible to proactively improve the situation or be prepared for disadvantageous circumstances should they appear.

There is a de facto unwritten rule in the business world that a company must put the customer first because customers are key to a company's financial success. But does this common business concept contain flaws? When a company always puts its customers' interests first, where does it put its employees' interests? The answer may reveal that this universal perception has some cracks. At least one company questioned this rule and designed its business practices differently. According to *Business Insider*, Southwest Airlines has been putting its employees first.[7] The company puts more of a direct emphasis on employee happiness than it does on customer satisfaction. They did this by developing a fun and inclusive culture that inspired employees to give their best in their jobs. The company believes that if it treats its employees well, in turn the employees will treat its customers well, too. The practice of putting the employee first has paid off well financially and in terms of customer satisfaction. Southwest has been ranked as one of the best airlines with top customer service in the US.

Despite the fact that most companies highly praise the slogan "always put the customer first," Southwest Airlines doesn't follow the idea blindly. In fact, its policy of putting the employee first is quite clever. Good customer service is not just a slogan, it's a team effort that requires employees to perform. If a company has dissatisfied employees, how can it presume its employees will provide top-notch services to its customers? When a company overly emphasizes customers, ignoring the employee's interests, the phrase becomes an empty saying. Hence, the true focus should be on what is the best way to provide superior customer service, using either the "Put the customer first" or the "Put the employee first" approach.

Summary

Things almost always have two sides to them. The good and the bad normally coexist. Life is not always smooth, and adverse situations inevitably occur. Conversely, there are few completely adverse situations where there is no possibility to reduce the negative impact. Confronted by an unfavorable situation, open-minded thinkers will try to convert an adverse situation into a favorable one, or at least attempt to generate some favorable results out of it. On the other hand, favorable things may have unfavorable factors as well. Open-mindedness exposes multiple ways to deal with both favorable and unfavorable situations, such as:

- ☐ When evaluating an unfavorable situation, change the perspective to a viewpoint where it can be treated as advantageous.
- ☐ Transform an unfavorable factor into a favorable factor.
- ☐ Treat an unfavorable situation as a challenge and create a favorable situation by overcoming it.
- ☐ Focus purely on the favorable aspects of an unfavorable situation and ignore the unfavorable parts.
- ☐ Examine the unfavorable aspects of a favorable situation so the situation can be improved or adverse circumstances can be avoided.

19

Try Reversed Approaches

As with anything, people usually find it relatively easy to come up with and adopt a traditional approach to reaching their goals. However, people with open minds will not be satisfied by only considering traditional approaches, but by also examining unusual approaches. Reversed approaches, which are 180 degrees in reverse to traditional approaches, are one way to handle something in an unusual fashion. Under many circumstances, reversed approaches can be beneficial in reaching the desired goal. When considering a traditional approach, don't forget to evaluate the opposite approach. If the effect of the opposite approach seems better than that of the traditional approach, then give the reversed approach a try.

Reverse It

Reversed approaches, which are complete opposites of traditional approaches, should be examined if traditional approaches don't work or do not work well enough. When a traditional approach cannot reach the desired goal, it implies that the traditional approach doesn't contain all the elements needed to reach your goal. Taking an opposing approach may create new conditions that are favorable in reaching the original goal.

The common potato was introduced from its origins in the Andes of South America to Europe as early as the sixteenth century. Potatoes are a good food resource for humans. However, convincing Europeans to grow and eat the new kind of food was a very slow process. One important reason was that at the time only seed crops were grown in Europe and people were not familiar with crops like the potato, which are planted by cutting harvested potatoes into pieces and burying the pieces in the ground. Europeans felt that the strange plant could potentially be harmful to humans. They refused to grow and eat potatoes for themselves and only grew small amounts for animal feed.

However, the rulers of many European countries came to realize the benefits of potatoes. They considered them to be a good source of nutrition to help avert famine, which was quite common back then. But because of the widespread aversion to potatoes, few common people ate them. King Frederick II of Prussia had to enact harsh laws to force his people to plant and eat potatoes. He even threatened to cut off the ears and noses of those who refused his orders. Under threat of punishment, Prussians had no choice but to obey. As a result, potatoes became one of the major food sources of a Prussian diet by the Seven Years War (1756-1763).

Potato's popularity in France was later than that in Prussia. The potato's popularization in France is attributed to Antoine-Augustin Parmentier (1737-1813), a French chemist and a vocal promoter of the potato as a valuable food for the French. Parmentier served as a French army pharmacist during the Seven Years War. He was captured by the Prussians and spent years in a Prussian prison. While in prison, he ate potatoes almost every day. From that experience, he learned the values of potatoes and later returned to France and tried to help King Louis XVI make potatoes popular. He tried many ways to promote potatoes and to encourage people to plant and eat them. Through his efforts, the Paris Faculty of Medicine eventually declared that potatoes were edible by humans. The potato advocate hosted many banquets that served mostly potato dishes and invited prominent guests to taste them. He even sent potato flowers to the queen so she could pin the flowers in her curls.

Parmentier remained unsatisfied with the result, however, and eventually decided to take a unique approach to convince the French people to voluntarily plant and eat potatoes. He requested fifty acres of land in suburban west Paris from King Louis XVI. The entire parcel was planted with nothing but potatoes. He then had the field patrolled by armed guards and didn't allow anyone to get close. It appeared that he had planted a highly valuable crop and was afraid someone would steal it. This aroused the public's curiosity about the type of plant that was growing there, thinking that only a very valuable plant would be so heavily guarded. People came to feel that it would be great if they could steal some plants from the land and grow it in their own fields. So, people started bribing the guards to allow them to steal just a few plants. Actually, Parmentier had already instructed these guards to accept the bribes and let people steal the plant. As a result, many people stole the plant and grew the plant not only on their own land but also shared the plant with their friends and relatives. The practice of growing and eating potatoes thus spread quickly. Perhaps the adoption of the potato wasn't all due to Parmentier, but less than ten years after Parmentier cultivated them in the Parisian field, potatoes became one of most popular foods in France.[1]

Parmentier used his creative mind to devise the strategy of using armed guards to protect the planted potatoes. Since the conventional approaches he had used to try persuading people to grow and eat potatoes were not very effective, he came up with an idea utilizing reverse psychology, turning 180 degrees from pressuring people to grow potatoes to pretending to prevent them from growing the crops. Through this deception, people became motivated to grow and eat potatoes, and the king's original goal of spreading the production and consumption of potatoes in France was realized. Just think, without Parmentier's idea of reversing a conventional approach to the problem, perhaps we may never have known the awesome taste of French fries!

Using an opposing approach is not only helpful in encouraging people to do constructive things, but also can play roles in preventing people from doing harmful things.

About 2,500 years ago, there were many independent states in China. Among the strongest was the state of Chi that was ruled by Duke Jing. The Duke's prime minister was Yan Ying (578-500 BC), who was considered to be the most creative thinker of his time. One day, the Duke heard that his favorite horse had suddenly died, and the news made him very angry. The horse's groom was ordered to the Duke's court immediately. Still in a rage, the Duke ordered his guards to execute the groom by butchering him alive into small pieces to punish him for the death of the horse. The Duke also warned the ministers in the court that if anyone tried to stop the execution, they would be executed in the same grisly manner. Everyone in the court, except the Duke, knew it was very unfair to execute the groom so brutally just because he may not have done his job well. But no one spoke up to defend the groom because they would suffer the same fate.

Just then, Yan Ying left the silent group and went over to the condemned man. He pushed the groom's head down with his left hand, while his right hand drew his sword. It appeared as if he was going to slice the man to pieces in accordance with the Duke's order. Before he swung his sword, Yan turned to the Duke and asked him, "When great rulers in ancient times butchered a person, which part of the body did they sever first?" The Duke thought for a time about the question and finally stood up and said, "Wait . . . I have changed my mind and have decided to let him go." The groom was then set free.[2]

Yan Ying lived up to his reputation of being a creative thinker. When he realized that the traditional approaches to keep the Duke from cruelly killing the groom would be ineffective, he abandoned them. Instead, he turned the tables and acted as if he was going to carry out the Duke's irrational order to punish the poor groom. Yan's surprising reverse approach made the Duke reconsider his order after realizing that a great ruler should not brutally kill a person for a serious mistake. Duke Jing decided he didn't want to be remembered as a brutal ruler stemming from this incident, thus making Yan's unusual approach effective in preventing a tragedy.

When conventional approaches don't provide the desired results, consider experimenting with approaches that are completely opposed to the conventional approaches. Use this alternative method to explore another route to reach the original goal.

When Conditions for a Conventional Method Are Not Met

There are situations where a conventional approach cannot be applied, since the conditions to use it aren't present. This poses a big challenge, and many people give up searching for an effective solution. In this kind of situation, approaches which are totally reversed from conventional ones should be considered. If the conditions for applying a conventional approach don't exist, it doesn't mean that the conditions for applying a reversed approach don't exist, either. Since there is no other alternative, why not try the opposite approach? A silver lining might be found after all.

Taitzu was the first emperor of China's Song dynasty, reigning from

960-976. Under his rule, each state was required to send tributes to him to show its loyalty. The annual tributes were escorted from each state to the capital by a prestigious local scholar assigned by the state governor. The emperor would also dispatch a member of his court to accompany the local scholar to the state prior to the tribute being sent. To show the people that the emperor had many intelligent members in his court, the emperor would normally dispatch a courtier with knowledge equaling that of the local scholar, so that they could have interesting conversations during the journey to the capital.

On one occasion, a southern state chose a famous local scholar named Hsu Hsuan for the trip to the capital. Hsu was not only very knowledgeable, but also had a reputation for being pompous and very competitive. The courtiers in the capital knew this well and were thus intimidated by him. Since no one in the emperor's court could match Hsu's intellect, the journey would likely lead to taunts and humiliation by Hsu. As a result, the minister in charge of dispatching the emperor's representatives couldn't find anyone to accompany Hsu. He had no choice but to report the problem to the emperor. Taitzu understood why no one wanted to travel with such an arrogant person and thought hard about finding a solution. Soon, he got an idea.

Emperor Taitzu told the minister make a list of his royal bodyguards who were illiterate. When Taitzu got the list, he glanced at it off-handedly, quickly selected a name, and told the minister, "Send him." The minister looked at the emperor's selection and immediately knew that the bodyguard couldn't even write his own name. The minister was baffled as to why Taitzu would send a totally illiterate person to accompany Hsu and his powerful intellect. But he couldn't disobey the emperor and sent the bodyguard to meet Hsu anyway.

After the fleet carrying the tribute started its journey to the capital, Hsu began boasting and showing off his knowledge to the entourage that included the emperor's representative. Hsu spoke eloquently, using scintillating witticisms that awed the company. People surrounding him all complimented his amazing abilities, except the emperor's representative. The royal bodyguard wasn't at all moved by Hsu's words and didn't say anything, since he understood nothing in what Hsu had said. The bodyguard just listened, smiled, and nodded occasionally with a simple "Yes."

Hsu became puzzled and wanted to know how deep the representative's knowledge was. So, he became determined to stimulate a discussion with the representative so he could show off his superiority. But, no matter how hard Hsu tried, the bodyguard just stood quietly. The situation remained this way for several days, and eventually Hsu became bored and trailed off into silence as well. From then on, the two had almost no communication. The tribute eventually arrived at the capital without incident. This was the first time Hsu had not been able to accomplish domination in a discussion since he had become famous.[3]

Taitzu's problem was indeed difficult. To have a highly intelligent discussion with Hsu, the emperor's representative would have to possess a knowledge level equal to or above Hsu's. But unfortunately, Taitzu had no such resource available. So Taitzu couldn't use the conventional approach: sending a highly knowledgeable person to compete with Hsu. What else could he do? If he could found a dynasty, he should be able to solve this much smaller problem. He decided to take a completely opposite approach to conventional thinking. He chose to send an illiterate bodyguard, who had almost no education and had no hope of competing with Hsu. This would create a new situation that might be beneficial, because the bodyguard couldn't understand any aspect of Hsu's harangue; he could only stand mute except for an occasional nod. This situation effectively prevented the competition that Hsu would easily win. Unlike earlier confrontations, Hsu could not gloat over a new victory. Therefore, when conventional approaches can't be applied to a situation, try the opposite approach. The situation might become significantly improved.

A Reversed Approach May Be Better

Even when a conventional approach can be applied and its results are satisfactory, there is no harm in looking at a reversed approach to see if its results are even better. Successful conventional approaches are not guaranteed to produce optimal results. However, other approaches only have the opportunity to be better if they're identified. A reversed approach is an example of another approach. In short, it will expand opportunities for better solutions if reversed approaches are considered in addition to conventional approaches.

In 1912, Theodore Roosevelt was campaigning for president again.

When his campaign team was preparing his final campaign tour before the election, one team member found a problem in the pamphlets they had prepared for the tour. The team had printed a few million pamphlets to distribute to the crowds. The cover of the pamphlet contained Roosevelt's portrait, but the team neglected to get permission from the studio that owned the photo copyright. Millions of the pamphlets had been printed and the name of the studio was clearly included beneath the photo. If the pamphlets were distributed in public, it would not only become a legal copyright violation, but also could turn into a scandal. Roosevelt's campaign would clearly lose the lawsuit and could not afford a huge fine. Unfortunately, there was no time to reprint the pamphlets with a different photograph. Withdrawing the pamphlets was not a choice, either, as that would negatively influence the results of the campaign tour. What was the solution? It seemed the only way was to negotiate with the studio to determine the price for permission to use the portrait. Permission would probably be expensive because so many pamphlets had been printed. What should they do?

The problem was given to the campaign manager, George Perkins. After learning about the situation, he quickly sent a telegram to the studio saying that the campaign team was planning to distribute millions of pamphlets with Roosevelt's picture in it during the upcoming campaign tour. It would be great publicity for the studio who supplied the photo for the pamphlet. He further asked how much the studio would *pay* if the photo was used in the pamphlet, and said he needed an immediate response. The studio hastily responded, offering to pay $250 for the publicity opportunity. The campaign manager quickly accepted the studio's offer. Consequently, the campaign team not only got to use the photo and avoid a lawsuit, but they also made some money too![4]

George Perkins' thinking was interesting. In this situation, it would be typical to use a conventional approach to negotiate with the studio to see how much the campaign should pay to use the photograph. He wasn't satisfied with the conventional approach, even though it might've solved the problem. Perkins took a reversed approach that had better odds of generating a better result. He flipped the approach from the campaign paying money to the studio to getting the studio to pay the campaign by recognizing the value of the photograph to both organizations. Since the owner of the studio didn't know the pamphlets had already been printed and instead thought the process was in the selection stage, he agreed to pay Roosevelt's campaign team for advertising his studio. As a result, George Perkins' innovative thinking produced good results for everyone. Therefore, when a viable conventional approach is available, still compare it to the opposite approach. The latter may produce better results.

Thinking about Reversing Expands Your Mind

Employing an opposite approach isn't necessarily confined to situations where a normal approach doesn't work, or when an opposite approach is better than a normal approach. It can be used in searching for new opportunities as well. It's valuable to think about the feasibility and advantages of using a reversed approach; new, previously unnoticed opportunities and ideas may have already emerged from an open mind through the practice of actively thinking about opposites.

People today are used to most online photo-sharing services being free, so few people consider paying for this service. However, in 2008 a *BusinessWeek* report described a California startup company, SmugMug, that had introduced a subscription-based, online photo-sharing service where its subscribers were charged annual fees.[5] In the face of intense competition from large competitors, this small startup won significant business with its high-resolution photo-storage services and attracted both professional and amateur photographers who demanded these services. The company's subscribers often touted their exceptional quality photos on the website to their families and friends. By the time *BusinessWeek* published the report, the website had already gained more than a hundred thousand paid subscribers.

While major photo sharing websites were providing free services, fee-based online photo services were rare. Using an approach that was opposite of the norm provided the seed for the startup to develop and grow a new business. As long as the new photo service satisfied its customer's needs, it didn't matter if its business model was 180 degrees reversed from that of other companies. Therefore, when seeking new opportunities, be sure to consider approaches that are directly opposed to the prevailing practice.

Summary

Under normal circumstances, people usually pursue traditional approaches to solve problems. However, conventional approaches may not be feasible or don't necessarily produce the best results. Therefore, remember to likewise examine your approaches in reverse to explore more choices. Perhaps a solution can be found where there previously was none, or a better solution can be found using this kind of open-minded thinking. Here are some situations where opposing approaches best play their roles:

☐ Check to see if a reversed approach can provide the desired results when traditional approaches show little or no ability to achieve the objective.

☐ Try an opposing approach especially if traditional approaches can't be applied at all.

☐ Even if a traditional approach works, still compare the benefits of a reversed approach in order to select the better one.

☐ Always explore opposite approaches to see if they can provide potential new opportunities.

Check Other Easily Overlooked Aspects

Discover Missing Factors

We can consider every factor related to something as a member of the full set of factors corresponding to it. For example, all countries that have a trade relationship with the US can form a set of factors corresponding to the total, or set, of the US's international trade. Each country is a *factor* and the total set has more than a hundred factors. When there's a large set of factors involved with something, it's difficult to identify every possible factor in the set without missing some of them. This is almost always the case.

When making a list of factors, the most obvious factors are usually at the beginning, but the less noticeable factors may not even be on the list. People pay more attention to factors if they're interested in them, but usually pay much less attention to the other factors. Since these overlooked factors may not be included in the total, seeing an incomplete list of factors makes it less likely for a person to create fresh ideas. Searching for these neglected factors and thinking about what new ideas can be triggered by a more complete list will almost certainly produce better results. Therefore, discovering overlooked factors and adding them to your object's set will help expand your open-mindedness. To accomplish that, it's important to develop the ability to identify missing factors effectively and efficiently.

Missing Factors

The simplest and most direct way to find neglected factors is to employ the "exhaustive method." When the number of factors related to something is limited, it's relatively easy to identify the factors one by one and then check each factor to find the potential missing outliers. You can use the following process as an example. First, list all of the possible factors, or as many as you can think of, that are associated with your set. Then, read down the list from the beginning and for each factor ask yourself this question: Is this factor a *commonly* considered aspect? If the answer is yes, move on to the next one. If the answer is no, then ask: Why is this factor unusual? Is it worthy of more attention? What new areas can be explored based on the factor? These questions should reveal to you the potential value of spending more effort thinking about that particular factor. Continue in this way until the whole list has been finished. After this has been done, choose the unusual factor that seems to have the highest potential value and work on it first.

In July 2007, three young Swedish businessmen, Jakob Ohlsson, Tor Rauden Källstigen, and Jacob Aström, got the idea to import jeans from North Korea and sell them in Stockholm.[1] At the time, few people knew that jeans were also made in North Korea, due the country's isolated nature. The Swedish men came up with the idea one night over drinks at a bar. Later that night, they went to North Korea's official website on foreign trade and discovered that there were many goods North Koreans wanted to establish trade in, including jeans. After discovering this, they sent an email to the contact address on the website asking about the possibility of importing jeans from North Korea to Sweden.

They didn't have high hopes for any kind of answer, but they were pleasantly surprised to receive a friendly response within twenty-four hours. The reply expressed strong interest in their business proposal. Seeing a good business opportunity emerging, the young men sent several pairs of jeans to North Korea as samples and subsequently planned a visit to the country to survey potential manufacturing partners. A year later, they finally arrived in Pyongyang, the country's capital. The young Westerners received a warm welcome in North Korea. Accompanied by local officials, they visited several places and inspected a few textile factories. After considering their options, they struck a deal with a textile factory in Pyongyang, signing a contract for the company to produce black jeans for them. The entrepreneurs named their first two jean designs "Kara," a slim fit, and "Oke," a loose fit, after the happy evening with their hosts at a karaoke bar on the first day they arrived at Pyongyang. They returned to

Pyongyang a year later to check on the production schedule and the quality of the jeans. Finally, the first shipment of jeans arrived in Stockholm in November 2009. These young men opened their own store in Stockholm selling the jeans and displaying cultural items from North Korea. This was the first time consumers in Western Europe were able to buy jeans from North Korea. These three young men provided a win-win solution for both countries' needs.

Since North Korea is such a closeted country, many businesses automatically avoid it when considering countries for importing goods. This makes North Korea a blind spot in the international trading scene. Perhaps searching for blind spots was the starting point for the three young men when they were thinking about foreign manufacturing and imports. If they opened a world map and crossed out countries which had normal trade relationships with Sweden, the remaining countries on the map were the countries which were intentionally or unintentionally overlooked in the business world. Selecting one of the blind spot countries and trying to build a business relationship led to a breakthrough, culminating in importing the first batch of jeans from North Korea. So, using the exhaustive method for searching for overlooked factors can be very effective.

The Subject of an Action Can Be Its Object as Well

For an action, its objects form a set. Different actions have different sets of objects. Interestingly, when people consider a list of objects that make up an action, they tend to forget one possible component—the object that executes the action. People usually think of the consequences of an action as externally directed manifestations, not inwardly directed at the one who performed the action. In fact, the action taker can be an object of the action, too. But most people don't think that way. Thus, for any action, look at whether the action taker can be considered as an object of the action. Thinking in this way can open undiscovered avenues for you.

A news segment in 2010 about a small company's reduction in force provides an example of how to find a certain missing object of an action. Lola Gonzalez, the owner of a small Floridian firm specializing in background checks, faced a market downturn and the accompanying pressure to sustain the company. To save the company, she felt she had to lay off one employee. Who should be fired? This caused her a lot of stress because

every employee played a critical role in the small company. It would severely impact the company's business if any of them were laid off. How
should she resolve this dilemma? Eventually, Gonzalez made up her mind.

On a Monday morning, she called a company meeting. She told her
people that due to the financial situation she had to make a difficult and
painful decision to lay off one member of the nine-member company.
When her employees heard this, they were scared. The economy at the
time had an unemployment rate of 14 percent in that area, which was one
of the highest unemployment rates in the state, and it would be very hard
to find a new job. While fearfully waiting for the owner to announce who
the unlucky person would be, the employees heard an unexpected answer.
Gonzalez told her employees, "The person to be laid off . . . will be me."
To everyone's surprise, Gonzalez explained that for the sake of the company's best interests she could not afford to lay off any of her employees.
The only choice left was to lay off herself. She also felt it would probably
be easier for her to find a new job than her employees. After the meeting,
Gonzalez was true to her words and left her six-figure job, subsequently
taking a social worker position.[2]

It's hard to believe that a company's owner would lay herself off. The
story made the news because of its rarity. In considering the employee
components of her layoff action, Gonzales' biggest difference in her thinking and that of other company owners was that she did not overlook an
important, but uncommonly considered, component: herself. In retrospect,
this was a smart decision. After the owner left, the company survived. Even
though she no longer worked there, she remained the owner and was the
ultimate beneficiary of her own selfless, yet clever, decision.

Therefore, from now on don't forget to include the action taker into the
set of objects of the action.

Temporary Factors

A set of factors related to something is not necessarily fixed in number and
may change over time. A factor may belong to the set at one time and not
at another time. Temporary, time-dependent factors are easily overlooked.

Here is a story I heard when I was a young boy. During the Tsarist period in Russia, most criminals were sent to frigid Siberian prisons. Bored
in their cells, prisoners craved some form of amusement, such as playing

chess or cards, to pass the time. Prisons, however, had strict rules that prisoners were not allowed to have entertainment in their cells. In one prison cell, however, the inmates did not follow the rules like the other prisoners. When the jailers weren't watching through the hole in the door, they would play cards. This small luxury was very much enjoyed by the prisoners who were able to get away with it.

When the warden of the prison found out, he was angry and decided to raid the cell and catch them playing cards. One day, the inmates were playing cards in the cell yet again. A jailer found out and reported it to the warden. The warden gathered more guards who immediately opened the cell door and rushed in. However, as the warden and his guards ran into the cell, the inmates had already stopped playing and the deck of cards was gone. Obviously, the deck of cards must have been hidden somewhere in the cell, so the warden ordered the prison guards to search the cell thoroughly, including the inmates' bodies. Surprisingly, the guards could not find the cards after searching everywhere. Since there was no evidence, the warden could not punish the inmates for violating the rules. The warden left the cell even angrier than when he had come in. Days later, the guards reported that the prisoners were playing cards again. The warden raided the cell again but couldn't find any cards as before. From then on, the inmates continued playing cards in a cat and mouse game with the warden's repeated searches. The warden just couldn't find the deck of cards to confiscate, and he was puzzled for long time.

The secret was exposed by a released inmate years later. He revealed that the inmates hid the deck of cards in a place the warden never expected. Whenever they heard the warden and his guards approaching, they immediately collected the cards into a deck and handed it to a prisoner standing by the door. This inmate quickly slipped the cards into the warden's coat pocket just as he walked into the cell. Because of the cold weather in Siberia, the warden always wore a thick, heavy coat that prevented him from feeling the deck in his pocket. When the warden was done searching and about to leave, the inmate near the door secretly retrieved the deck from the warden's pocket. After the cell door was closed and locked again, the prisoners resumed their game. As the deck of cards was hidden in such a "safe" place, how could the jailers find it?

The crafty inmates used the warden's erroneous assumption that he had searched all possible places in the cell where the deck of cards might be hidden. By not including *all* the possible hiding locations *while he was in the cell*, he missed an important place—the pockets of his very own coat. Yes, his coat pockets were not a part of the cell most of the time, but after he entered the cell his coat became a part of the cell while he was there. The inmates made good use of the *temporary* place to hide their cards and escaped the warden's repeated searches. Obviously, the warden did not realize that the number of hiding places could change from time to time. He completely overlooked his own pockets. Therefore, when searching for missing factors by making a complete list of all factors, don't just focus on permanent factors but also pay attention to the relative factors based on time.

Factors Considered Only in Special Situations

When listing all the factors related to something, people often believe they have included a complete set. While a set is complete under *normal* circumstances, it may be incomplete under *unusual* conditions—something a lot of people overlook. Some factors that do not belong to the set normally may become members of the set under special scenarios. These factors can be easily missed. Even if others seem quite sure they have taken into account every relevant factor about something, continue to think about what other factors may come into play in specific situations.

In twelfth century Germany, the Duke of Welf living in Weinsberg Castle declared his loyalty was no longer tied to King Konrad III because of a conflict. This betrayal angered the king greatly since the castle contained much wealth, causing him to order his massive army to surround the castle and demand that it surrender. The castle came under siege and relied on supplies from secret tunnels connecting to neighboring towns. The siege persisted for several weeks without resolution and the king started to lose his patience. He decided to solve this problem by force, since negotiations weren't working. He ordered his soldiers to find all the secret tunnels connected to the castle and block them. The castle wouldn't be able to survive for long without supplies. Then, the king sent a message to the duke saying that if the castle surrendered, he would spare the women and children, but all men must face the sword. If the castle did not surrender by nightfall, he would set the castle on fire and burn everyone inside.

The castle residents seemed to have only two horrible choices. Either everyone would be killed or all the men would die. Both choices were unacceptable to the duke so no response was sent to the king. Just before the king was ready to attack and burn the castle that night, a messenger from the castle came into the king's camp. The messenger carried an important letter that he was required to deliver to the king personally. The king's guards brought the messenger to the king.

The king opened the letter and discovered that it was written by the duke's wife, Lady Uta. She wrote that she knew that the duke had offended the king greatly and the duke's actions were unforgivable. She knew the castle was in grave danger and the king's army would break the castle's walls very soon. She begged the king to forgive the women and children in the castle, and asked for his mercy to let the women leave the castle peacefully with their children at sunrise the following day. The last sentence of the letter had a small last request, pleading that the king allow the women leaving the castle to carry a few treasures out with them, at least what they were able to carry on their backs. The letter persuaded the king to let the women and children leave, since killing unarmed women and children was not an honorable deed, and also agree to the Lady Uta's requests, including the last one. The king figured that the women could carry very little treasure on their backs and the bulk of the vast treasures of the castle would be left behind for him.

When the sun climbed over the hills the following morning, the king's soldiers stood ready at the gate of the castle. The gate gradually opened with creaks and groans. Appearing out of the light fog, the soldiers watched the women and children walk slowly out of the gate. They were astonished to find that each woman had a rather large load on her back—a man! Wives carried their husbands, sisters carried their brothers, and single women carried their male neighbors or relatives. The women staggered and paused to adjust the weight, but kept moving forward. After the shock wore off, the king's soldiers became angry that they were duped. They drew their swords, ready to kill everyone, but the king stopped them. As a king, a promise is his solemn word and he would suffer greatly if he broke it, even though he was the one that had been responsible for being duped. Why didn't he think that a husband or relative could be considered a treasure as well? The king let them go. Because of Lady Uta's clever letter, the king did not kill the castle occupants and the duke eventually reconciled with the king.[3]

In this German legend, the clever wife of the Duke of Welf saw a factor which others did not consider and caused a mighty king to abandon his horrible plan, saving the people in her castle. Obviously, when the King read of the "treasures" the women might carry, he only thought of what valuables people would normally carry when they were facing life and death choices: gold and silver, jewelry and mementos, or even articles for daily life. However, Lady Uta thought differently. She realized that in such a special case, the castle women's most valuable belongings were not necessarily limited to the list of material objects a woman typically had. Another factor could be included in the list that would not normally be considered. Lady Uta worded her request so that the women could carry anything, including an unusual factor—their men. The king didn't make the effort to think about what other things could be considered treasures. Perhaps it was because the king appreciated Lady Uta's guile that he stopped his soldiers' intervention.

Therefore, when looking at a complete list of factors belonging to something, don't forget there may be other factors which aren't normally related to the matter but can be included in special circumstances.

Summary

When we consider a set of factors related to something, it's easy to overlook some elements of the set, especially those which are unusual or hidden. Searching for overlooked factors in a particular set helps us to expand our minds, since new ideas may come into being when missing factors are discovered. Here are some ways to uncover overlooked factors:

☐ Use the exhaustive method of searching for the complete set of factors. Try to identify as many factors as possible in a set. Then, examine all of the factors, especially the uncommon ones that are frequently overlooked by others.

☐ Realize that the one who performs an action can receive the action as well. Within an action's set of objects, there is usually one factor that stands out as easy to miss: the one performing the action.

☐ Explicitly look for temporary factors of a set because sometimes the factors belonging to a set are not necessarily fixed. They may vary, and the temporary ones can be overlooked quite easily.

☐ Try to find factors which aren't normally in a set but could be included in particular situations.

20. Discover Missing Factors   183

☐ Particularly look for important factors. If you're not focused on the
core technology, you have to survey all the necessary fixed costs and
variable and the temporary ones that can be overlooked quite easily.

☐ Try to find factors which aren't necessarily in a set but could be
included in particular situations.

21

Dig into the Essence

Knowing the essence of something is critical to thoroughly compre-
hending it. Different things have different fundamental cores. To
solve a problem, it is important to grasp what the root cause of the problem
is. To formulate a solution, it is essential to determine what key element
the solution requires. To observe a person, it is crucial to understand the
fundamental motivation behind the person's actions. The root cause of a
problem, the key element of a solution, and the fundamental motivation for
an action can all be considered parts of the *essence*.

Understanding the essence of something allows people to grasp the most
important information more easily. This insight provides guidance for future
actions. Unfortunately, the essence of things is usually not apparent and requires
significant effort to discover it. The process of looking for a core idea is an exercise in extending one's thinking. If the exploration isn't wide enough, the search
for the fundamental core won't be comprehensive enough. If the search isn't
comprehensive enough, then the essence may be missed. Vague and incomplete
understanding is the result of not having the precise knowledge of your particular thing's essence. Consequently, it's helpful to practice searching for essences
to hone your mind in this respect. The more experience with searching for the
essence of situations, the more effective you become in deep, broad thinking.

The Root Cause of a Problem
There may be many factors causing a problem to occur, but its fundamental
causes are likely to be few. Frequently, there is only a single root cause.

Knowing the root cause of a problem is key to solving the problem. When a root cause is known, solutions can be formulated much more easily and the problem basically dissolves into a single-point solution. Expend effort on searching for root causes, and don't be distracted by less critical factors. Try hard to figure out what has really caused the problem. Generating solutions for problems with identified root causes is perceived to exhibit creative thinking to others, but it is in fact a natural consequence after identifying the root cause.

Mergers and acquisitions (M&A) of companies is a common practice in the business world. M&A helps a company to grow, enhance synergy, eliminate overlaps, reduce costs, and increase revenues. It's considered to be a positive event not only for shareholders, but also for the company's overall growth. That's why a lot of company executives are enthusiastic when they find a synergistic M&A opportunity. For example, in 2005 American companies performed M&A deals worth about one trillion dollars.

However, not all M&A deals are successful. The risk of doing an M&A deal is actually quite high. Based on market analysis, only about a third of all M&A deals can be considered successful while the rest fail to meet their original goals. The lawnmower giant Toro's approach to minimizing the risks of their M&A deals has won the praise of a lot of people, thanks to the ideas from its chairman Ken Melrose. Before the leadership would make a decision on an M&A proposal, the company CEO would appoint a due diligence team to make the case to the board of directors of the company, just like other companies would. At the same time, however, the CEO would also appoint a "contrarian team." The contrarian team was composed of high-level management just like the due diligence team. The main job of the contra team was to search for evidence for not doing the deal. This way, there would be two reports presented to the company's board when a decision had to be made for the M&A project; one was for the case and one was against the case. Thus, the probability of making the best decision on an M&A project was much higher with both perspectives being presented. This approach has played a very positive and central role in Toro's business growth.[1]

When the leadership of a company is seriously pursuing an M&A deal, voices of dissent are normally unpopular. Many times, people will follow the predominant executive level perspective, even though they may see problems that don't lie in favor of a merger. Toro's leadership might have realized that the lack of an official channel to let voices against a merger be heard was a fundamental root cause of the problem that caused many M&A deals to fail. If that was true, then forming a team focusing solely on finding reasons *not* to do the M&A would be a good way to solve this problem. Since the contrarian team was formally appointed and tasked by the CEO of the company, the team members had no fear of giving their best efforts to collect information on what would have a negative impact on the deal. This way, the CEO, the chairman, and the board would be presented with both favorable and unfavorable statements from the two teams that had done their jobs thoroughly. When a decision was made, it was much more informed than in the cases which didn't use a contrary team. Being knowledgeable about both sides of an opportunity is highly worthwhile to a company since the final M&A decision will usually have multimillion-dollar impacts. Therefore, identifying the root cause of your problem helps find effective solutions.

The Key Step in a Solution

Any solution, no matter how many steps it may contain or how complex its structure is, in many cases will have only a single critical element that is key in determining success or failure. If the key element is included, the solution can be expected to be successful. Conversely, without the key element, the probability of finding a successful solution will be significantly diminished. The key element is often unapparent, however. It often requires an extensive thinking effort to search for it. The more accurately the key element is identified, the higher the likelihood of the solution's success.

There was a popular tourist area in South America. However, part of the area had a dangerous section of highway that passed through the mountains. The highway was not very long, only a couple of miles, but it had many sharp curves and hairpin turns. If a driver was not keenly alert to road conditions or did not maintain a safe speed, accidents could easily occur. Data collected by the local highway department indicated that the accident rate was very high in this section of road, and many of the accidents were fatal. Consequently, it became known as "The Road of Death." The highway department considered various ways to reduce the accident rate on this road. They installed speed cameras to detect speeding drivers. They also set up a large warning sign at the entrance and along the dangerous part of the highway. However, even though these warning signs were quite visible, many drivers ignored the warnings and car accidents continued to happen.

While the department continued the struggle to find a better solution, a story about a retired cab driver appeared in the local newspaper that gave them some fresh ideas. The retired driver had spent a lifetime of driving buses, limousines, and cabs. In spite of his long driving history, he had an outstanding driving safety record. In his more than forty years of driving, he had no traffic accidents and never had received any traffic tickets. What was his secret? When the newspaper reporter asked him how he had been able to drive safely for so long, his answer was quite simple. "Whenever I get behind the wheel, I always think about my family," he said. "I know my family is thinking about me as well and waiting for me to come home safe and sound." That was true; when he was thinking about his family while he was on the road, he couldn't help but remind himself to drive safely. It seemed that always thinking about his family was a big reason why he had such an impeccable driving record.

Learning about the story gave new inspiration to the highway department still struggling to find an effective way to reduce the accident rate on the dangerous highway. The department saw the true meaning of the driver's story: connecting with the love of one's family could be the key to safer driving. That association could be used to reduce the chance of accidents on the road. Soon after, the department changed the billboards along the road to read something like "Drive carefully, don't cause your elderly parents heartbreak!" and "Pay attention to the road, your family is waiting to see you for dinner!" and "Your safety is the best gift you can give to your children!" and so on. The result of the changes surprised everyone. Traffic accidents on this risky road dropped sharply. For a few years, it was even accident free! As a result, people started to call this road "The Road of Love."[2]

Obviously, the initial measures the highway department had taken to curb the high accident rate didn't contain the key element that solved the problem: that is, to remind drivers to think about their families and their responsibility to their loved ones. Only the idea of caring about loved ones stimulated drivers to change their behavior and drive more cautiously. People typically pay more attention to the wellbeing of family members than of themselves. This may explain why the billboards with only warnings signs weren't as effective as the new billboards reminding drivers to pay attention to the effect an accident would have on their loved ones. Fortunately, the department eventually found the key element of the solution inspired by the retired taxi driver's experiences. If the department had identified the key element in solving the unsafe driving problem earlier, they would've found this powerfully effective approach sooner. This case clearly shows that early focus on searching for and finding the key element of a solution can be very important.

The Fundamental Reason for Why Something Happens

In general, things happen for a reason. Among potentially many reasons, usually one is fundamental, and knowing the fundamental reason helps you understand the event in depth. For example, when people learn the essential motivation for an action, they acquire a deeper understanding of the person taking the action and will have a good indicator for future actions.

Planet Honda, a car dealership in Union, NJ, implemented a new customer-friendly policy: it invented a "Just Looking (JL)" sticker. When a customer walked into the shop, the receptionist would ask the customer if the customer needed any assistance. If the customer's answer was "Thanks, I'm just looking," the receptionist would give the customer the "JL" sticker. With the yellow "JL" sticker on the client's lapel, the customer could wander around the showroom without pressure from a salesperson to buy a car. When the customer made up his mind and was ready to move forward, he could peel off the sticker and find a salesperson to help him. It may seem that the "JL" sticker lowered the chance of the sales team being able to introduce cars to customers and that might lead to lower sales volume, however, it achieved the opposite effect. After implementing the measure, the sales revenue didn't fall at all, but rather, it enjoyed a substantial increase. People were surprised by the miraculous power of the tiny yellow sticker.[3]

When people visit car dealerships, they're normally annoyed by salesmen's overbearing marketing, especially when the customer hasn't made up his mind yet. This dealership understood a customer's perspective very well. They knew the fundamental reason why customers don't like salesmen, not because they don't need sales help, but it's the fact that they don't like to be disturbed when they are weighing their options. After understanding why customers behave that way, it became obvious that they needed to create a JL sticker.

This story shows that searching for the fundamental reason behind something may be related to the characteristics of having an open mind. Hence, it's a good exercise in creative thinking to consider fundamental reasons when observing events.

The True Meaning of Words

The true meaning of what people say is another type of essence. The true meaning of what is heard quite often differs amongst people depending on their contextual understanding. To understand what is really meant by a statement, it's necessary to find its true meaning. Discovery and confirmation of a statement's true meaning requires extensive thought, and that process helps to sharpen one's mind.

One day, an old monk and a young monk were traveling together and begging for alms for the poor. As they walked along, they encountered a shallow river. There was no bridge over the river so they decided to wade across it. When they were about to enter the water, they saw a young woman who also wanted to cross the river. She had paused at the river bank and was trying to figure out what to do to keep the beautiful clothes she wore dry. The old monk, seeing the young woman's difficulty, walked up to her and offered his help. The young monk didn't move, since he knew it was taboo for a monk to touch a woman. The woman accepted the old monk's kind offer, after which the old monk carried her across the river on his back. When they reached the other side, the old monk put the woman down on the river bank. After thanking him, she said good-bye to the monks and walked off. The monks then continued on with their journey, but didn't talk much to each other after the encounter with the woman. After a lengthy silence, the young monk suddenly asked, "The rules of our temple clearly say that we shouldn't touch a woman at any time, and you just carried a young woman across a river. Haven't you violated the rules?" The old monk replied with a smile, "I left her at the river bank a long time ago, but you are still carrying her around with you!"[4]

On the surface, both monks were compelled to comply with the rule to not touch women. However, helping people in need was an important part of a monk's mission, too. The key to the issue was what was really meant by the rule beyond its literal meaning. If a monk really understood the essence of the rule, he would understand that it meant that he should not harbor any lustful ideas about a woman, rather than that he could not have any physical contact. When the old monk carried the young woman across the river, he was focused on offering help to someone in need. It didn't make any difference to him that the person was male or female. It was merely an innocent offer of assistance in the old monk's mind. But the young monk, though he didn't physically touch the young woman, began to think lustful thoughts after seeing the woman being carried on the old monk's back. For a long time after the monks parted ways with her, she was still very much on the young monk's mind. In this context, the old monk, who had physically carried the woman, actually hadn't "touched" her, but the young monk, who didn't physically touch the woman, had actually been "touching" her in his thoughts. If the young monk had really understood the true meaning of the rule, he wouldn't have shown his ignorance to the elder monk by asking such a question. Sometimes profound things can be difficult to fathom and require detailed examination to discover.

Summary

The quest to find the essence of things is a process of examining something more thoroughly and comprehensively with the help of an open mind. Therefore, don't forget this way to expand one's thinking. Most everything contains a certain fundamental core, or *essence*, which plays a decisive role in determining its traits. Knowing something's foundation is helpful in forming a clear and accurate understanding of it and making related judgements. Many times, it's not trivial to discover and grasp the essence of something. Focusing on the central component is a good exercise for deeper thinking. Here are several ideas that can help you find the essence:

- ☐ When facing a problem, always try to identify its root cause.
- ☐ When searching for a solution, think about what key step the solution should contain.

☐ When something occurs, look for the fundamental reason causing the event.

☐ For any statement, always try to identify its true meaning, not just the surface or literal meaning.

☐ Identify key components such as the fundamental difference between things, the true effects of a plan, the real purpose of an action, the actual reason of a rule, and so on.

☐ Always explore situations at their deepest level, asking questions such as: What is the most important part? What is the fundamental issue? What is most appealing to others?

Conserve Resources

Everyone wants to do more with less. Figuring out how to save your resources is a great way to help search for new ideas. Conserving resources results in productivity increases, which motivates people to seek out new approaches for further improvements. This motivation also drives people to find more ways to utilize existing resources, especially if the resource is on hand or low cost. The word *resource* in this chapter represents many things, not just material resources. As long as it can be used to create value, anything tangible or intangible can be considered a resource. The topic of conserving resources is quite broad. By thinking about resources in this manner and how to better use them, new ideas can emerge for you.

Low-Cost Replacement
Given an existing solution, think about how to find a less expensive approach that costs less but is still able to serve the same purpose, giving the same or better results. Frequently, an existing solution is overkill and a lower-cost solution will do just fine. Perhaps new technologies or products in the market can provide you with new opportunities to create cost-saving solutions. Searching for a lower-cost replacement is a common way to find better solutions. This search process will stimulate effective brainstorming.

In 2009, a small group of MIT students wanted to capture images of the curvature of the Earth, but only had a meager budget. They decided to use a weather balloon to carry an ordinary ice chest to high altitudes. Inside the chest was a secondhand camera and a mobile phone for communications.

They cut a hole in the cooler for the lens of the camera, which was programmed to automatically take pictures at five-second intervals. The camera took hundreds of pictures during the ascent before the balloon burst at a height of about seventeen miles. The package was recovered using GPS signals sent by the mobile phone. The pictures the group obtained were astonishingly good and looked similar to ones taken by NASA. Even more astounding was that the total budget for the project was only $150![1]

When people see pictures of Earth's curvature, most assume that a giant space shuttle or a huge rocket carried the camera into space. While pictures like these are normally taken from space, the group of MIT students conceived a way that didn't require space shuttles or satellites. The students thought about how they could find an extremely cost-effective way to take nearly NASA-quality pictures. Clearly, they found a way to accomplish their goal with much cheaper equipment.

In 2005, while driving, I heard another story from radio about saving costs. The police department of a large city replaced a high-cost solution with a lower-cost one when dealing with speeding drivers. Speeding was a big headache for the police department, and they couldn't afford to hire more officers to monitor and enforce their speed limits. But then the department got a brilliant idea. They hired civilians to drive police cars in their spare time. The civilian's only job was to keep the police cars constantly visible on the streets. When drivers spotted a police car nearby, they would usually check their speed and slow down to be within the speed limit. The police department didn't have to pay the civilians much for driving, so the new program didn't create a major budget issue. After this new approach was implemented, the city's accident rate dropped significantly.

The department's idea was interesting. Since drivers naturally lower their speed when they see a police car, increasing the visibility of police cars on the streets would be an ideal approach to reduce speeding. Drivers typically can't see clearly who is driving a police car, so the effect is similar to having a police officer driving the police car. A civilian driver costs much less than a police officer does, saving money. Civilian drivers were just a portion of the entire police car fleet, so even if drivers knew the department's trick, they would not risk a ticket by assuming the driver was a civilian.

College students and policemen aren't the only ones who know how to use low-cost substitutes. According to a *Daily Mail* report in 2008, Kaoru Otsuka, the owner of Tokyo-based restaurant Kayabukiya, hired two special waiters: a pair of clever monkeys.[2] The monkeys wore a normal restaurant uniform while moving among the tables, taking orders and performing other common table-waiting services. Many patrons really liked being served by the monkeys. They felt the monkey waiters did surprisingly well when compared with their human counterparts. The restaurant owner enjoyed even more benefits from the monkeys than his customers. The owner probably felt that the monkeys required far fewer resources than hiring human waiters because monkeys didn't need to be paid and only wanted bananas as their tips.

The examples above show that expensive approaches can be replaced with practical, low-cost approaches. The high-altitude balloon example particularly shows that it can be quite effective to search for solutions with much lower costs than that of the obvious solutions.

Be Frugal

Unnecessary resource consumption can be found in many areas. To explore new ideas for saving resources, examine existing resource utilization by asking a question such as, "Does this solution require this resource to fulfill its purpose?" Fresh thoughts may emerge when considering the question. Here's an example.

Today, almost all corporate internal networks are connected to the Internet via communication channels such as optical fibers, copper wires, or wireless radio waves. The Internet is mission critical to almost all businesses. To guarantee dependable and reliable Internet access, businesses usually employ two redundant channels from two separate service providers. Each channel only carries data at half of the channel capacity. In case one channel has a problem, the other channel can carry the whole data traffic. This fail-safe solution requires companies to pay twice as much as they would for a single, full data channel. A start-up company has proposed using an unbalanced channel setup for Internet connection, where one main channel carries all the data traffic and one much smaller channel is used for backup. The rationale behind the idea is that when the main channel has a problem, only critical data, which usually is a small fraction of the total traffic, needs to be continuously connected to the

Internet. Non-critical data can be delayed until there is no critical traffic to pass. Using this scheme, a company pays a relatively small amount for the backup connection. This approach can save a lot of money when compared to a balanced Internet backup connection.[3]

The observation that not all data is critical in an emergency is the key to this approach. The backup channel's capacity doesn't have to be as large as the normal working channel, as long as it is large enough to handle the time-critical data flow. This observation was the catalyst for the asymmetric backup channel design that greatly reduces the cost of maintaining dependable data communications.

Use Available Resources

Another important way to conserve resources is to make as much use as possible of resources that are already available. That way, the cost of new resources can be minimized. If one looks hard enough, many times there are already existing, available resources that can be used to your advantage.

On August 18, 2011, Lieutenant Anastasia Bagdalov of the Israel Defense Forces rode a bus home from the air force base where she was stationed. Unexpectedly, the bus was ambushed by militants, wounding her in the arms and legs. She didn't tend to her own injuries, but instead rushed to save a fellow passenger whose leg was bleeding seriously. To stop the hemorrhaging, she urgently needed a tourniquet, but there was no tourniquet or obvious alternative available. At that moment, she got the great idea of using a woman's brassiere as a tourniquet! The bra-tourniquet and the pressure of her hands finally stopped the bleeding, saving the man. In April 2012, Lieutenant Bagdalov received a military commendation decoration for her heroic acts on the ambushed bus.

When she couldn't find a tourniquet, Lieutenant Bagdalov thought about using anything she could find to save the man's life. Most people would probably do the same. What was uncommon was that the lieutenant thought more broadly than most people would while she was searching for alternatives. Otherwise, she might not have thought about utilizing an intimate garment to help the dying man. The award she received was not only a noteworthy recognition of her valiant actions, but was also a validation of her out-of-the-box thinking.[4]

In an emergency, all available resources must be quickly discovered and evaluated, but the same principle can also be applied under less critical circumstances. Hillary Clinton's book *Hard Choices* includes a picture taken in 2011 of her with German Chancellor Angela Merkel and Vice President Joe Biden at the State Department.[5] The picture shows Chancellor Merkel presenting then Secretary of State Clinton with a gift. The gift was a framed front page of a German newspaper featuring a photo of the chancellor and Clinton standing side-by-side, one wearing a blue jacket and the other wearing a crimson one. The newspaper photo didn't show a full view of both women, but rather just two pairs of hands. The newspaper challenged its readers to guess which hands were the chancellor's and which were Clinton's. This newspaper clipping gift made both Clinton and Biden laugh a lot. They never expected that the chancellor would present such a humorous gift.

The gift meant a lot to Clinton, otherwise the event would not have been included in her book. Thanks to the chancellor's insight, she made great use of an available resource—a common newspaper clipping of little apparent value—and turned it into a priceless and memorable gift. From this example, who can say that thinking seriously about how to best use readily available resources isn't important?

Other Resource-Conserving Methods

There are many other ways to conserve resources. Here are several other methods that can be considered.

Prolonging use of something is a common way to conserve resources. A resource has a time period in which it is normally used. If the time period can be extended, the resource can be indirectly conserved. In 2007, it was reported that scientist Paul Smith at the Xerox Research Centre of Canada had invented an amazing type of paper. The paper looked like normal, letter-size, white paper but it was embedded with a special material that changed color when exposed to a moving beam of light inside an inkless printer. When the printer printed a document on the special paper, the printing disappeared after twenty-four hours. Documents could then be printed for temporary use, and the paper reused multiple times. If this paper was used on a large scale, many trees could be saved.[6]

Another approach is to turn the resource consumer into a resource conservationist as well. If a resource consumer can be made to conserve the resource at the same time as using it, one can reduce the expenditure of the net resource. For example, when a library was in the process of moving to a new location, the staff decided to ask for the public's help. The library posted a notice that before the readers visited the library to borrow a book, they should check online to see whether the book was located at the old address or at the new address. If the book was located at the old address, the reader was asked to return the book to the new address when they were finished with it. Not long after the notice was posted, many of the books in the library had been moved to the new address by readers. The library saved a significant amount of time and money they would have lost by moving those books themselves. In this case, the users were consumers of library resources in normal circumstances, but this time they also became contributors to saving the library's resources.[7]

Choosing the location or time to save more resources can be also helpful. The amount of resources needed to accomplish a job can be location and time dependent. Sometimes it's wise to try to find a different location or time which requires fewer or less costly resources to get the job done. Manufacturing outsourcing is a prominent example. When manufacturing a product is expensive in developed countries, businesses move manufacturing to developing countries where less costly resources are available. This principle can be applied to many other fields as well.

Be Persistent in Resource Conservation

Conserving resources should be a continuous process for improving productivity. Oftentimes when a resource-saving approach is implemented, a new opportunity appears to save even more. When conserving resources is kept in mind, new ideas for this purpose may appear spontaneously. Even though the following story is humorous, it reveals the principle of constant improvement in resource conservation.

A company's executive mentored his facility manager to continuously reduce the operational costs of warehouse security. The company had a remote warehouse, so the facility manager assigned a full-time employee as a security guard to monitor the warehouse at night. After the warehouse didn't have security issues for a period of time, the executive suggested that the manager replace the full-time employee with a part-time contractor who would only work three randomly chosen nights a week. After more time passed, the executive learned that the warehouse was still issue free. To further save resources, he then suggested that the manager replace the part-time contractor with a dog. A year later, the manager told the executive that the dog worked out just fine and that there were no security breaches. The manager didn't expect that the executive would have yet another new suggestion to save costs, but he did! The boss suggested replacing the dog with a recording of the dog's barks![8]

The executive was not satisfied in reducing the cost of warehouse security just once but again and again, suggesting that the facilities manager continually adopt a new approach to replace the previous one. This shows that when a lower-cost solution is implemented, other solutions with even lower costs may still be waiting to be found. Therefore, after finding an initial, effective, resource-saving approach, continue to search for even better improvements.

Summary

We can stimulate new ideas by paying attention to conserving resources. It should be emphasized that the meaning of *resource* is quite broad in this context. Besides things like effort, money, materials, information, and skill sets, many other things can be considered resources, such as physiological or psychological phenomena, well-known names, natural forces, laws and rules, historical events, and so on. Think about familiar situations to discover more opportunities to save resources and produce additional new ideas during the process. Here are a few ways of thinking about how to conserve resources:

- ☐ Substitute with a lower-cost item if it will serve the same purpose.
- ☐ Use resources only in areas where they are truly required.
- ☐ Take advantage of resources that are already available or employ idle and free resources as much as you can.
- ☐ Extend the useful lifetime of a resource.
- ☐ Redesign a resource consumer to also generate resources.
- ☐ Shift the location or time to where or when fewer resources are needed.
- ☐ Sacrifice a small amount of a resource to generate a larger return.
- ☐ Conserve resources constantly.

23

Take Indirect Paths

When we strive for a goal, it's ideal to have a clear and direct path to it. A direct path is normally the shortest path and takes the least amount of energy and time. However, reality is not always so ideal. Many times, when people want to accomplish a task, there are obstacles blocking the way that must be overcome. If these obstacles can be overcome, the original path may still lead to a solution. But sometimes an obstacle cannot be removed. In these cases, think about taking a detour and reaching the goal in an indirect manner. Find an outside source to help reach the goal. This method can also be used in cases where a direct path yield results, but an indirect path may yield better results. Anything can be considered an outside source, whether animate or inanimate, tangible or virtual, as long as it can help achieve the goal.

When Unable to Reach the Goal Directly, Get a Helper

When an especially challenging task needs to be accomplished, there will likely be daunting problems associated with it. However, no matter how difficult the task, there's usually a way to overcome the problems and reach the goal if other resources are brought in. In these situations, searching a wide expanse of outside opportunities for help can prove very fruitful.

Using an inanimate object as a tool is probably the most common approach to using an outside source to reach a goal. Viganella, a village in the Italian Alps, sits in a deep valley where mountains block the sunlight completely for three months every winter. Being cut off from sunlight for so long caused many villagers to feel like they lived in Siberia. To fix their problem, the village people got their heads together and installed a huge mirror at the north side of the valley where there's plenty of sunlight in the winter, per a BBC report.[1] The four-hundred-square-foot mirror, financed by the local government and a bank, reflects sunlight into the main square of the village. The mirror is controlled by a computer that tracks the sun and compensates for its movement, so the reflected sunlight always falls into the square. Now on sunny winter days, everyone in the village can enjoy the warm sun shining in the square. In some sense, the sunlight in the square fits the villagers' needs even better than sunlight directly from the sun, since the light from the natural sun moves, and doesn't consistently shine on the same spot. Using the mirror, the people in the village have finally escaped the feeling of being in Siberia.

Limited by its shadowed location between mountains, the village couldn't get sunlight directly in the winter. The villagers couldn't change this unfortunate fact. However, it didn't prevent them from seeking an outside source to help them. In this case, the villagers called for outside help from a computerized mirror. When they opened their minds and thought about how to get sunlight *indirectly*, it wasn't too difficult to come up with the idea of getting sunlight via a large, computer-controlled mirror.

Besides inanimate objects, living creatures can also be outside helpers for finding solutions. Living creatures include human beings *and* animals. Frequently, not only can humans provide help, but animals, too.

John Downer was a British wildlife photographer. Several years ago, he produced a BBC series about a young tiger family in the Indian jungle. He wanted intimate, close-up pictures of the tigers, requiring his crew to be physically very close to them. Needless to say, it was heart-pounding and very dangerous work. Tigers are territorial and ferocious animals that are not fond of potential human threats. In order to get the job done well without taking too many risks, Downer began to think about alternative approaches. An idea came up: why not get help from some of the other animals in the Indian jungle such as an elephant? Elephants are the largest animals in the jungle, and as herbivores with a docile temperament, they typically aren't a threat to or the prey of other animals. Because of this, other animals don't avoid them when they cross paths in the jungle.

If elephants could take pictures, they could easily get very near the tiger family without problems.

Realizing this, Downer and his team quickly leaped into action. They hid cameras in common things that elephants carry around, like rocks and logs, and picked several elephants from an Indian nature park for the special task. After a simple training session, they released the elephants carrying the camouflaged cameras into the jungle. Sure enough, the elephants exceeded Downer's hopes. When the elephants returned, they brought in many exciting pictures. The giant helpers had not only taken a lot of breathtaking, close-up photos of the tiger family, but also captured many surprising pictures of other exotic animals. Since these photos were taken by elephants, the animals' behaviors in the pictures were completely natural without any trace of human disturbance. Many of these pictures provided people with a new perspective on wildlife, because they couldn't have been taken by a human photographer at such close distances. Using elephants as photographers turned out to be a revolutionary way to capture wildlife on camera in their real habitat without external influences. A lot of photos recorded interactions of the elephants with other animals in the jungle. The animals stared at the elephants, played with them, or posed for them. Now the elephants' photos are appreciated by viewers all over the world and are greatly valued for their unique perspectives and authenticity.[2]

John Downer wasn't able to reach his goal directly using his own capabilities alone, but he didn't resign himself to his own limitations. He came up with a plan by taking a detour to accomplish his goal. Maybe he came up with the idea by chance, maybe not. But, if he hadn't had the idea, we may not have been lucky enough to see these amazing photos. Before his discovery, many wildlife photographers encountered similar difficulties in trying to capture close-up photos of animals without disturbing them by their presence. Most probably focused on disguising themselves through camouflage or shooting from a downwind location. Why didn't other photographers think of using an outside helper like an elephant, who has the ability to roam freely in the jungle while simultaneously taking pictures? It appears that these earlier photographers could have used a lesson in reaching goals indirectly. Otherwise, they would have thought of this method of taking breathtaking photos of wild beasts a long time ago.

A computer-controlled mirror and an elephant are touchable things that can provide outside help to attain a goal. But don't exclude abstract things from consideration. Abstract things can include facial expressions, gestures, movement and so on. These things may also be opportunities to help us reach our goal.

An Indirect Solution May Be Better Than a Direct Solution

The method of reaching a goal indirectly doesn't have to be used only when a direct route is unattainable. An indirect path can actually be a good choice in situations where we already have an acceptable solution. The essential idea is to use an indirect path when it proves to be better than a direct path. It's human nature for people to disregard indirect paths if they already have a direct path in mind, but discounting indirect approaches provides opportunities for others who do consider the potential benefits of the indirect path. Build a habit of thinking about indirect approaches even if there's an existing direct approach, and there will be more opportunities for you to discover new ideas than for those who ignore them.

When Margaret Thatcher's former Parliamentary Private Secretary was blamed for stealing books from a bookstore, she displayed strong support for her loyal former aid. After the man was accused, Thatcher asked him to stay beside her in the Parliament for the whole day. She wanted to show everyone that she was quite sure her former aid was innocent. Her judgement turned out to be right, and the man was eventually acquitted on appeal.[3] In this incident, Thatcher could have claimed that her former Private Secretary was guiltless. Instead, she chose to demonstrate her support and confidence by having him by her side for a whole day in full view of Parliament. Thatcher showed her superior leadership skills and accomplished her goal of supporting the gentleman using an indirect path.

Occasionally, we all make excuses. An excuse is basically a weak explanation attempting to hide reality. At times, when we aren't comfortable revealing our true intentions, excuses may be used to help reach goals indirectly. While this may sound dishonest, there is a positive side of excuses, on those occasions when using an excuse usually sounds better than telling the truth.

In a German village during WWII, an old farmer met a stranger wandering into the village near dusk. He looked like an important business-man carrying a briefcase, apparently without a destination and not knowing where to stay that night. During that time, there were many refugees who came from cities to find a haven and escape the war. The farmer wanted to help him out, but he hesitated. He approached the businessman, but instead of asking him to stay in his home, he asked him for a favor.

The farmer explained that he was getting old and lacked strength. He would really appreciate it if the businessman could help him move a pile of logs in his yard. The gentleman agreed without hesitation, even though he was wearing a suit. He followed the farmer to his home, took off his suit, and rolled up his sleeves. There was a large pile of logs in the east corner of the yard. The farmer wanted him to move the logs to the west corner of the yard. The man said "No problem," then got to work. He moved the logs one by one, from the east corner to the west corner, following the farmer's instructions. Although it took him a while to finish, he put all the logs neatly in the new location. After the businessman accomplished the task, the old farmer was very satisfied and invited him to have dinner with him. The farmer also told him he could stay with him overnight if he wanted. The businessman readily accepted his invitation, since he had nowhere else to stay. That evening, the old farmer entertained the stranger with his best hospitality. After a hearty dinner, the businessman had a good night's sleep before he continued his journey next morning.

The businessman never knew that the pile of logs didn't need to be moved. This was only an excuse that the old farmer used on many occasions so that the refugees who came through the village needing shelter and food would accept his help. The poor logs had been shifted from the east corner to the west corner, back and forth by many different strangers.[4]

The old farmer had a very kind heart. He wanted to help those who were escaping from war-torn cities through providing free meals and a place to stay the night. At the same time, he was also considerate and wanted to respect those people's self-esteem. Even though being a refugee was tough, these people still held on to their dignity. They might have refused assistance from the old farmer if they couldn't provide something in return. To help the refugees, the old farmer came up with an idea and used moving the pile of logs as a deception. With this excuse, the people wouldn't feel guilty accepting the old farmer's hospitality after they helped him. They probably would never know their labor was just a trick invented by the farmer for an excellent reason.

Summary

Ideally, there is a direct path to reach a goal. However, reality quite often has the direct path blocked by obstacles that are too heavy to remove. In such cases, try to get help from outside sources and reach for the goal indirectly. Explicitly remembering to check potential, indirect paths can provide many more opportunities to generate new ideas. Here are a few areas you may consider:

- ☐ Think about finding a solution by taking an indirect path if it is too difficult to reach a goal directly.
- ☐ Investigate an indirect path to see if it achieves a better result, even if the original goal can be reached directly.
- ☐ Remember, almost anything can act as a helper for indirect paths. This could be a person, a living creature, a place or location, a moment in time, an action, a motion, an excuse, a piece of information, a set of data, a fictional object, an analogy, and so on.

Imagine the Impossible

The act of imagining forms a picture or a concept in our minds. Even though imagination is used most of the time to preview something before it happens, imagination isn't always confined to reality. Imagination can reach far beyond the real world. In this chapter, the focus is not on imagination in general, but on imagining something that appears to be impossible. Normally, people reject things that aren't realistic because it seems that there can be no gain. But actually, the chance of finding a new idea among apparently unrealistic things may not be as rare as we think. When imagining impossible things, don't think about how they happen, but instead focus on what might turn out if they *did* happen. Don't let logic and pre-conditions limit imagination. Even something that's never happened before and looks like it won't happen in the future can contribute to new ideas. There are lots of impossible things to consider, including such works created by the human mind as books, movie plots, advertising, and so on. Certainly, imagination can't change something that has already happened, but it may help in certain other ways.

The Impossible Can Stimulate Imagination

Imagination is powerful because it has no limitation besides those that are self-imposed. "Imagination" is often thought of as thinking about things that have never happened before but might happen in the future. In that case, however, the words *conjecture* or *prediction* are probably more suitable. In this chapter, the term *imagination* is reserved for thinking about something that's impossible in the real world. This kind of mental activity can really expand our field of view when looking for ideas.

In the book *The World Without Us*, Alan Weisman described an extremely unlikely scenario where humans suddenly disappear from the Earth, leaving everything behind. Assuming this had really happened, he discussed how nature might react to this unexpected situation. The book included many interesting consequences that would be caused by this event if it actually occurred. For example, animals would quickly take over cities, and vegetation would occupy residences. Without human maintenance, infrastructure would gradually deteriorate. Buildings would collapse and oil refineries would burn down. Natural forces would eventually wipe out evidence that people ever inhabited the Earth, though traces of human activity wouldn't vanish completely. Stainless steel cookware, for instance, might survive for millions of years after the event. Even when the Earth reaches the end of its lifetime, signs of human presence would still be preserved through items like the *Pioneer* Plaque and the *Voyager* Golden Record as the spacecraft continue their separate journeys into deep space. Translated and published in many countries, the book garnered a lot of interest after its publication and was high on several 2007 best seller lists. Two documentary films based on ideas from the book were very popular spinoffs. *Life After People* and *Aftermath: Population Zero* aired on the History and National Geographic Channels.[1]

The book's premise that the Earth's entire human population suddenly and completely disappears one day is impossible to believe for us. Why did the author choose this impossible beginning from which he based his analysis? It's likely that he intentionally simplified how humans disappeared so he could then quickly move readers toward the main theme of the book: what would happen if people abandoned a large geographic area, like humanity abandoning the Earth? Propelled by vivid descriptions of the aftermath, readers captured a visual impression of the consequences suffered by the abandoned area. If the author had spent a lot of time describing details of how human beings had vanished, the primary message of the book would have been severely weakened. Therefore, for something that couldn't happen even in the distant future, using imagination may be helpful.

The Impossible in Media and Arts

Imagination has been widely used to create fictional works. Here, creative works are not limited to literary and artistic works, such as novels, dramas, movies, and TV shows, but also other kinds of creativity, such as advertising designs. Since these works are products of people's minds, their contents are not necessarily limited to what can rationally happen, but can expand as far as the thinker's mind can stretch. Therefore, imagining impossible things can help to extend the range of thinking much farther than only reality can provide. This is yet another approach to cultivating creative minds.

A funny stage show once had a scene in it where an argument between two "magicians" was performed by two comedians. Let's call them John and Dave.[2] In the show, John performed a magic trick called "the shot from a cannon," similar to the one performed by magician Melinda Saxe in Las Vegas in the 1990s.[3] Dave played the "bad guy" who was trying to expose John's trick to the audience. When John was about ready to put a girl into the cannon as a human cannonball, Dave stopped him. Dave didn't want the girl to act as the cannonball because he was afraid that the girl might be John's confidant. Dave told John that he wouldn't believe in his magic powers unless John would use his (Dave's) wife as the cannonball. Unexpectedly, John immediately agreed to Dave's request. So, Dave called his wife up from the audience. The wife walked on stage wearing an attractive red and black sports outfit that made her look like a beautiful human cannonball. Then, under Dave's angry glare, John roughly stuffed Dave's wife into the barrel and pulled the cannon trigger. The audience heard a loud bang and saw a lot of smoke coming from the barrel, implying that the woman had been shot from the cannon.

Onstage, Dave fretted about his wife's fate. Suddenly, she emerged from the back of the theater and walked towards the stage. Overwhelmed with relief, Dave asked the woman how she got to the back of the theater. She told him that she had no idea how she got there. Dave was then convinced that John's magic was truly amazing. Just when Dave was about to congratulate John for his performance, John pulled the trigger of the cannon again. Then, another lady who looked exactly like Dave's wife, also wearing a red and black outfit, appeared at the back of the theater and walked towards the stage. Now Dave was confused. He never expected he would see an exact duplicate of his wife. Onstage, the two ladies began to argue about each other's fidelity. This was only the beginning of Dave's nightmare.

While Dave was still baffled about this shocking conundrum, John pulled the trigger for a third time! Unsurprisingly, a third wife showed up at the back of the theater and came to the stage. When the third woman arrived and saw her husband already had two other wives with him, the woman became quite angry and pulled Dave over to punish him before he could explain the escalating confusion. At the end of the show, Dave had no choice but to flee from the stage, resulting in roaring laughter from the thoroughly entertained audience.

It's impossible to suddenly turn a person's wife into three wives. However, a comedy skit is a writer's artistic work and isn't necessarily bound to realism. In this show, three similar-looking young ladies were selected to wear the same outfit to play the role of Dave's wife. During the performance, each subsequent appearance of Dave's wife astounded practically everyone in the audience. No one suspected that Dave could have three wives simultaneously. The comedic effect was pretty much perfect. Obviously, the writer of the show utilized the "imagine something impossible" approach and created a hilarious situation which left a vivid impression on the audience.

Literary and artistic works aren't the only fields that use the approach of getting value out of something that's not realistic. There's a popular picture online advertising an aerosol insecticide. The picture shows a man lying on the floor of a storage room without any sign of life. Only his still arm is visible because the rest of his body is concealed behind a wall. This man, however, wasn't just anybody. Seeing the distinctive covering on his arm and hand, he can immediately be identified as the famous Spiderman. Could the supposedly invincible Spiderman be dead? What led to the mighty superhero's fall? The insecticide spray in the picture implies that it's the spray that caused the deadly result. The picture's message is clear. No matter how tenacious an insect may seem, even if it's as strong as a super-hero, they won't survive so long as people have the spray at their disposal.[4]

The picture's artist cleverly used the experience of the powerful and famous Spiderman to publicize the capability of the insecticide spray. Spiderman, as a super hero, could never die. If the super bug couldn't survive the spray insecticide, are words needed to explain the effectiveness of the spray on regular bugs? The artist clearly created the fictional image to produce a stunning visual effect in the real world.

In instances related to works created by human minds, consider scenarios that aren't rooted in reality. This may help expand the range of useful solutions.

What Already Is Can Benefit from the Impossible as Well

Normally, the practice of imagining the impossible is confined to things that have never happened. If something has already happened, it then becomes a reality and leaves no room for imagination. However, building on things that have already happened by imagining a related, impossible scenario can produce useful benefits as well.

Here's a legend about Mark Twain. As an editor of a small Missouri newspaper, Twain one day received a strange letter from a reader. The reader had found a spider in his newspaper and wondered if that portended good or bad luck. Twain pondered the odd question and then wrote his response. He told the reader in his letter that the spider in the newspaper was not an indication of good or bad luck. He continued by saying the spider was just searching for a merchant who didn't advertise in the newspaper so it could find a store where it could build a web across the front door without interference.[5]

The reader's question presented an initially awkward situation. If Mark Twain had not used humor in his response, he would have had difficulty answering this seemingly bizarre question. Twain used his imagination to connect the spider and the advertising in the newspaper. Of course, in reality, spiders can't read advertising, but that fact did not keep Twain from giving the spider human characteristics. After receiving such a humorous and witty answer, the reader was unlikely to have bothered Twain with such a smart-aleck question again.

Summary

Imagination is an important way to improve creativity. This chapter focuses on one branch of imagination: imagining things that appear to be impossible. It's common to imagine things that are about to happen. However, things that are considered impossible are more likely to be overlooked without explicitly thinking about them. Imagining impossibilities clearly helps to open minds. Here are a few suggestions to consider:

☐ Consider something that won't happen in the foreseeable future, and think about how it could evolve if it did happen.

☐ Realize that the contents of creative works don't necessarily have to be aligned with logical reality. Something that cannot exist in the real world can surely occur and perhaps even thrive in a fictional world.

☐ Imagine impossibilities with existing things for producing benefits.

Let Facts Speak for Themselves

Every day, we sense many things happening around us. Everything that has happened is a fact. A fact is a stated piece of reality, and no one can change it. Therefore, although some people may argue about why something happens or what the consequences are, most of us agree that facts are indisputable. Facts are powerful. During the process of seeking new ideas, letting facts speak for themselves is frequently a powerful aid in reaching a goal. For example, disclosing a fact can influence people to believe in something or to agree with a statement. In this case, facts don't just refer to events that have happened, but also include data or clues that represent valid information. For instance, the statement "two presidential candidates had a debate at Hofstra University on September 26, 2016" is a fact. On that evening, 84 million people watched the debate. Here, the quantity of 84 million is also a fact, a quantitative fact. Further, letting facts and data speak on their own doesn't only consist of simply declaring the facts or data to be true, but also includes checking other properties related to the facts or data, such as their statistical patterns, to generate new concepts. Facts and data can sometimes help in amazing ways.

Facts Speak Louder Than Words

A famous proverb says that seeing is believing. This illustrates that people tend to believe only what they see with their own eyes, but don't necessarily believe what they hear. In the past, people were afraid that the information might have been altered during the word-of-mouth communications. The essence of the proverb is that people want to be confident that communication is true and factual. Because people rely so much on the accuracy of information, using facts consistently produces dependable results when dealing with situations requiring belief or trust.

The invention of the elevator deserves closer study. Before the time of Elisha Otis, elevators, or "hoisting platforms" as they were called at that time, were used for lifting goods only. They broke down quite often and were generally too dangerous for carrying people. Safety was an issue because if a suspension cable broke, the platform would free-fall to the ground, certainly causing injuries or death to any elevator passengers. In the 1850s, Otis took on the challenge to improve elevators and make them safe enough for passengers and not just cargo. He designed a spring device for his elevators that would be triggered if a suspension cable broke. The device would lock the elevator platform to the rails, preventing the platform from falling. After manufacturing his safe elevator design, Otis got no orders for several months. To convince people that the new elevator was safe to carry people, he took his elevator to the 1854 American Institute Fair in New York. In front of a large crowd at the New York Crystal Palace, Otis stood on the platform of the elevator while it hung much higher than the Crystal Palace pavilion. He then told a man to cut the suspension cable using an ax. The watching crowd was surprised to see that the elevator only dropped a few inches before it stopped descending. This demonstration gave people a new feeling of confidence that riding an elevator was no longer a dangerous experience. After the Fair, Otis's elevator business began to take off. By the beginning of the twentieth century, his elevators had become an indispensable part of high rise buildings.[1]

Otis was smart. He created an extremely unusual situation by ordering the cable to be cut while he was standing on the platform. Without steadfast faith in his new device, he couldn't have done it. His dramatic demonstration replaced countless hours of trying to convince people that his invention worked. He not only achieved a convincing demonstration, but also used it to establish an undisputed fact while giving people an unforgettable experience. After seeing Otis's demonstration, the fear of riding passenger elevators began to evaporate. Thanks to Otis, today we don't even think about walking aboard a high-rise elevator.

The seeing-is-believing paradigm is still playing its role, even today. In June of 2016, the longest and highest glass-bottomed bridge was completed in Central China's Zhangjiajie Grand Canyon. The bridge is about twenty feet wide, fourteen-hundred feet long, and a thousand feet above the floor of the canyon. Walking on the bridge feels like being suspended in air. Visitors can see beautiful panoramic views from the bridge in a uniquely thrilling experience. The common assumption that glass is fragile could have made visitors apprehensive about walking on the bridge. To prove the bridge was strong enough, the bridge builder invited a BBC reporter to test the strength of the glass floor. The journalist used a sledge hammer to repeatedly batter the glass floor in an effort to shatter it. The test result was astonishing! After receiving several severe blows, only the top layer of the glass displayed a few small cracks, while the two reinforced layers beneath remained intact. The video of the test was posted online for the world to see. Knowing about this test, a visitor to the bridge is much less likely to worry about their safety and can enjoy viewing the exciting new world wonder.[2]

Convincing anxious potential visitors of the bridge's integrity was not easy. Visitors were concerned that the glass floor might shatter while running and jumping on the bridge. Falling a thousand feet from the bridge would, of course, be catastrophic. It was a straightforward idea to use a large hammer to test the safety of the bridge. The pressure generated by the hammer's blows to the bridge floor was much larger than any caused by a visitor running and jumping on it. When potential visitors watched the video clip showing that the bridge could withstand the crushing blows, worries about the safety of the bridge were eased because the visitors considered the hammer test result to be a fact. Showing the video clip was more powerful than explaining the safety of the bridge to convince potential visitors. So, when ideas are needed to convince someone or win someone's trust, consider creating inspiration by presenting the facts.

Charts and Data

Letting facts speak for themselves is done by demonstrating reality, as in the previous cases, or by presenting fact-based data. Data can be expressed in various forms such as numbers, diagrams, or charts. People tend to believe reality-based data more than long-winded explanations because the data itself is objective. Therefore, when searching for new solutions, don't overlook the power of data.

On October 2, 2009, in Copenhagen's Bella Center, members of the International Olympic Committee were voting in the third and final round for the host city for the 2016 Olympic Summer Games. Rio de Janeiro, Brazil was selected over Madrid, Spain by the large margin of sixty-six to thirty-two. It's said that a world map had played an important role in Rio's campaign for hosting the Games. During meeting sessions, the Rio delegation displayed the map to the committee members, showing all the cities that had previously hosted the Olympics. The total number of hosting cities on each continent was also put on the map using a large font. The map showed that Europe had hosted thirty-two times, North America twelve times, Asia five times, and Australia twice. Only South America and Africa had had no host cities. The map clearly showed that it was time to give the honor to one of the two continents that had never had a chance to host the Olympics. Despite the impassioned pleas of Juan Antonio Samaranch, the Spanish-born longtime Olympic chair, Rio won the Committee's vote.[3]

The Rio delegation had a brilliant idea to show the total number of Olympics hosting cities on each continent on the world map. Even at a cursory glance, the map data presented a clear picture to the committee members. The map was much more concise than any verbal description. Also, since the map represented just pure facts, it didn't overtly pressure the committee members one way or another. No one could argue about the fact that South America never had a chance to host the Olympic Games. The map obviously made an important contribution to the success of Rio's bidding. Maybe next time, when an African country wants to bid to host the Olympic Games, its delegation might use the same tactic.

Data is also useful in converting a bad situation into a good one. In 2012, a blogger posted a comment on Twitter, saying that one day he saw a bird defecate on a Smart car, destroying it. Obviously, this was a joke with an implied negative bias toward the car. When the director of Smart's social media department saw this disparaging tweet, he was surprisingly not angry. The department decided to respond to the blogger's tweet and refute the blogger's statement. They posted a response online soon there-after saying that based on a careful calculation, the department had deter-mined that it would take about 4.5 million pigeon droppings to destroy a

Smart car, so a single dropping could never do any damage. It's interesting that the blogger's original tweet didn't actually gain much attention, but Smart's response went viral. For the first time, people learned how many bird droppings could destroy a car. The bird-dropping incident effectively increased the marketing power of the Smart brand.[4]

Encountering an unfavorable and unreasonable comment towards the company's product, Smart's social media department took it seriously. It presented the calculated data to its online audience in a non-confrontational manner. People of course didn't believe the blogger's story that a single bird dropping could destroy a car. After Smart provided the new data, people had clear reasons to think that birds could never destroy a Smart car. The director and department staff were smart. They successfully converted a negative comment into a prominent public relations opportunity, just by presenting real data.

Sometimes even simple numbers can produce unique effects. La Tour d'Argent (The Silver Tower) is a French restaurant in Paris with a long and rich history. It sits on the south side of the Seine River, and its customers are able to see the tall towers of the Notre Dame Cathedral from its windows. The restaurant is famous for its special duck dish. Around 1890, its chef at that time created a duck dish called "pressed duck." The restaurant only uses ducks from its own farm to guarantee the quality of this delicacy. This isn't the most important point, though.

The biggest difference between this restaurant's duck dish from that of other restaurants in Paris is that every duck consumed in this restaurant is registered and has a serial number. Each time a customer finishes a pressed duck dish, they receive a certificate with the serial number of the duck they ate. Receiving a certificate after dining at a restaurant is quite a rare experience. No wonder many famous people are drawn to the restaurant to experience the duck dish and to collect the legendary certificates. The restaurant's guest book includes many famous figures, including King Edward VII, who enjoyed duck #328 in 1890; US President Franklin D. Roosevelt, who tasted duck #112,151 in 1929; and the former Soviet Union President Mikhail Gorbachev, who consumed duck #938,451 in 2001.[5]

Any restaurant serving duck automatically uses a sequence of ducks since the first day a duck dish was sold, whether or not the chef records that sequence of numbers. This sequence number really exists and is a fact. The restaurant La Tour d'Argent chose to use the serial numbers in a unique way. When the trivial serial number of a duck is presented in a nice package with a fine certificate, the delicious dish becomes even more distinguished. Presenting the serial number to diners from all over the world makes the restaurant's customers feel that it is an honor to dine on duck at the establishment. It's amazing that a simple number can have so much power.

Take Advantage of Statistics

One important property of data we often see is statistics. Statistics represent patterns of groups of data, not single pieces of data individually. Along with checking individual elements of a collection of data, it's sometimes useful to examine the trends of the data as a group, because statistical insights are usually not apparent otherwise. Statistical features can remain hidden or be overlooked if only singular elements are examined. Therefore, exploring statistical aspects of data may help in creating new ideas as well.

A team headed by astronomer Craig Mackay of the University of Cambridge in England has produced high-quality astronomical pictures with conventional, ground-based telescopes. In an unexpected achievement, the pictures were even sharper than those taken by the space-based Hubble telescope. The expensive Hubble telescope was launched into space because, due to air density fluctuations in the atmosphere, ground-based telescopes couldn't produce very clear pictures of the heavens. Flying above the atmosphere, the Hubble telescope can capture very clear images, even though many ground-based telescopes are larger and have more capabilities. Because air density fluctuations happen randomly, the impact on picture quality constantly changes. Occasionally the impact of the fluctuation may drop to nearly zero. If a picture was taken at that exact moment, it would be very sharp, but predicting when that lucky moment will happen is almost impossible. To capture the opportune moment, the Cambridge team took a fairly simple approach. They set up their ground-based telescopes to continuously take pictures of an astronomical object of interest, ten photos each second. After collecting thousands and thousands of pictures, the team selected the clearest ones and discarded the rest. Some of the best pictures are sharper than even Hubble's. The approach developed by the team became a new method to obtain high-quality space images at very low costs. The method was chosen as one of the best inventions of 2007 by *Time* magazine.[6, 7]

The probability of obtaining a sharp space photograph from the ground is very small. However, taking many pictures over a long enough period of time made it likely that at least a few clear pictures would be captured. The award-winning technique must have been found by using the principle of statistics.

Summary

Paying more attention to facts and fact-based data is another way to open one's mind. The most valuable property of facts is that they are real and indisputable. Facts, therefore, are very powerful, since they represent the absolute truth. The following are a few concepts to pursue when searching for fact-related new ideas:

- ☐ Let facts speak for themselves when trying to convince people of your idea or stance.
- ☐ Use fact-related data, diagrams, charts, and more to improve the understanding of facts.
- ☐ Understand the magic power of numbers and think about different ways to present them.
- ☐ Take advantage of statistics, paying particular attention to events with very large or small probabilities.

Make Perceptions More Effective

How something is described affects how it is perceived and shouldn't be overlooked when seeking new insights. People usually try to understand an object through the characteristics it exhibits. An object that has value may not be understood as valuable if it's not described appropriately. Thus, improving the perception of something is another effective way to pursue new ideas. This concept aims to create a more persuasive perception than the existing one. A more accurate perception promotes easier and more effective understanding of the associated information. There are many aspects to think about when attempting to improve a perception of something: making it simpler, clearer, more appealing, more easily visualized, more pleasant, more shocking, and so on. Particularly in areas where the current perception fails, trying to improve perception may generate new solutions.

A Picture Is Worth a Thousand Words

A simple way to improve a perception is to determine whether a picture can be used to replace an assortment of words. As implied by the title of this section, the information contained in a picture is frequently much greater than that of written words occupying the same space. When something can't be described clearly in words, representing the thought in a simple drawing may quickly convey the concept.

One of the advantages of using pictures is that images usually have no communication barrier. Two people that speak different languages may not understand each other in words, but it's likely they will have the same understanding of a picture. Therefore, pictures are useful tools to build bridges of communication between people of different nations. Recently, CNN reported that a team of Swiss men from the company ICONSPEAK developed a "talking" T-shirt to help travelers.[1] On the front of the T-shirt are forty printed symbols. The symbols are designed to meet basic needs of someone traveling in an area where there may be a language barrier. Wearing this T-shirt in a foreign country can make communication a lot faster and easier. If a traveler wants to express something to a local inhabitant, they just need to point to one or more symbols on their T-shirt. For example, if the traveler needs to call a cab, pointing to the car symbol should communicate the idea. If he wants to find a restroom, he can point to a symbol depicting a person sitting on a toilet. Isn't that convenient and effective? Many international travelers love this T-shirt.

It's common to use gestures to communicate when there is a language barrier. The unique aspect of the "talking" T-shirt is the idea of using recognizable symbols as a tool to help travelers communicate in foreign countries. According to CNN, the idea was hatched when the members of the team were riding motorbikes through Vietnam and one of the bikes broke down. After they realized they couldn't verbally ask for help from the local people, they switched to drawing pictures to get their point across. That was the moment the T-shirt idea was born. Printing symbols on T-shirts doesn't require advanced technology. So why hadn't anybody invented this useful travel tool until recently? If someone had purposely searched for a better way to communicate when traveling internationally, this "talking" shirt would probably have been invented generations ago.

Graphic depictions can help improve perceptions in many other areas as well. In 2007, a newspaper article in *People's Daily* reported that the Beijing Drug Education Center had created a new program to help people stop using illegal drugs.[2] The program used video game software and artificial intelligence to implement its important message. When someone sat down in front of a screen and started the program, a camera on top of the screen took a picture of the player's face. During the game, if the player encountered an illegal drug and tried to get high, the program would modify the image of the person's face to show how they would look based on the number of years of drug use in the game. For example, if the player chose to use heroin and pushed the "3" button on the screen, the screen would display an altered picture of the player's face reflecting the result of taking heroin for three years. The longer the drug was used, the more the player's face would show signs of deterioration. After five years of virtual heroin use, the program would show the person looking seriously ill. After eight years, the person would appear to be dying. People that used the program were alarmed by the drugs' effects because they saw the consequences of drug use with their very own eyes. The program helped many people give up drugs and stay clean.

There are many media formats used to spread the anti-drug message. This AI-based software appears to be one of the most effective ever seen. It seems clear that written anti-drug material isn't as powerful as vivid images. The Beijing Drug Education Center provided an excellent example on how to take advantage of graphical perception to improve the effectiveness of the message.

Make Perceptions Easy to Understand

When a perception is difficult to understand, people often wonder why it can't be formed in a way so its meaning is easy to grasp. Unless a perception is related to a topic in a very specialized field such as mathematics or physics, ordinary people should be able to comprehend it without struggling. Of course, guessing at riddles is an exception. Because many perceptions in our daily lives are imprecise, it's worthwhile to try to improve them, potentially stimulating new thinking.

John Wanamaker was a Philadelphia merchant who invented the price tag in 1861. At that time, stores didn't show prices of the goods they were selling to their customers. Instead, people commonly haggled over the price of wares. For the first time in American history, Wanamaker put price tags on goods to explicitly tell customers how much the goods cost, relieving customers from struggling to guess the price. They could know the price by just glancing at the item. This was an important invention in the retail industry. Thanks to Wanamaker's great contribution, using price tags eventually became a standard practice. Nowadays, it's rare to see something for sale in a store without a price tag on it.[3]

Before Wanamaker's introduction of the price tag, knowing the price of goods in stores was difficult. Displaying a price tag on an item is a concise identification of the price of the item, and both stores and customers greatly prefer the certainty brought by the price tag. Why did Wanamaker, and not some other merchant, invent the price tag? Perhaps Wanamaker had a more open mind than his peers.

Applying the principle of making a perception easy to understand isn't just limited to alphanumeric information. They may also include other forms of information. Appliances in houses draw electricity from electrical sockets, but people typically have no idea how much power is flowing in their wires because the electric current in wires is invisible. If people were able to "see" the electrical power flow in wires, they might be more inclined to conserve energy when they see a lot of power being used. Recently, a non-profit Swedish organization, The Interactive Institute, developed a power cord that does exactly that. The power cord emits a flashing light when electric current flows in its wires. The brightness and flash rate of the light are proportional to the electric power flowing in the wires. The larger the power flow, the brighter and faster it flashes. Experiments showed that when people were able to "see" the electric power flow, they were more likely to save energy. When people see the cord rapidly and brightly flashing, they were more liable to check to see if any unused devices were on and turn them off. This power cord became a new tool to remind people to conserve energy. If more consumers adopt the use of this power cord, significant reduction of overall electricity usage will result. The Swedish power cord was selected as one of the 50 Best Inventions of 2010 by *Time* magazine.[4]

The cord employed a unique way of intuitively showing electric power consumption by using the brightness and frequency of a flashing light. This form of communication is so evident and clear that it's almost impossible to miss. Since the technology required to develop the cord is relatively simple, the most important step in the cord's invention was creating and developing the idea to make invisible electricity visible and easily interpreted.

Make the Outside Reflect the Inside

Another way to look for ideas to improve people's perception of something is to make an external trait reflect the important meaning or value

of internal content. People normally are exposed only to the outward appearance of something, but can't see what's inside it. If the hidden internal
content is of value, then it's critical that the external appearance reflect it.
Without an effective outward representation of the unseen value, the value
will remain hidden. The following story provides an excellent example.

Intel has a memorable marketing slogan: "Intel Inside." The slogan
can be seen on many types of computers. The origin of this marketing
effort is very interesting. According to *Fortune* magazine, when the head
of Intel's marketing first presented the slogan idea to a group of executives
in 1990, he ran into a lot of criticism.[5] Their reasoning was that Intel's
processing chip was merely one component of many inside a computer.
Placing Intel's name on the outside of a product seemed preposterous. Andy
Grove, Intel's CEO at the time, didn't agree. He felt it was a great idea and
told the marketing chief to make it happen. The result shows that Grove
was right, as "Intel Inside" became one of the most successful marketing
slogans in history.

No one had ever before used a component manufacturer's name on the
outside of a product to promote that product, but in this case the computer
was different from traditional products. Even though the processing chip
is just a component, the performance of a computer is largely determined
by the performance of its processor, and as the "brain" of a computer, it
is arguably the most important component. In this sense, explicitly exposing the brand name of its processing chip on a computer seemed to be
an intelligent choice. This way, a customer would feel his expectations of
performance of the computer would be fulfilled based on the small "Intel
Inside" sticker on the outside of the computer.

Appearances Influence Perceptions

There is yet another area to consider for improving perceptions: people's
moods. Colors, shapes, and patterns all can influence a person's feelings.
They can make people feel comfortable, excited, calm, or agitated. So,
think about changing colors, patterns, or shapes of something to influence
people's feelings when they see it.

Almost everyone uses an adhesive bandage after getting a scratch
or a small cut. Ever since this basic first aid item was invented, its plain,
skin-colored exterior hasn't changed much. The appearance of such a simple

item doesn't seem to have much room for improvement. However, there are companies with a passion for innovation which continue to explore new directions for these products. For example, according to the website Inventor Spot, a Japanese company, Nichiban, developed new looks for bandages.[6] The new designs targeted the exposed side of the bandage, abandoning traditional plain designs for colorful print patterns. The patterns included cartoon figures for kids, and traditional cultural drawings and modern abstract art for adults. Amazingly enough, the new designs seemed to reduce users' discomfort from their injuries, indicating that the outside surface design did impact their feelings. The new adhesive bandage received overwhelmingly positive feedback from the market, and sales are still growing.

The company's challenge was to figure out a way to improve the design of the bandage to make it more attractive to consumers. Traditional designs had nothing functionally wrong with them, they were just a bit dull to look at. The original thought was probably that printing interesting patterns on the bandages would be a unique design that make people feel more at ease. The new look of the bandage was able to reduce discomfort as well as be more attractive, so the external appearance improvements turned out to have a positive result.

Summary

Paying attention to improving the perception of something is another way to think about new ideas. Whether the perception of something is good or bad is directly influenced by the effectiveness of the transfer of information from itself to the external world. Therefore, this is an important area to examine when thinking about something. The following are some areas to pay attention when considering improving perceptions:

- ☐ Use pictures instead of words to convey information more easily and efficiently.
- ☐ Improve the clarity of a perception to make it easier to comprehend by others.
- ☐ Tighten connections between an external perception and an internal meaning or value.
- ☐ Strengthen perceptions to influence people's feelings.
- ☐ Know how to package something more effectively.

Include Areas People May Try to Avoid

27

Be Open to Options Outside of the Common Scope

In Chapter 1, we discussed how to go beyond a normal range that was bound by numerical values. However, not all ranges can be fully described by just numbers. Many ranges, which are called "scopes" here, are determined by the characteristics of the situation, not particular numerical values. For example, most teachers normally have a common scope with blurred boundaries for what they can and what they cannot say in front of students in a classroom; how a company employee is treated normally has a common scope of rules for most managers; and what a politician is asked by a news reporter during an interview normally has a common scope of topics. The common scope of what a teacher normally says, what a manager normally does, and what a politician is normally asked are hard to define effectively using the kind of hard numbers we discussed in the first chapter of this book. However, we can "sense" the existence of the common scopes affiliated with these settings. These common scopes are usually widely accepted and people consciously try to confine themselves to the scopes. However, common scopes can be surpassed as necessary to enable people to explore solutions outside the usual extent. Two key points are worth highlighting here: (1) common scopes are not the only scopes to consider; (2) going beyond common scopes should focus on bringing in positive values. These two concepts provide another opportunity to cultivate a creative mind.

Beyond the Common Scope of Action Implementers

Decisions are made every day that establish who should and should not take a particular action. These decisions typically involve guidelines that define a common scope or have some common rules. Frequently, these rules are hidden or obscure and are only defined by common practices. For example, formal banquets have invisible rules that govern where guests should sit in proximity to the host. However, rules that determine who may perform an action (in this case where to sit) are not necessarily unbreakable. In situations like this, think about how to break the rules to allow actions that are normally forbidden to improve the outcome.

There are many legends about the origin of the cocktail. One legend claims that cocktails originated from a Mexican girl's clever thinking. In the beginning of the nineteenth century, the fighting between Mexico and the southern states was approaching an end.[1] To honor the signing of the treaty, King Axolot VIII of Mexico invited the American general to the king's tent to celebrate the peaceful resolution and to start a new chapter in their relationship. As a gesture of goodwill, the king and the general would enjoy a drink together at the ceremony. A beautiful girl entered the tent holding a magnificent, emerald-encrusted gold cup with an unknown drink she had concocted herself. The gold cup was the king's heirloom and would not have been used except for such a special occasion as this toast.

Just as the girl was about to raise the cup and suggest that the king and the general drink its contents, everyone gathered in the room realized there was a problem: who was going to drink first? There was only one cup. If either of them drank first, the other would be snubbed. Thus, neither of them could drink from the cup without one of them losing face. The girl immediately saw the impending breach of etiquette, and instead of offering the cup to one of them, she nodded with a knowing smile toward *both* the king and the general. She then promptly emptied the cup herself. By breaking normal protocol, the girl had cleverly defused the awkward situation. The general was particularly grateful for the girl's fast thinking in preventing potential humiliation. When the general asked who she was, the king replied, "She is my daughter Coctel." The general decided that he would bring the mysterious drink back to America and would name the drink after the king's daughter to show his respect for her cleverness. Henceforth, the cocktail has become a popular drink in the United States and throughout the world. Many people to this day believe the popular drink was named after the girl, Coctel.

In this diplomatic situation, only the king and the general were supposed to drink the mysterious liquid from the cup brought by the girl. Everyone else was excluded, including the king's daughter. Her responsibility was only to deliver the cup to the two VIPs. But, suddenly, "who shall drink first" became a problem and there seemed to be no solution. People were trapped by the common notion that the only people able to drink the toast on this occasion were the king and the general. The girl knew well the importance of the toast and decided that she would abandon tradition. Perhaps someone else could represent the king and general to drink the cup so one of them would not have to defer to the other. It was much easier and faster for the girl to empty the cup herself, so she went outside the bounds of the normal scope and resolved the stalemate. Imagine if she had not used her ability to think outside the box—this situation may have had troubling results. Worse yet, perhaps we never would have had a chance to enjoy cocktails! What we can learn from the girl is not to limit ourselves to thinking about implementing actions only within their common scope.

Beyond the Common Scope of Action Recipients

Just like the common scopes of those initiating actions, common scopes for those who *receive* actions also exist. For example, a person usually only tells intimate secrets to his most trusted friends, not others. There are conventions where an action is normally applicable and where an action is not applicable. However, another technique for encouraging an opening mind is to examine potential benefits of looking outside the common scope of receivers of actions to find out if there are better results available than staying inside the common scope.

Netflix co-founder Reed Hastings once recalled his unexpected experience in a startup company, according to *Business Insider*. As a young programmer fresh out of Stanford, he worked very hard for the new company and seemed to never have time to wash his coffee mugs. There were often dirty coffee mugs scattered on his desk. Once in a while, when he came to work in the morning, he found all his dirty mugs had been mysteriously cleaned. One day, he came to work earlier than usual and saw a man washing his mugs in the bathroom. The man turned out to be the CEO of the company! Hastings was surprised and asked the CEO if he had been cleaning his mugs for the past year. The CEO admitted that indeed he had been, after which Hastings asked him why. The CEO said that it was the one unique thing he could do for Hastings to show his appreciation for the hard work he had done for the company.[2]

It is rare to hear of a CEO washing an employee's coffee mugs. He might do so for his family, but not at his company. However, this CEO went beyond the normal scope of people who he would consider washing mugs for to include the young programmer who had contributed so much to his company. The CEO had perhaps asked himself, why can't I reward him by washing the mugs to show my appreciation? The CEO didn't limit his action to those he would ordinarily consider. After Hastings saw his CEO's unprecedented act of appreciation, the young programmer was probably even more inspired to spend more time coding in his office. This example shows that going beyond the ordinary bounds of the action can pay off with significant value.

Beyond the Common Scope of Action Contents

Besides the implementers and receivers of an action, the contents of an action usually have a common scope as well. For a given action, there are invisible rules that influence what people normally do and what they normally don't do. For example, when a teacher creates a final exam at the end of a semester, normally the concepts contained in the test are those directly related to the course. Sanctimonious politicians normally want to show their best public faces and don't want to appear like clowns to the public. In general, people decide on the elements of an action based on the characteristics of the action itself. They instinctively know what to say and what not to say, what to do and what not to do. The good side of this is that people can make sure their actions are in line with the norm. However, the bad side is that people may tend to fall into stereotypes, thus limiting their range of thinking.

In the mid-1950s, an inquisitive photographer working for the *Washington Times-Herald* was tasked with interviewing people chosen at random off the street and photographing them. The questions and the responses would then be published in the newspaper along with the pictures. She showed her unique abilities by asking creative questions that were quite unusual for a normal reporter. The questions were quite revealing and often very innovative. Sometimes her questions were very personal, such as "Do you consider yourself normal?" or "If you had a date with Marilyn Monroe what would you talk about?" She asked a lot of surprising questions like that. Once she posed a question to housewives, asking, "Which US president's first lady would you want to be?" The responses varied, but one answer left a deep impression on the reporter that she would remember vividly in later years. The woman replied that she would choose to be Lincoln's First Lady, because she could have had stopped him from going to the Ford theater the night of his assassination. When the reporter's series of interviews were published, people really enjoyed reading them. Even today, some people still remember her interesting articles. The reporter later married one of the most influential politicians in the US history. She was subsequently referred to as "America's Queen" Jacqueline Kennedy Onassis. Her unique thinking ability was probably one of the reasons that John Kennedy married her.[3]

In general, news reporters design their interview questions to focus on the immediate situation of the interviewee. It isn't usually considered appropriate to go purposely beyond the obvious questions and asking seemingly irrelevant questions. Thinking more about it, though, people were probably tired of reading other interview articles containing cliché questions and stereotypical responses. Reading how ordinary people answer unexpected questions was an interesting and attractive break from the norm. This demonstrates that an open mind can explore uncommon actions within a common activity to produce valuable benefits.

Deviate from Normal Personalities

Another type of uncommon action a person can take is one where the action doesn't fit a person's particular identity. A person's behavior has an associated common scope, and what a person says or does typically follows their identity traits. Scopes of people's "normal" behaviors do exist, but people aren't constrained to those common behavioral scopes. In special situations, unusual behaviors may shed light on great insights which are not apparent within "normal" behaviors.

If we want to pick an event where unusual behavior solved a major issue in a country's history, nothing demonstrates the concept better than that created by the former German Chancellor Willy Brandt (1913–1992).

In December 1970, Brandt visited Poland's capital Warsaw as the head of state of West Germany. His mission was to mend the strained relationship between the two countries, which stemmed from the Nazi occupation in World War II. While visiting a memorial to the Nazi-era Warsaw Ghetto Uprising, without any warning, he suddenly knelt in front of the monument. He remained silently kneeling for a while, ignoring to the scores of reporters swarming around him. This totally unexpected gesture surprised everyone attending the ceremony. To many Poles, Chancellor Brandt demeaned himself by kneeling on the land of a former enemy of Germany. Photos of Chancellor Brandt's unusual behavior quickly spread throughout the world on the front pages of prominent newspapers. However, the effect of Brandt's astonishing behavior was to the benefit of both Germany and Poland. His heartfelt humility largely eliminated the hatred between the people of the two nations. This event showed Poland and other countries that suffered under Nazi brutality that Germany was capable of sincere repentance for its past atrocities. This led to quick normalization of relations between Germany and these countries. Chancellor Brandt explained why he did this for his country: "Under the weight of recent history, I did what people do when words fail them. In this way, I commemorated millions of murdered people." Brandt's behavior was very creative and resulted in significantly better relations between nations. Because of his innovation that helped heal old wounds of decades past, Brandt won the 1971 Nobel Peace Prize. In 2000, the square in Warsaw where the memorial is located was renamed the Willy Brandt Square in commemoration of his demonstration of empathy.[4]

Before Brandt, it's hard to remember any public figure in modern history that knelt to make an apology in such a manner. It is an unusual behavior for any politician. Like Brandt showed, to make the people in the victimized countries believe that Germany had recognized its mistakes and was sorry for them, a verbal apology alone would not have been enough to soften such egregious violations of human rights. Knowing this, Brandt probably searched for better solutions to this problem that took him outside the behaviors of a conventional politician. As a result of looking outside the ordinary political comfort zone, he found this extraordinarily successful approach. If such an unusual behavior could solve a difficult political problem, why not use it?

Well-known people like Chancellor Brandt aren't the only ones who can achieve a difficult goal by showing "abnormal" behavior—an ordinary person can benefit from this tactic, too. According to a report in *The New York Times*, in December 1970, an eighteen-year-old freshman at Ohio State University wrote a letter to President Nixon expressing complaints regarding his high-rise dormitory. The letter also praised the president and requested a meeting with him. Surprisingly, President Nixon replied to his letter promptly, inviting him to visit the White House. On his subsequent visit, the young college student had a twenty-minute meeting with the president in the Oval Office. It's obvious that the meeting must have strengthened the student's determination to pursue a career in politics. He's now the governor of Ohio and was a major candidate in the 2016 Republican presidential campaign—John Kasich.[5]

College freshmen have many things they feel they need to accomplish, but writing a letter to the President of the United States to ask for a meeting in the Oval Office probably wouldn't be one of them. Most people would generally think that requesting a meeting with the president of the United States could only be possible with someone at least at the level of the head of a university. No wonder Mr. Kasich's mother thought something was wrong with her son when he told her he needed an airline ticket to go to Washington to have a meeting with President Nixon at the White House. However, it was his courage and boldness, which might not fit his place as a college freshman, that may well have driven him to become who he is today.

Expand Common Scopes from Various Angles

Besides categorizing common scopes according to the implementers, the receivers, and the contents of an action, you can also use different viewing angles to look at how to expand common scopes. You can easily consider many different scopes, such as the scope of your choices to make, fields to target, words to use, levels to set, requests to put, and so on. The next two examples illustrate this principle.

Author James Michener once received an invitation from President Eisenhower to have dinner at the White House. Coincidently, three days before he received the president's invitation, he had promised his high school English teacher to give a speech at a dinner honoring the educator.

He still remembered that the teacher had taught him how to write creatively when he was a student, and wanted to honor him. However, the two events conflicted and he could only choose one to attend. Which one would it be? What happened was that he wrote an honest letter to President Eisenhower telling him that he would not be able to attend the dinner at the White House. His reason was quite simple: throughout a person's lifetime, that person might have experienced more than a dozen presidents, but knowing a great teacher is very rare. President Eisenhower understood Michener's explanation and probably agreed with his unconventional thinking process.[6]

If you were James Michener, what decision would you have made? Because of the importance of the president of the United States, common sense for most people would be to accept the invitation without thinking. But Michener thought beyond the common-sense reaction to find the real value and made his decision accordingly. This is a lesson in thinking out of your ordinary scope of choices.

Here's another example about a house design that's way beyond the common scope of house shapes. According to Fox News, there's a special house in Suwon, South Korea that was built by its mayor, Jae-duck Sim. This two-story building is a steel, concrete, and glass structure of over four thousand square feet. It has four bedrooms and three bathrooms. Functionally, it's not considerably different from other houses. Its biggest distinction is its external appearance. It's called the world's only toilet house—that's no mistake, yes, *toilet* house—because it looks just like a gigantic, white toilet! When visitors want to go up to the balcony, they have to use the stairs inside the "toilet drain." Mr. Sim spent his whole life promoting sanitation through bathroom hygiene and advocating the improvement of living conditions for the two billion people worldwide who live without toilets. The purpose of building this toilet house was to remind people that sanitation is very important to people's health. Now, the toilet house has become a special landmark in Suwon and continues inspiring South Korea's modern toilet initiatives.[7]

When someone decides to build a house, there are endless external designs available. However, I would bet there aren't any sample design books that contain homes that look like a toilet. Clearly, such a crazy house design could only be created by a mind without boundaries. The design wasn't just intended to be audacious, but rather to remind anyone who sees the huge toilet house about improving sanitation. Wasn't this precisely Mr. Sim's original intention?

Therefore, in addition to the common scopes of actions and behaviors, consider the common scopes in other aspects of daily activities.

Summary

The boundaries of various common scopes may not be represented by numerical values. People normally have a reasonable feeling, however, of what should be inside the borders and what should be outside. Therefore, there are common scopes associated with many areas. Look for and understand these common scopes first, then try to find options beyond these scopes to discover new opportunities for solutions. These factors outside the scope boundaries are frequently beneficial. The following are a few areas to consider:

- ☐ Pay attention to possibly going beyond the common scopes of implementers, receivers, and contents of activities, i.e., think beyond those who normally do the activities, those to whom the activities are normally done, and what the contents of the activities normally contain.
- ☐ Remember that a person's behavior does not necessarily have to always be consistent with their personalities.
- ☐ Consider elements outside other common scopes encountered in daily life and look for potential benefits from that perspective.

28

Remove Unnecessary Mental Constraints

Thinking is the motivation for most actions. Thinking is a process where a person decides what he or she will or will not do. Deciding against doing something often comes from self-imposed constraints. Many of these constraints are indeed legitimate, frequently taking the form of necessary constraints such as obeying laws or following social norms. Unnecessary constraints may exist either consciously or unconsciously and can hinder people from thinking as freely as they're able. It's better to clearly realize that not all constraints are necessary, and removing unnecessary constraints is helpful for opening minds and creating new solutions. The more you remove unnecessary constraints, the more room you have for imagination, and the first step to removing these mental constraints is to identify them.

Their Constraints Aren't Yours
Mental constraints are different for different people. John's constraints are not necessarily the same as Bob's constraints. If a constraint is identified, check first to see if it applies to you. Ask yourself, Do I really need to follow this restriction? Apply this question especially toward those constraints that seem universally applicable to the general population. Your answer will uncover more information about the constraint and help you decide whether to follow the restriction or reject it based on the particular

situation. Identifying those constraints that most people have but don't apply to you will make it easier to create new ideas since you're not burdened by those constraints.

In 2003, Andy Riley published his self-illustrated comic book *The Book of Bunny Suicides: Little Fluffy Rabbits Who Just Don't Want to Live Any More*. The book depicts cute little bunnies that do nothing but try their best to kill themselves in a myriad of ways. Particularly striking was the unexpected methods they use to end it all. The inventive twist was that many of the cartoons don't explicitly tell readers how the bunnies die. It allows readers to imagine the specific methods of death based on the reader's own imagination. In one cartoon, a bunny uses superglue to stick himself onto the hull of a submarine about to submerge into the ocean. Even though the cartoon doesn't tell readers how the bunny was going to die, most readers were able to figure out the method by just glancing at the cartoon. In another cartoon, a few bunnies sit under the gigantic space shuttle rocket engines at a launch pad and quietly wait for the moment when the shuttle will blast off into space. The book's cartoon about Noah's Ark particularly worried readers. When all the other animals were lining up to board Noah's Ark to avoid the imminent flood, two fluffy, cute little bunnies refused to go. They instead had fun sunbathing and reading books at the beach. It didn't take much imagination to figure out the bunnies' fates when the flood arrived. In summary, the bunnies used their ingenuity and came up with many ways to end their lives. Readers were intrigued by the bunnies' dedication, persistence, and inventiveness, and were even more fascinated by how such a morbid topic could be turned into a humorous book. When the book was published, it was no surprise that the peculiarly dark topic drew instant attention from avid readers and curious passersby alike. It quickly topped many bestseller lists. In 2004, the sequel *Return of the Bunny Suicides* was published, and in 2007 a special edition was released which contained every bunny suicide. The books are so popular that unauthorized copies of the cartoons are still circulating on the Internet today.[1]

Suicide is an unpleasant topic. General George S. Patton once found when he was chatting with some women that he could talk to them about almost any topic except death on the battlefield. Clearly the women just didn't want to hear about this morbid subject.[2] Most cartoonists may

unconsciously avoid the topic of suicide. Riley was likely the first cartoonist who was successful in using this subject matter in his work. He
might have realized that avoiding the topic of death might be a constraint
for cartoonists, but it was *not a constraint for him.* Just the opposite, he
used it as a wonderful opportunity. The idea may have come to him when
searching for an original topic that no cartoonist had thought of before.
If another cartoonist had thought about drawing a series focused on the
topic of suicide and had recognized and removed the unnecessary taboo
constraint, Riley's success would have probably been achieved earlier. So,
when constraints limit other people's thinking, first check to see if new
ideas are limited by that constraint and then determine whether the constraint is really necessary or not.

Only Accept Real Constraints

Another category of unnecessary constraints is that of voluntarily adopting
a restriction which doesn't actually exist. People sometimes inadvertently
make assumptions, expecting that there are some inherent constraints.
Actually, these constraints may not exist at all. People who accept these
phantom constraints put themselves in an unfavorable situation that dis-
courages an open mind. Here are two classic examples that illustrate this
point.

The story of Columbus's Egg is a great example.[3] The story goes that
Columbus was once at a dinner with some Spanish nobles and challenged
them to make an egg stand on its end without using any outside assistance
to balance it. None of the nobles were successful, even though the answer
turned out to be quite simple. The solution to the challenge was to slightly
crush one end of the egg shell so it would stand by itself. Columbus had
not indicated there was a constraint that the egg had to survive totally
intact. Everyone at the dinner *assumed* the egg had to balance on its end
undamaged when that was not the case! The undamaged egg constraint
was purely a fabrication of the nobles' imagination. No one took the time
to think about the fact that it was a nonexistent constraint.

The old story of the Gordian Knot has a similar lesson.[4] In the ancient
world, the oracle of Telmissus prophesized that the one who could untie
a special, highly intricate knot would rule all of Asia. Since the knot was
so complicated, many people tried and failed. All those people who had

tried to untie the knot, however, didn't recognize that *the oracle didn't say that the knot's rope had to stay intact* while it was untied. The constraint that the rope be undamaged was invented only by the people themselves. This unjustifiably assumed constraint caused all who tried to fail. Then, Alexander the Great came to try to untie the knot. He quickly recognized the phantom restriction was invalid and drew his sword and severed the knot in a powerful stroke, making it easy to untie the remainder of the rope. It could be said that this example of thinking outside the box made him the Ruler of Asia!

Although you may not discover a new continent or become the next Ruler of Asia, removing mistaken assumptions in your thinking will surely be beneficial to your career and everyday activities.

Constraints Can Be Flexible

Social norms bring with them many constraints. For example, most people feel comfortable with close interactions with others at the same or similar social levels, or with those that participate in same circles, but are cautious to build relationships with people at somewhat different levels or in different circles. In some sense, these mental constraints are rational. However, such restrictions are not necessarily inflexible, and in many circumstances certain constraints are not even necessary.

In November of 1948, Bud Ince, a midshipman at The Naval Academy, found out that his girlfriend Jean was coming to the east coast to visit him. So, he decided to take the opportunity to ask her to marry him. He wanted to make it a big surprise by proposing in an elegant location with a romantic atmosphere, but high-class, romantic places were very expensive. However, he was not intimidated by this hurdle. Instead, he wrote a letter to the manager of the famous Waldorf Astoria Hotel in New York City and described how important this moment would be to him. He hoped to impress his girlfriend and create a cherished memory for his soon-to-be fiancée. Ince dreamed of a lavish dinner with her in the gorgeous hotel before proposing to her. He admitted that as a cadet he couldn't afford it, but asked the price anyway. Surprisingly, the manager and maître d'hôtel were moved by his sincerity and decided to help him. When the cadet and his girlfriend arrived at the Waldorf, a special table was reserved for them in the restaurant. During dinner, not only were there gourmet dishes, wine, and candles, but also an orchestra led by a famous musician who played "Navy Blue and Gold" at midnight for them. After the sumptuous dinner, the hotel only charged a small fraction of the usual price to its special guests. Undoubtedly, when the young cadet asked his girlfriend to marry him at midnight, the girl was visibly moved and answered with a definitive "Yes." The couple were married the following year and returned to the Waldorf on their thirtieth and fiftieth wedding anniversaries to celebrate their love and show their appreciation to the kind and warmhearted staff at the famous hotel.[5]

A student without much money normally wouldn't have been able to make a dream that was so far outside his means come true. When confronting this type of situation, most people would probably assume the constraint that a lack of money would prevent them from having a wonderful experience. But why should the cadet be limited by this constraint? Why not think positively and try to get around it? Could it be possible that the grand hotel would be moved by the young cadet's sincere letter? Ince's decision to contact the manager of the hotel stemmed from ignoring the commonly assumed constraint based on social norms. Of course, there was no guarantee he would get help just by asking, but it was *guaranteed* that if he didn't ask, no one would help. Others can't help if they don't know help is needed. Therefore, it is very important to look for flexibility in assumed constraints.

Timely Constraints

Unnecessary constraints also come from not realizing that constraints can change over time. Constraints on thinking are not always static. Over time, the basis for a constraint can dwindle and disappear, making the constraint invalid. Identifying this type of constraint evolution allows mental constraints to be lifted and actions taken to exploit the changes.

To understand how an old restriction can become out of date over time, no better example comes to mind than China's economic reform led by Deng Xiaoping. Deng was the de facto leader of China from 1978 through 1992, and his influence was felt even after his death in 1997. Before 1978, China had a planned economy. According to classical economic theory, a country with a communist political system must operate under a planned economy, not a capitalistic market economy. This was a commonly accepted rule at that time. Because of the poor efficiency of a planned economy, slow growth in living standards was common in communist countries. After Deng became China's leader, he realized the old restriction was out of date in modern times and put aside China's thirty-year-old planned economic model. In turn, he opened up China to the world and introduced a market-based economy to China. Under his leadership, China started to access foreign investment, global markets, and private competition. Deng's decision improved China's economy immensely. During the two decades from 1978 to 1997, China's GDP average annual growth rate shot up to nearly 10 percent. That's a great achievement. Deng's new policies made China one of the fastest growing economies in the world and significantly increased the standard of living for hundreds of millions of Chinese.[6]

Deng was obviously a person who knew how to think innovatively. He observed that the world was changing and China must adapt to it. He knew that the economic constraints of a classical communist political system were gradually fading away. New global economic realities provided the stimulation that drove market-based economic systems beyond capitalistic countries into communist countries. The obsolete classical restrictions were no longer valid. Fortunately, Deng saw this change and removed the constraint in time to update China's economy, otherwise the modernization process in the country would have been delayed for many years. This example shows that examining constraints for signs of aging can be very important.

Don't Assume Something Is Impossible

Often, we hear claims that something is impossible. Certainly, a lot of things can't occur in a specific way or at a specific time. However, it's unwise to assume something is *totally* impossible. Assuming that something is impossible will automatically create boundaries in one's mind, which limits further exploration of potential opportunities. Perhaps the impossibility isn't real, or it can be transformed into a possibility, but ignoring something because you initially felt that it is impossible will hinder you in finding these opportunities. Therefore, don't accept that something is impossible too readily. When confronting a situation where something seems impossible, first ask, "Is that really true?" and then see if there are circumstances where the situation can be changed.

For a long time, people believed that plastic could not conduct electricity, otherwise how could it be used as insulation materials for electric wires? Therefore, it was widely accepted that it was impossible for plastics to conduct an electric current. In the 1970s, Professor Hideki Shirakawa, a Japanese chemist, was studying plastic thin films in his lab. One day, he mistakenly added too much catalyst to the reaction vessel. To his surprise, the resulting synthesized film shined like silver. After more experiments, he found that he was able to produce plastic films with different metallic colors by adjusting the temperature and quantity of the catalyst.

At a seminar in Tokyo, Professor Shirakawa met Professor Alan MacDiarmid, who was also working on plastic films with metallic colors. After learning that Professor Shirakawa was working in the same area of research, Professor MacDiarmid invited him to visit his lab at the University of Pennsylvania in Philadelphia. There, they worked together and produced improved metal-like plastic films using a modified method. At that time, Professor Alan Heeger also joined their research.

One of Professor Heeger's students discovered unusually high electric conductivity in the films in his measurements. The measured conductivity of the films was ten million times higher than that of a normal plastic film! This was an unprecedented breakthrough in plastic materials research. It proved that, under certain conditions, plastic materials are able to conduct electricity just like metals. The three professors jointly published their important findings. Since the discovery, research in this field has grown tremendously and many applications for the new plastic materials have been conceived. For example, light-emitting wallpaper based on thin, conductive plastic films could replace light bulbs in houses of the future. The three professors received the Nobel Prize in Chemistry in 2000 for their discovery.[7]

It was formally well-known that plastic was an insulator, so the "impossibility" of conducting electricity in plastics was a strong constraint. However, the professors didn't limit their activities because of the so-called impossibility. When they saw thin plastic films with metallic colors, they probably thought that since the plastic's color looked similar to a shiny metal, could it be possible that other properties, such as conductivity, were similar to that of metals, too? By ignoring the constraint of impossibility, the researchers created a new situation which led to a significant discovery. Actually, anyone can develop this kind of attitude of breaking through perceived obstacles to overcome the impossible, whether they are researchers winning prestigious awards or regular people wanting to make a difference.

Summary

People are hindered by many self-imposed mental constraints when they think about something. Most of these constraints are necessary and deeply rooted, but some of them are unnecessary and avoidable. Unnecessary constraints limit the scope of our thinking. Remember to try to identify unnecessary constraints to thinking and remove them. If you are success-ful, it can be quite beneficial. Here are several ways to identify unnecessary mental constraints:

- ☐ Don't simply take other's constraints as your own.
- ☐ Identify constraints resulting from misunderstandings and remove them.
- ☐ Realize that many constraints are based on social norms and are thus flexible. They become unnecessary in many circumstances.
- ☐ Notice how constraints may have evolved. Yesterday's necessary constraints may have become unnecessary today.
- ☐ Don't easily accept constraints based on an "impossibility."

Accept Imperfect Solutions

Everyone strives to find an ideal solution when seeking to reach a particular goal. But the real world is not perfect and there may be no ideal solution. The known solutions may not be very good or they may be defective. Worse, people may not identify *any* acceptable solutions at all. When a situation like this is encountered, people may just give up because it's the easiest route. However, those with open minds have a tendency to explore a wider variety of choices that include imperfect solutions. They are more willing to accept an inferior solution or solutions with a few defects rather than have no solution at all. When a completely suitable solution cannot be found, those with creative minds will take the next best thing: an imperfect, but feasible, solution.

Take Baby Steps

Frequently, goals cannot be satisfied in the near term due to constraints such as the social environment or technical issues. In these situations, it's helpful to set a near-term goal, which approximates the long-term goal. Going after the near-term goal can be considered a small step in the process of realizing the original goal. The difference is that the near-term goal may be achieved much more quickly than the original goal and the effort is not wasted because it represents a positive step in achieving the original goal. Achieving the near-term goal may bring immediate benefits with it as well.

In 2009, *Time* magazine recognized teleportation as one of the 50 Best Innovations of that year.[1] This feat was accomplished by a research team from the University of Maryland who successfully transported the state of an atom in one chamber to another atom in another chamber one meter away, changing the second atom's state to that of the first atom while the original state of the first atom disappeared. In the atomic world, the state of an atom is the most fundamental characteristic in its identification. When the state of an atom in a location is transferred to another atom in another location, it is considered that the atom at the first location has been "transported" to the second location, since same type of atoms are indistinguishable except by their states.

This type of teleportation isn't the kind people normally associate with the word *teleportation*. Mankind has long dreamed about the ability to instantaneously transfer material things from one location to another location. This concept can be seen in *Star Trek* movies where "transporters" are used to move people and objects from a starship to another starship or a planet.[2] A crew member may stand in a fictional transporter and start the transfer by saying "Beam me up, Scotty." Then the person gradually disappears as they are converted to an energy pattern and beamed to the destination a long distance away. At the destination, the energy is converted back into matter and reassembled into the original crew member.

Today, this is just science fiction and a practical teleporter is only a dream. Although a physicist predicted in 2008 that similar teleporters will appear within a hundred years, it may never become a reality. The success of the experiment at the University of Maryland, however, showed that the research team cleverly chose to work on teleporting tiny atoms as a near-term goal that may be a stepping stone to the real teleportation goal (that is unlikely to be realized any time soon). In the experiment, the team chose simple atoms instead of larger pieces of matter. They also chose a short distance of one meter to transport a state of an atom instead of trying to achieve it over thousands of miles. By setting a simpler, much less challenging near-term goal as the focus, it helped the team achieve one type of teleportation for the first time.

Another example of incrementally approaching the goal of teleportation can be seen in three-dimensional printing technology. When an object is scanned, its three-dimensional data is collected and then electronically sent to a distant location over the Internet. Upon receiving the data, the 3D printer at the distant location reproduces the object by building it up from its local materials.[3] It's effectively as if the object was sent to a distant location without any physical transportation involved. This primitive teleportation tool is nowadays finding more and more applications in industry and in other fields.

Teleporting the state of an atom and three-dimensional printing both demonstrate the principle of pursuing a smaller piece of the overall goal when the larger, long-term goal is too big or too difficult to tackle today. Even though the solutions for the smaller goal will likely not be a complete solution to the larger goal, the smaller goal's solutions represent beneficial progress toward the overall goal.

Solutions with Shortcomings

When unable to find a proper solution to a problem, consider solutions that may contain obvious defects but can still be implemented quickly if urgency is a major factor. Many times, waiting to develop proper solutions is not desirable or possible. Using solutions with some defective parts allows you to still make progress even though some sacrifices have to be made.

Going to Mars and colonizing it has been a dream for many years. One motivation for doing this is the potential need to save mankind in case a global disaster threatens to annihilate everyone on Earth. A Mars presence could represent a kind of lifeboat for the human race. Because no one can determine when such a disaster will happen, it would make sense to work toward Martian colonization as soon as possible. With today's existing technology, it's not too difficult to go to Mars, but it's very difficult to return from Mars. The gravity of Mars is more than double of that of the Moon's, and the distance from Earth to Mars is much farther than from Earth to the Moon. The resources needed to return from Mars are many times that of what it took to succeed in the Apollo moon-landing project. To deal with the difficulty space activists have proposed one-way trips to Mars. Since the long-term goal is to colonize Mars anyway, why not let the astronauts fly to Mars to stay there and build settlements? This way, there's no longer a need to solve the problem of how to bring them back, and the proposal can be implemented much more quickly. Of course, some of the defects of the proposal are obvious. Once the astronauts leave Earth, they will no longer be able to visit their home planet and will never see their loved ones again.[4]

If the problems surrounding a round trip to Mars cannot be solved for many years, a one-way trip to Mars may be feasible, even though the one-way trip has some serious drawbacks. The thinking that resulted in the idea for a one-way Mars trip shows the characteristics of an open mind. The originators of the idea didn't confine their thinking only to full solutions like all other manned space exploration solutions to date, but expanded their search for solutions to include a one-way trip that had some defects in favor of achieving the goal more quickly. Therefore, when good solutions cannot be found, think about solutions with defects or even with some serious defects. Using this approach, you can create many more opportunities rather than waiting, perhaps forever, for a perfect solution or stopping the pursuit of the goal altogether.

Solutions That Partially Fulfill the Goal

Once a goal has been established, the next step is to find solutions that satisfy the goal. Sometimes solutions are evident but aren't practical because you don't have the ability to carry out the solutions. For example, a solution may be too expensive and is unaffordable. In these circumstances, consider the next best thing: focus on *partially* achieving the original goal. You can try to modify the goal to make the new solution more cost effective so that it is affordable.

Today, private space travel is available and relatively safe. Businessman Dennis Tito was the first space tourist. He paid $20 million to the Russian space agency to visit the International Space Station for about a week.[5] Virgin Galactic has passengers booked for its future sub-space flights. The price for the space flight ticket is much cheaper than what Mr. Tito paid, only a "cheap" $200,000.[6] To the general public, however, such space tourist programs are still too expensive, even though many people dream of visiting outer space.

Recently, several space tourism companies have introduced some radically new programs that provides hope for dreams with smaller wallets. Those who join the programs can stay in space for a few years or longer. The fee for each passenger is priced surprisingly low, from about a few hundred to a few thousand dollars. Incredibly, there's even been a price tag reported as low as $49.95, according to *USA Today*.[7] These companies are not hoaxes but real businesses. So far, demand for these programs come from ordinary people including technicians, nurses, and college students, among others. Of course, such programs would be too good to be true if they didn't have some drawbacks. Yes, it's true that the inexpensive space-travel programs are designed to help people realize their dreams to go into space, but the fulfillment of those dreams won't happen during the passenger's lifetimes. These programs offer services only to those who have already passed away. The core service of these companies' businesses is to load a small amount of each passenger's cremated ashes into a specially designed capsule. The capsule is then loaded onto a rocket that goes into orbit. Once in space, the capsules of ashes orbit the Earth for years before reentering the atmosphere and burning up. The passengers will have been in space, even though only a part of the passengers' remains will have reached their goal. Nevertheless, for some people this achieves their dream of space travel.

Despite facing the very expensive costs of providing space tourism, these new companies didn't stop thinking about new product designs. Targeting prices at affordable levels for the general public, they designed alternatives with much lower costs to cater to ordinary people, although the alternatives only partially meet the consumer's desire for space travel. What can be learned from this example is that when the resources to execute a program are too constrained, consider modifying the program based on available resources to make the modified program work. Even though the modified program won't be an ideal solution and may only partially implement the original goal, it may be a practical solution that satisfies significant needs.

Incomplete Solutions

While searching for solutions to reach a goal, there is no doubt that the ideal result is finding a solution that attains 100 percent of the goal. However, uncovering an ideal solution isn't always possible. When a perfect solution isn't possible, or an ideal solution costs too much, it may not be a bad alternative to consider a non-ideal solution that nearly fulfills the goal. Including less-than-perfect solutions will expand the scope of your search.

In 2015, *National Geographic* reported that the Los Angeles Department of Water and Power (LADWP) released approximately a hundred million four-inch black plastic balls into the Los Angeles Reservoir in an effort to fight California's drought problem.[8] The balls float on the water and cover the entire water surface of the reservoir, making it look like black velvet. The balls provide shade from the sunlight, cooled the water, and reduced evaporation. They also protected the water quality from dust and other harmful materials. Cleaner reservoir water in turn lowers the cost of treating it to become drinking water. Based on experimental results, the specially designed black balls reduce evaporation by 85-90 percent, decreasing water loss by 300 million gallons annually, which is about 10 percent of the reservoir's total capacity. LADWP hopes this innovative approach can help mitigate the water shortage problem in the area.

Using floating plastic balls is not an ideal solution to stop water evaporation. A flat sheet covering the entire surface of the reservoir would be even better. Because the plastic balls are round, there are unavoidable spaces between the balls and thus they can't cover the whole surface. But they can cover more than 90 percent of it. Considering the low cost of using them and the associated water treatment savings, LADWP probably found the black ball solution to be imperfect but still the best solution for the problem. The beauty of this example is that the creator of this approach didn't reject this less-than-perfect solution, which doesn't prevent water evaporation completely, when considering solutions. Therefore, don't forget to examine slightly flawed results in the process looking for solutions.

Solutions That Involve Additional Costs

When searching for solutions to reach a goal, include solutions which require extra costs to allow success. In this case, compare the extra cost to execute the solution with the cost incurred if the goal is not fulfilled. If the extra cost is less than the cost of not having a solution, the extra expenditure may justify itself.

Here's a story that happened more than a thousand years ago in the Tang Dynasty of China. At that time, people used hand carts to transport goods in mountainous areas. Once, on a dangerous mountain trail, there was a line of hand carts that contained various goods. This section of the narrow, one-lane trail was especially dangerous, as one side of the trail was the mountainside and the other was a sheer cliff. Usually, the carts moved forward in single file at normal speed, but that day the convoy moved especially slow because the first cart, which paced the entire line, was moving very slow. This cart was going so slow because it carried several large and fragile pottery jars. The cart's owner was afraid the jars would break if he pulled the cart too fast over the bumpy road.

Seeing that the sun was setting, other cart pullers in the line began to worry. If the carts couldn't pass the dangerous section by sunset, it would be much more dangerous for them to move in the dark. But what could they do? Then Liu Po, the leader of a group of several carts in the middle of the line, shouted to the owner of the first cart and asked what was the total cost of the pottery jars. When the owner answered with the price, the leader managed to move to the front of the line and pulled out his wallet. He took out several silver coins and handed them to the owner of the first cart, saying, "I want to buy all your pottery jars."

The first cart owner accepted the money, after which the new owner of the jars tilted the cart and dumped all of the jars into the river below the cliff. The first cart, now empty, could proceed at a normal pace, thus speeding up the entire line. Eventually, all the carts passed through the dangerous section by sunset. Other cart owners were very grateful to Liu since his clever thinking probably saved some lives that day.[9]

While many cart owners wanted to quickly pass this dangerous section, the slow-moving cart at the front of the line prevented them from doing so. The cart owners couldn't make the first cart go faster, nor could they pass it, so it seemed they would have to pass the dangerous section at night and incur high risks. Liu wasn't discouraged with the difficult situation even though there seemed to be no solutions. In his quest for a solution, he included one that incurred extra costs. The first cart moved so slowly because its owner was afraid of losing money if he broke the jars. But if the line of carts weren't able to pass the dangerous section in daylight, the problem of safety would've become a much bigger issue. This led Liu to think about compensating the owner of the first cart for the risk of money loss in order to gain the safety of the entire column of carts. Spending extra money enabled him to find a feasible solution to a situation with seemingly no solutions.

So, when there isn't an ideal solution, or no solution at all, examine whether solutions that require extra costs exist. Even though they may be imperfect, they can be the optimal choice in special circumstances.

Summary

It's clearly best to find an ideal solution when pursuing a goal. However, many times people aren't able to find a perfect solution or even any solution at all. Don't give up easily when a perfect solution is not available. Be open to accepting imperfection and proactive in searching for less-than-ideal solutions. Using these techniques, an open mind will become even more flexible. Imperfect solutions still can be solutions, they just don't fully meet the goals that were originally envisioned. The following are several directions to consider when pursuing non-ideal solutions:

☐ If there appears to be no way to reach a goal in the near term, consider taking a small step first to maintain progress toward the goal. Or, set a goal similar to the original goal to pursue in the near term.

☐ When an existing solution is not realistic, think about solutions which partially satisfy the goal but are feasible and practical.

☐ If a solution can't be applied on a larger scale, find out if it can be implemented on a smaller scale first.

☐ Between an adequate solution and a sub-optimal, quickly implementable solution, choose the latter if it is more beneficial.

☐ Include solutions that don't quite reach but fall near the ultimate goal.

☐ Don't overlook solutions that cost more.

30

Remember Everything
Has Exceptions

$\mathbf{M}$ost people have a pretty good idea about how they should behave in a civilized, modern society. People generally believe it's okay to do or say acceptable things, while it's wrong to do unacceptable things. But the world we live in is complex. Although this norm usually indicates good behavior, this perspective may not be the optimal choice in some circumstances. Certain remarks that people think shouldn't be made should perhaps be made in some cases, just as some situations may require certain activities that people don't normally believe one should partake in. The conditions in these situations can be considered as exceptions. A person with an open mind who realizes that everything has exceptions will recognize that sometimes doing what normally shouldn't be done can be beneficial. Likewise, when making statements, remarks that shouldn't be made in normal circumstances may also prove helpful. Someone who understands this concept has a wider range of thinking than those who can't recognize the flexibility brought on by deviation. These people can only see the conventional, allowable prospects.

Clearly, caution and prudence must be used when introducing exceptions. After all, they are contradictory to what is commonly accepted. A good guide for whether or not you should pursue an action that conflicts with the norm is to determine if the action is done for legitimate reasons and results in no harm to others. The rest of this chapter presents cases where an open mind can be expanded by properly employing exceptions.

Exceptions to Social Norms

There are many social norms. For example, people know that they should take good care of their possessions and not waste resources when replacing them. These simple ideas seem obvious to everyone, and we follow them without much thought. However, exceptions can be made in some circumstances when it comes to complying with social norms. Not following a social norm may lead to a more useful result. To accomplish this though, common mindsets must be put aside so that the possibilities associated with not complying with social norms can be explored. If these other possibilities are not recognized, how can exceptions to complying social norms be considered?

Sima Guang was a scholar and historian in eleventh century China during the Song dynasty. A story is told about a childhood incident he experienced. One day, when he was about six or seven years old, he was playing with several friends in a garden when one of his friends accidently fell into a large fish cistern. The cistern was huge and the water was so deep that the small child was in danger of drowning. When the other kids saw their friend fall into the cistern, they got scared and all ran away, except Sima. Sima stayed behind because he wanted to save his friend's life. The wall of the cistern was too high for Sima to climb. Even if he could, he wasn't strong enough to pull his friend out of the water. He thought for a moment and got an idea. He picked up a big rock and used it to hammer the side of the cistern over and over until the side wall shattered. The water quickly drained out through the hole he had made, and his friend was saved. After hearing about this episode, the whole community was surprised that such a young child had used such highly creative thinking during the emergency. Drawings depicting the rescue were widely publicized, and even today parents are still telling the story to their children.[1]

Sima Guang was in a dilemma because he wasn't able to perform the rescue by pulling his friend out of the cistern from the top. Then he got the clever idea to break the cistern to save his friend. A giant fish cistern is a valuable item, and ruining such a large and important item is out of the question under ordinary circumstances. The uncommon part of Sima's idea was that he didn't exclude the option of damaging property. If damaging the cistern could save his friend's life, then the destruction was totally justified, even though it would never be considered in a normal situation. On the other hand, if Sima had not expanded his thinking to include exceptions to following social norms, he wouldn't have discovered this idea in time and his buddy probably would have drowned. The lesson that can be learned from this story is to always keep your mind open to opportunities that include exceptions when social norms are involved, especially in crisis situations.

Exceptions to Reality

In courtrooms, witnesses usually take an oath before testifying. They raise their right hand and swear "I will tell nothing but the truth." Truthfulness is very important in these circumstances, as many times they involve life or death consequences. However, by understanding that *everything* has exceptions, you can have exceptions relating to facts, for example, in circumstances when telling a white lie has a more positive result than being completely truthful.

A story about Winston Churchill's cleverness has circulated for many years. It's said that one evening Churchill attended a dinner with the dignitaries of the Commonwealth of England. In the middle of the dinner, the protocol officer contacted Churchill and whispered to him that one of the guests had placed a silver salt shaker into his pocket. The officer hoped Churchill would help stop the important guest from stealing the item. On hearing about the incident, Churchill decided to postpone action until the end of the dinner. When the dinner was over, Churchill walked up to the guest and secretly showed him a silver pepper shaker in his pocket, which matched the salt shaker in the guest's pocket. Churchill told the guest in a low voice that the two of them had been discovered and that they were better to put the shakers back. The guest had no choice but to follow Churchill's suggestion. None of the other guests ever knew that the incident had happened.[2]

According to the story, Churchill clearly lied to the guest. Churchill didn't steal the pepper shaker, nor had anyone seen him slip the pepper shaker into his pocket. All he did was communicate to the thief that someone knew the guest was trying to steal the item and that he would be caught if he refused to put it back. Churchill showed compassion when he privately pretended that he also occasionally stole things. This way, the guest could quietly return the item with his reputation still intact, thinking that Churchill was a confederate. If the incident had been handled typically, for example, if Churchill had walked up to the guest and demanded that he pull the item from his pocket in front of the other guests, a great commotion would have ensued and the man would have been totally humiliated. Fortunately, Churchill's harmless lie resulted in a win-win outcome. The item was returned with no one knowing the incident had occurred. Consequently, the practice of always presenting the unaltered facts can have certain positive exceptions.

Honesty is one of the basic characteristics of a person with integrity. A dishonest person won't only find it hard to win trust from others, but he or she also may cause trouble for themselves. However, due to the myriad events in life, absolute honesty isn't always without its exceptions, especially when dealing with evildoers such as criminals. In such special circumstances altering information or even fabricating facts can be permissible and perhaps even be necessary.

Here is an example. A bank was robbed and a large amount of cash was stolen. The police investigated the incident but found no leads. In order to help the police solve the case, the bank manager offered to be interviewed by a local newspaper reporter. In the interview, the reporter asked the manager how much money had been stolen. The manager said that after doing careful counting and auditing, the amount was $951,636. The bank manager then urged the public to provide tips on the case to the police and appealed to the thieves to turn themselves in as soon as possible to reduce their punishment.

Shortly after the interview was published, the police received several valuable tips. Based on the information, the police identified and arrested the thieves one after another. Most of the stolen money was recovered except for $150,000. Why the shortage? When the thieves were dividing their spoils, they found the total amount of money wasn't the same amount as the bank manager mentioned in the newspaper interview. The thieves fought fiercely among themselves because none of them admitted to secretly taking the extra money. The infighting led to information leaks about the robbery that allowed the police to solve the case. The amount of stolen money was actually not the amount the bank manager publicly stated in the interview. He had just made up the extra $150,000 to trick the thieves, and it worked!

Obviously, the bank manager didn't disclose the real amount of money stolen by the thieves to the interviewer. If the manager had revealed the actual amount of the stolen money that matched the total in the thieves' possession, the distrust between the thieves wouldn't have occurred and the police wouldn't have solved the case as quickly. The thieves had no idea that the manager had an innovative mind that understood the power of exceptions, and was playing a clever trick on them. Therefore, it's important to open one's mind to recognize the benefits of exceptions to total transparency in special cases like this, while still insisting on total honesty in normal situations.

Exceptions to Obedience

In general, an order from a superior should be obeyed. Disobeying an order can have severe consequences. Even if an erroneous order is carried out by a subordinate, the superior usually bears the consequences, not the subordinate. Theoretically, all a subordinate needs to do is follow the order, no matter whether the order is right or wrong. However, it's better to realize that following orders has its exceptions as well. In special cases, disobeying a command may be better than following it blindly, especially when the command is seriously flawed.

Matsushita Konosuke, the founder of Japanese consumer electronics giant Panasonic, once told a story about the shogun era while explaining his business philosophy. The story was about the third shogun of the Tokugawa dynasty, Tokugawa Iemitsu, and his top advisor, Abe Tadaaki, who had an impressive reputation. One day, the shogun came back from a hunting trip and was taking a bath. His servant, who was responsible for the bath, accidentally poured very hot water over the shogun's body. The shogun felt searing pain and his burned skin turned bright red. The shogun was furious and called Abe in immediately. Despite the servant's pleas for mercy, the shogun told Abe that the servant was to be put to death. Abe quickly replied, "Yes, sir." Abe had always obeyed the shogun's orders without question.

This time, however, after leaving the shogun's quarters, Abe didn't follow his superior's order to execute the hapless servant. Instead, Abe asked the shogun's attendants to tell him when the shogun's mood had improved. That evening after dinner, when the shogun's pain was abating and his mood returned to normal, Abe rushed into the shogun's room to see his master. He told the shogun, "Earlier today, you instructed me to punish the servant who poured the hot water on you. I'm sorry, but unfortunately I can't remember what you told me to do. Please remind me how you want the person punished."

The shogun thought for a while and told Abe, "He made a serious mistake because of his negligence; exile him to a distant island." To which Abe replied, "Yes, sir!" and left the shogun's room to carry out the order. Afterwards, the shogun's attendants were talking about the incident saying that they were surprised that Abe had forgotten the shogun's order. When the shogun heard of their discussion, he told the attendants, "How could Abe have forgotten my order? He was just using it as a clever way to oppose my order and to ask me to re-think my decision!" As a result, Abe's impressive reputation became even more acclaimed.[3]

Abe was very astute and insightful! Putting the servant to death wasn't a rational decision because it was made in the heat of anger. Luckily, Abe was very perceptive and created a situation where the shogun had an opportunity to reconsider without losing face. Although he usually complied with the shogun's orders dutifully, he seemed to always leave room for exceptions. While he couldn't directly disobey the shogun's order to put the man to death, he delayed the punishment with a trivial excuse, which allowed the shogun time to reconsider. Imagine if Abe had immediately carried out the shogun's order as he normally did. When the shogun recovered from his anger and had time to think after the execution, he would have been upset that Abe had followed his order so swiftly. Therefore, exceptions can be applied to many situations when directions from superiors are involved. Dealing with unreasonable orders or commands is a common situation.

Summary

There is nothing in the world that is absolute. Every activity has exceptions. Given that fact, it's prudent to examine perceived absolutes for opportunities to sharpen one's mind. Because exceptions may include actions that shouldn't be carried out normally, they may cause controversy. Therefore, when thinking about sensitive exceptions, there must be justifiable reasons to employ them. Here are a few areas where exceptional actions may be considered:

- ☐ Remember that complying with social norms isn't always required, particularly in situations where an exception provides clearly positive benefits.
- ☐ Think about whether distorting reality is more beneficial than being completely open in an unusual circumstance.
- ☐ Avoid exposing too much information when dealing with villains.
- ☐ Check to see if an exception to following a rule or an order can be considered in a special situation.

The Grand Checklist of Generalized Idea-Inspiring Approaches

1. **Go Beyond Traditional Ranges**
   - ☐ Look for values incrementally larger or smaller than the values in the normal range.
   - ☐ Think about values much larger than the largest value or much smaller than the smallest value in the normal range.
   - ☐ Examine extremely large values up to infinity or extremely small values near or equal to zero.
   - ☐ Consider expanding the range in various dimensions such as time, space, weight, quantity, grade, percentage, and so on.

2. **Consider More Than "One"**
   - ☐ When thinking about something normally associated with a singular instance, see if multiple instances are possible.
   - ☐ Try letting something that normally happens in one location happen in more locations, or something that normally happens once to happen multiple times.
   - ☐ Think about how to change something with only one function into something with multiple functions, or something that only serves one objective into something that serves multiple objectives.
   - ☐ See if something tightly bound to a singular form can be related to multiple forms.

☐ Pay attention to multiplicity, such as multiple meanings of a phrase, multiple expressions of an idea, or multiple interpretations of an action.

☐ Don't forget to try reversed scenarios. For a situation normally associated with multiple instances, see if there are potential benefits by reducing the number of instances to one.

3. Look at More Dimensions

☐ Consider more spatial dimensions. For example, consider adding a third dimension to a two-dimensional object.

☐ Think about transforming abstract characteristics into dimensions associated with various objects or situations. For example, think about a person's hearing when only his sight is normally considered, or think about the temperature of an object when only its color and weight are normally considered. Consider the following:

☐ Pay attention to the relationships and interactions amongst dimensions.

☐ Alternatively, think about how you might shrink the number of dimensions.

4. Add One More Type

☐ Try to add one more type that is distinct in at least one aspect from the existing types.

☐ Think of the Adding One More Type method in terms of content, function, appearance, format, category, platform, usage, effect, concept, a way to do something, as the target of an action, and so on.

5. Explore Relationships

☐ Search for hidden connections between different things to discover inconspicuous relationships, then think about their added benefits.

☐ Create a new connection between things from diverse fields. For example, build a connection between things that have happened at different times and/or locations, things that have similarities, opposite characteristics, or no relationships at all.

☐ Find a way to have two originally unrelated things match each other.

☐ When building a new relationship, consider having one end support the other, or both ends support each other.

6. Combine Things
☐ Combine things from different fields.
☐ Associate two widely contrasting things.
☐ Put totally unassociated things together.
☐ Marry two things with opposite characteristics.
☐ Fuse things with existing relationships.

7. Think About Differences
☐ Pay attention to the different results of an activity due to different implementers, different targets, or different processes of the activity.
☐ Note different effects caused by different times or locations.
☐ Recognize favorable differences in circumstances, conditions, situations, requirements, relationships, and so on.
☐ Be particularly careful to look for subtle differences since they are inconspicuous.
☐ Create a difference between two things which were originally the same, or, enhance their existing differences.
☐ Look for a measurable benchmark to create a positive difference. Search for opportunities to make valuable differences in efficiency, quality, performance, etc.
☐ Don't overlook reverse-case scenarios where differences can be reduced or removed for taking advantages.

8. Apply Diverse Concepts
☐ Adapt the same approach to a different category, field, or goal.
☐ Consider the result of the same action if it were applied to a different target.
☐ Think about using different content in the same format.
☐ Take the same concept into a different time, location, environment, or situation.
☐ Let a different thing assume the same function or capability.

9. Heed Both the Whole and Its Parts
- ☐ If something is typically only considered a whole, attempt to divide it anyway. Then think of it as an assembly of parts and handle the whole on a parts level.
- ☐ Treat each part differently and explore the individual parts for their unique merits.
- ☐ Try to convert a part into a whole.
- ☐ Attempt to transform a whole into a part of another whole.
- ☐ Focus on parts with the most benefits.

10. Rearrange Patterns
- ☐ Expose groups and reassemble their elements to form new groups.
- ☐ Adjust the relative size of segments belonging to an assembly or a procedure.
- ☐ Tune the sequence of segments in a process.
- ☐ Deviate from the regular pattern if it's more beneficial that way.
- ☐ Form positive-negative pairs to gain net benefits.

11. Set Reference Points
- ☐ Choose a proper reference to maintain an advantage.
- ☐ Adjust a reference point to improve a gain.
- ☐ Set a fitting reference point to produce a better outcome.
- ☐ Establish a new reference point to shift focus.
- ☐ Let things reference each other.

12. Look Back to the Beginning
- ☐ Reassess your justification of the starting point, even though you seem to be nearing a good solution.
- ☐ Check if the starting point can be improved, even if it seems valid.
- ☐ Verify if the original premise is still suitable with the possible situational changes.
- ☐ Frequently re-examine initial conditions to find opportunities to save time and energy.

13. Consider Changes

☐ Pay attention to hidden or unnoticeable changes, large or small, in processes or situations.

☐ Don't underestimate the importance of small changes, as they may have significant meaning.

☐ Introduce changes proactively if they are beneficial. For example, create and apply changes to quickly adapt to new situations.

☐ Alter something which is normally static so it becomes dynamic to produce an improved result.

☐ Don't assume that something which seems immutable can't be changed in a positive manner.

☐ Make changes by substituting an element in a process or a thing.

☐ Recognize the endless ways to introduce changes in life.

14. Take One More Step

☐ Think about what the next stage could be to explore new opportunities while most people continue to focus on the current stage.

☐ Contemplate what new benefits might arise during a concept's evolution.

☐ Identify future benefits or problems ahead by examining more stages down the road and take action to secure or prevent them.

☐ Consider additional steps to gain a more complete picture of your situation.

15. Notice What's New

☐ Be sensitive to things that are fresh and new. Frequently check up on what has become available recently.

☐ Investigate whether something new may present an opportunity to improve what exists.

☐ Find out if a newly discovered item may be the key to solving a longstanding, unresolved problem.

☐ Try to create completely new things that no one has ever thought of before with newly feasible resources.

☐ Pay attention to new concepts, new methods, new platforms, new trends, new products, new technologies, new situations, new theories, new viewpoints, and so on.

☐ Be timely in how you take advantage of new resources.

16. Think Symmetrically

☐ If someone performs an activity, see if his opposite counterpart that is able to perform the same action.

☐ When most people perform the same action, examine whether a symmetrical action may be carried out as well.

☐ An action is normally done relative to someone or something, so think about whether the action may be done relative to a symmetric counterpart.

☐ If something happens in a particular situation, imagine what would happen if it were in a symmetrical situation.

☐ If A takes an action toward B, consider what would happen if B took the same action toward A.

☐ Develop the habit of putting yourself in your counterpart's shoes.

17. Recognize Complementary Parts

☐ Explicitly think about identifying the complementary parts of everyday things.

☐ Choose the complementary part that delivers a better result.

☐ If using one aspect doesn't work, try its complementary part.

☐ Try adjusting the ratio between a complementary pair to favor the more advantageous one.

☐ Take the opportunity to improve the performance of an element when its complementary part changes.

18. Find Favorable in the Unfavorable

☐ When evaluating an unfavorable situation, change the perspective to a viewpoint where it can be treated as advantageous.

☐ Transform an unfavorable factor into a favorable factor.

☐ Treat an unfavorable situation as a challenge and create a favorable situation by overcoming it.

☐ Focus purely on the favorable aspects of an unfavorable situation and ignore the unfavorable parts.

☐ Examine the unfavorable aspects of a favorable situation so the situation can be improved or adverse circumstances can be avoided.

19. Try Reversed Approaches

☐ Check to see if a reversed approach can provide the desired results when traditional approaches show little or no ability to achieve the objective.

☐ Try an opposing approach especially if traditional approaches can't be applied at all.

☐ Even if a traditional approach works, still compare the benefits of a reversed approach in order to select the better one.

☐ Always explore opposite approaches to see if they can provide potential new opportunities.

20. Discover Missing Factors

☐ Use the exhaustive method of searching for the complete set of factors. Try to identify as many factors as possible in a set. Then, examine all of the factors, especially the uncommon ones that are frequently overlooked by others.

☐ Realize that the one who performs an action can receive the action as well. Within an action's set of objects, there is usually one factor that stands out as easy to miss: the one performing the action.

☐ Explicitly look for temporary factors of a set because sometimes the factors belonging to a set are not necessarily fixed. They may vary, and the temporary ones can be overlooked quite easily.

☐ Try to find factors which aren't normally in a set but could be included in particular situations.

21. Dig into the Essence

☐ When facing a problem, always try to identify its root cause.

☐ When searching for a solution, think about what key step the solution should contain.

☐ When something occurs, look for the fundamental reason causing the event.

☐ For any statement, always try to identify its true meaning, not just the surface or literal meaning.

☐ Identify key components such as the fundamental difference between things, the true effects of a plan, the real purpose of an action, the actual reason of a rule, and so on.

☐ Always explore situations at their deepest level, asking questions such as: What is the most important part? What is the fundamental issue? What is most appealing to others?

22. Conserve Resources

☐ Substitute with a lower-cost item if it will serve the same purpose.

☐ Use resources only in areas where they are truly required.

☐ Take advantage of resources that are already available or employ idle and free resources as much as you can.

☐ Extend the useful lifetime of a resource.

☐ Redesign a resource consumer to also generate resources.

☐ Shift the location or time to where or when fewer resources are needed.

☐ Sacrifice a small amount of a resource to generate a larger return.

☐ Conserve resources constantly.

23. Take Indirect Paths

☐ Think about finding a solution by taking an indirect path if it is too difficult to reach a goal directly.

☐ Investigate an indirect path to see if it achieves a better result, even if the original goal can be reached directly.

☐ Remember, almost anything can act as a helper for indirect paths. This could be a person, a living creature, a place or location, a moment in time, an action, a motion, an excuse, a piece of information, a set of data, a fictional object, an analogy, and so on.

24. Imagine the Impossible

☐ Consider something that won't happen in the foreseeable future, and think about how it could evolve if it did happen.

☐ Realize that the contents of creative works don't necessarily have to be aligned with logical reality. Something that cannot exist in the real world can surely occur and perhaps even thrive in a fictional world.

☐ Imagine impossibilities with existing things for producing benefits.

25. Let Facts Speak for Themselves

☐ Let facts speak for themselves when trying to convince people of your idea or stance.

☐ Use fact-related data, diagrams, charts, and more to improve the understanding of facts.

☐ Understand the magic power of numbers and think about different ways to present them.

☐ Take advantage of statistics, paying particular attention to events with very large or small probabilities.

26. Make Perceptions More Effective

☐ Use pictures instead of words to convey information more easily and efficiently.

☐ Improve the clarity of a perception to make it easier to comprehend by others.

☐ Tighten connections between an external perception and an internal meaning or value.

☐ Strengthen perceptions to influence people's feelings.

☐ Know how to package something more effectively.

27. Be Open to Options Outside of the Common Scope

☐ Pay attention to possibly going beyond the common scopes of implementers, receivers, and contents of activities, i.e., think beyond those who normally do the activities, those to whom the activities are normally done, and what the contents of the activities normally contain.

☐ Remember that a person's behavior does not necessarily have to always be consistent with their personalities.

☐ Consider elements outside other common scopes encountered in daily life and look for potential benefits from that perspective.

28. Remove Unnecessary Mental Constraints
☐ Don't simply take other's constraints as your own.
☐ Identify constraints resulting from misunderstandings and remove them.
☐ Realize that many constraints are based on social norms and are thus flexible. They become unnecessary in many circumstances.
☐ Notice how constraints may have evolved. Yesterday's necessary constraints may have become unnecessary today.
☐ Don't easily accept constraints based on an "impossibility."

29. Accept Imperfect Solutions
☐ If there appears to be no way to reach a goal in the near term, consider taking a small step first to maintain progress toward the goal. Or, set a goal similar to the original goal to pursue in the near term.
☐ When an existing solution is not realistic, think about solutions which partially satisfy the goal but are feasible and practical.
☐ If a solution can't be applied on a larger scale, find out if it can be implemented on a smaller scale first.
☐ Between an adequate solution and a sub-optimal, quickly implementable solution, choose the latter if it is more beneficial.
☐ Include solutions that don't quite reach but fall near the ultimate goal.
☐ Don't overlook solutions that cost more.

30. Remember Everything Has Exceptions
☐ Remember that complying with social norms isn't always required, particularly in situations where an exception provides clearly positive benefits.
☐ Think about whether distorting reality is more beneficial than being completely open in an unusual circumstance.
☐ Avoid exposing too much information when dealing with villains.
☐ Check to see if an exception to following a rule or an order can be considered in a special situation.

References

CHAPTER 1
1. Koch, Wendy. "Needy Students Given Food for Weekend." *USA Today*, September 14, 2007. http://usatoday30.usatoday.com/news/nation/2007-09-13-backpack_N.html.
2. *Wikipedia*, s.v. "Muhammad Yunus," accessed June 27, 2016. https://en.wikipedia.org/wiki/Muhammad_Yunus.
3. Frankel, Rebecca. "The FP Top 100 Global Thinkers." *Foreign Policy*, November 25, 2009. http://foreignpolicy.com/2009/11/25/the-fp-top-100-global-thinkers-7.
4. *Wikipedia*, s.v. "Rubber Duck (Sculpture)," accessed December 31, 2013. http://en.wikipedia.org/wiki/Rubber_Duck_(sculpture).
5. Whitehead, Kate. "Hong Kong's Giant Rubber Duck." CNN, May 2, 2013. http://www.cnn.com/2013/05/02/travel/hong-kong-giant-duck.
6. Farndon, John. *The Great Scientists*. New York: Metro Books, 2005, 12.
7. Lunine, Jonathan I., Clark R. Chapman, Raymond Jeanloz. "Earth." *Encyclopedia Britannica*, December 3, 2015. https://www.britannica.com/place/Earth/Basic-planetary-data.
8. Stewart, Will. "Lusha the Chimpanzee Outperforms 94% of Russia Bankers with Her Investment Portfolio." *Daily Mail*, January 12, 2010. http://www.dailymail.co.uk/news/worldnews/article-1242575/Lusha-monkey-outperforms-94-Russia-bankers-investment-portfolio.html.
9. Hanlon, Mike. "Land-Mine Detecting Plants Created." New Atlas, June 4, 2004. http://newatlas.com/go/2568.
10. *Wikipedia*, s.v. "Liu Ling," accessed January 23, 2017. https://en.wikipedia.org/wiki/Liu_Ling.

CHAPTER 2
1. McGregor, Jena. "The Other Indian Outsourcer." *BusinessWeek*, November 6, 2006.
2. *Wikipedia*, s.v. "Bernard Montgomery," accessed July 14, 2014. http://en.wikipedia.org/wiki/Bernard_Montgomery,_1st_Viscount_Montgomery_of_Alamein.
3. Flannery, Sean. "Our Story." CAMiLEON, accessed December 21, 2016. http://www.camileonheels.net/About_Us_s/1670.htm.
4. Sterling, Toby. "'Second Life' 3-D Digital World Grows." Fox News, October 9, 2006. http://www.foxnews.com/story/2006/10/09/second-life-3-d-digital-world-grows.html.

5. Kiviat, Barbara. "Travel: Locked Up." *Time,* December 15, 2003. http://www.time.com/time/magazine/article/0,9171,1006471,00.html.

6. Roberts, Steven V. "Reagan and the Russians: The Joke's on Them." *The New York Times,* August 21, 1987. http://www.nytimes.com/1987/08/21/us/washington-talk-reagan-and-the-russians-the-joke-s-on-them.html?pagewanted=all.

7. *Wikipedia,* s.v. "American Airlines fleet," accessed October 5, 2016. https://en.wikipedia.org/wiki/American_Airlines_fleet.

8. "The Secrets of Southwest's Continued Success." *The Economist*, June 18, 2012. http://www.economist.com/blogs/gulliver/2012/06/southwest-airlines.

CHAPTER 3

1. della Cava, Marco R. "For Couples Who Love the Chaise." *USA Today*, February 10, 2006.

2. Piore, Adam. "Haptic Computer Interface." *Scientific American*, September 1, 2011. http://www.scientificamerican.com/article/patent-watch-sept-11.

3. *Wikipedia*, s.v. "Mehmed II," accessed August 9, 2009. http://en.wikipedia.org/wiki/Mehmed_II.

4. Fox, Margalit. "N. Joseph Woodland, Inventor of the Bar Code, Dies at 91." *The New York Times*, December 12, 2012. http://www.nytimes.com/2012/12/13/business/n-joseph-woodland-inventor-of-the-bar-code-dies-at-91.html.

5. *Wikipedia*, s.v. "Force Touch," accessed July 10, 2016. https://en.wikipedia.org/wiki/Force_Touch.

6. Gao Weijie. "A Special Movie Theatre for the Blind." [In Chinese.] *Readers*, No. 6, 2009.

7. Jobson, Christopher. "Rashad Alakbarov Paints with Shadows and Light." *Colossal* (blog), January 20, 2012. http://www.thisiscolossal.com/2012/01/rashad-alakbarov-paints-with-shadows-and-lights.

CHAPTER 4

1. Koeppel, David. "Nurses Bid with Their Pay in Auctions for Extra Work." *The New York Times*, June 6, 2004. http://www.nytimes.com/2004/06/06/jobs/nurses-bid-with-their-pay-in-auctions-for-extra-work.html.

2. *Wikipedia*, s.v. "Noise Map," accessed June 11, 2015. https://en.wikipedia.org/wiki/Noise_map.

3. "Best Inventions of 2007: Water Works." *Time,* accessed August 15, 2010. http://content.time.com/time/specials/2007/article/0,28804,1677329_1678083_1678067,00.html.

4. Klages, Karen. "Student Design Competition Winners Strut Their Stuff." *Chicago Tribune,* January 19, 2003. http://articles.chicagotribune.com/2003-01-19/news/0301190024_1_student-design-competition-international-housewares-show-industrial-design.

5. Snyder, Steven James. "The 50 Best Inventions of 2010: Sarcasm Detection." *Time,* accessed November 11, 2010. http://content.time.com/time/specials/packages/article/0,28804,2029497_2030615_2029717,00.html.

6. Bruno, Laura. "Web Levels These Dating Fields." *USA Today*, January 17, 2006.

7. Lahrichi, Kamilia. "Hospital Clowns Get Serious." *USA Today*, October 9, 2015.

CHAPTER 5

1. Whitehorn, Mark. "The Parable of the Beer and Diapers." *The Register*, August 15, 2006. http://www.theregister.co.uk/2006/08/15/beer_diapers.

2. "Chupa Chups Sugar Free: Ants." *Business Insider*, accessed December 20, 2016. http://www.businessinsider.in/The-18-Most-Hilarious-And-Clever-Print-Ads-Ever/Chupa-Chups-Sugar-Free-Ants/slideshow/33459006.cms.

3. Jiang Guangyu. "Madonna Effect." [In Chinese.] *Readers*, No. 3, 2009.

4. Wanxisha. "Trade Used Mobile Phones for Forests." [In Chinese.] *Readers*, No. 16, 2008.

5. Associated Press. "Virginia Synagogue Doubles as Mosque for Ramadan." Haaretz, September 18, 2009. http://www.haaretz.com/jewish/news/virginia-synagogue-doubles-as-mosque-for-ramadan-1.7715.

6. Zheng Youyou. "West Lake: Fu Yongjun Photography Works." [In Chinese.] Xitek.com, August 29, 2012. http://vision.xitek.com/books/201208/29-99848.html.

7. Stone, Alex. "Why Waiting Is Torture." *The New York Times*, August 18, 2012. http://www.nytimes.com/2012/08/19/opinion/sunday/why-waiting-in-line-is-torture.html?r=0.

CHAPTER 6

1. "We Pioneered DNA Art." DNA11, accessed November 20, 2007. http://www.dna11.com/about.asp.

2. *Wikipedia*, s.v. "Dominique Boivin," [In French] accessed September 13, 2014. http://fr.wikipedia.org/wiki/Dominique_Boivin.

3. *Wikipedia*, s.v. "Angry Birds (video game)," accessed August 30, 2016, https://en.wikipedia.org/wiki/Angry_Birds_(video_game).

4. Gallos, Peg. "Innovation Gains Educator US$500,000." *IEEE Institute*, Vol. 28, No. 2, June 2004.

5. White, Daniel. "Google Wants Pedestrians Hit by Self-Driving Cars to Stick Around... Literally." *Time*, May 20, 2016. http://time.com/4343175/google-driverless-car-glue-patent.

6. Yu, Roger. "Hotel-to-Plane Transition Eased." *USA Today*, March 1, 2006.

7. Li Yinhe. "Sakura's Love." [In Chinese.] *Readers*, No. 24, 2007.

CHAPTER 7

1. "Ask the Inventors: About Us." AsktheInventors.com, accessed January 2, 2015. http://www.asktheinventors.com/about.html.

2. "Mouse Feces in Honey." [In Chinese.] Baidu.com, accessed December 21, 2016. http://baike.baidu.com/view/1210562.htm.

3. Balfour, Frederik. "Catching the Eye of China's Elite." *BusinessWeek*, February 11, 2008.

4. Boccaccio, Giovanni. *The Decameron.* New York: Oxford, 1985.

5. Zhang Huijun. *Admitted to Beijing Film Academy.* [In Chinese.] Beijing: China Youth Publishing House, 2014.

6. Zhang Huan. "Making Money Faster than Printing It." [In Chinese.] *Southern People Weekly*, December 1, 2007.

7. "How Did Yang Lan Get Hired by CCTV?" [In Chinese.] TSCTV.net, November 30, 2010. http://www.tsctv.net/node/53824.

8.   Stein, Perry. "A D.C. Cop Tried to Break up a Group of Teens. It Ended in This Impressive Dance-off." *Washington Post*, October 28, 2015. https://www.washington-post.com/news/local/wp/2015/10/28/a-d-c-cop-tried-to-break-up-a-group-of-teens-it-ended-in-this-impressive-dance-off.

CHAPTER 8
1.   Fuson, Ken. "More Instructors Make Lectures, Notes Available for Downloading." *USA Today*, March 15, 2006.
2.   Lee, Jennifer 8. "Using Lasers to Zap Mosquitoes." *Bits* (blog), *The New York Times*, February 12, 2010. http://bits.blogs.nytimes.com/2010/02/12/using-lasers-to-zap-mosquitoes/?em.
3.   "Fully Dedicated to Luggage Development." [In Chinese.] CCTV.com, February 5, 2006. http://www.cctv.com/program/twwx/20060127/101833.shtml.
4.   Wilson, Craig. "An Experience You'll Dine out on for Decades." *USA Today*, January 11, 2006.
5.   *Wikipedia*, s.v. "Surfing," accessed September 27, 2014. http://en.wikipedia.org/wiki/Surfing.
6.   *Wikipedia*, s.v. "Skysurfing," accessed September 1, 2008. http://en.wikipedia.org/wiki/Skysurfing.
7.   Harrell, Eben. "The 50 Best Inventions of 2010: Deep Green Underwater Kite." *Times*, November 11, 2010. http://content.time.com/time/specials/packages/article/0,28804,2029497_2030623_2029802,00.
8.   Weise, Elizabeth. "'Noah's Ark' of 100 Million Seeds Opens in Permafrost of Norway." *USA Today*, February 27. 2008.

CHAPTER 9
1.   "The 50 Best Inventions of 2009: The Personal Carbon Footprint." *Times*, accessed February 27, 2015. http://www.time.com/time/specials/packages/article/0,28804,1934027_1934003_1933957,00.html.
2.   Yang Hui. "Working with Foreign Police Officers." [In Chinese.] *Readers*, No. 11, 1990.
3.   Adee, Sally. "Spy vs. Spy." IEEE Spectrum, August 1, 2008. http://spectrum.ieee.org/computing/software/spy-vs-spy.
4.   Brook, Tom Vanden. "Military Pay, Life to Get Reboot." *USA Today*, March 30, 2015.
5.   "Advert on Oxford Street Shown Only to Women," BBC News, February 20, 2012. http://www.bbc.com/news/uk-england-london-17099518.
6.   *Wikipedia*, s.v. "Photographic Mosaic," accessed August 2, 2015. https://en.wikipedia.org/wiki/Photographic_mosaic.

CHAPTER 10
1.   Wang Yaowen. "Fundamentally I Am a Farmer." [In Chinese.] *Readers*, No. 20, 2003.
2.   Speroni, Charles. *Wit and wisdom of the Italian Renaissance*. Berkeley: University of California Press, 1964, 35.
3.   *Wikipedia*, s.v. "2010 Winter Olympics Closing Ceremony," accessed March 1, 2010. https://en.wikipedia.org/wiki/2010_Winter_Olympics_closing_ceremony.

CHAPTER 11
1. "Scholar of Skinny Sheep." [In Chinese.] Baidu.com, accessed December 21, 2016. http://baike.baidu.com/view/439049.htm.
2. Morgan, Tom. "Revealed: How a Homesick Wife Nearly Blew It for the British Double Agent Who Fooled Hitler." *The Telegraph*, September 28, 2016. http://www.telegraph.co.uk/news/2016/09/28/revealed-how-a-homesick-wife-nearly-blew-it-for-the-british-doub.
3. *Wikipedia*, s.v. "Wang Pang," [In Chinese] accessed October 14, 2016. https://zh.wikipedia.org/wiki/%E7%8E%8B%E9%9B%B1.

CHAPTER 12
1. Wang Guangyue. "Story Behind the Plaque of 'Upright and Bright'." [In Chinese.] The First Historical Archives of China, July 17, 2016. http://www.lsdag.com/NETS/lsdag/page/article/Article_869_1.shtml?hv=965.
2. Clinton, Hillary. *Living History.* New York: Simon & Schuster, 2004.
3. "You Yu." Baidu.com, accessed August 21, 2014. http://baike.baidu.com/view/390596.htm.
4. *Wikipedia*, s.v. "Laconic Phrase," accessed August 4, 2016. https://en.wikipedia.org/wiki/Laconic_phrase.
5. Active Power. "UPS System," ActivePower.com, accessed November 26, 2012, http://www.activepower.com.
6. "Harry Leichter's Jewish Humor." Haruth.com, Haruth Communications, accessed June 25, 2016. http://www.haruth.com/jhumor/jhumor61.htm.

CHAPTER 13
1. Mahurkar, Sakharam. "The Smart Syringe." SmartSyringe.com, accessed January 13, 2015. http://www.smartsyringe.com.
2. "Dew-Covered Damselflies Glitter Like Jewels in the Morning Sunshine." *Daily Mail*, December 29, 2010. http://www.dailymail.co.uk/news/article-1342448/Dew-covered-damselflies-look-like-jewels-morning-sunshine.html.
3. "The Art of Naming Something." [In Chinese.] *Readers*, No. 18, 2006.
4. *Wikipedia*, s.v. "Suite Vollard," accessed January 21, 2015. http://en.wikipedia.org/wiki/Suite_Vollard.
5. *Wikipedia*, s.v. "Dynamic Tower," accessed January 21, 2015. http://en.wikipedia.org/wiki/Dynamic_Tower.
6. "A Schoolboy Saved the Olympic Games." Olympic Games Museum, accessed January 22, 2015. http://olympic-museum.de/john_wing/jwing.html.
7. San Pedro, Emilio. "Cuban Internet Delivered Weekly by Hand." BBC, August 10, 2015. http://www.bbc.com/news/technology-33816655.
8. *Wikipedia*, s.v. "Hong Yi," accessed November 30, 2016. https://en.wikipedia.org/wiki/Hong_Yi.

CHAPTER 14
1. Mizokami, Kyle. "Germany's Got a 4-Barrel Laser Gatling Gun." *Popular Mechanics*, September 21, 2015. http://www.popularmechanics.com/military/weapons/news/a17425/germanys-got-a-4-barrel-laser-gatling-gun.
2. *Wikipedia*, s.v. "reCAPTCHA," accessed January 6, 2017. http://en.wikipedia.org/wiki/ReCAPTCHA.

3. *Wikipedia*, s.v. "King Zhuang of Chu," [In Chinese] accessed August 8, 2014. http://zh.wikipedia.org/wiki/%E6%A5%9A%E5%BA%84%E7%8E%8B.
4. *Wikipedia*, s.v. "Pioneer 10," accessed April 15, 2016. https://en.wikipedia.org/wiki/Pioneer_10.
5. *Wikipedia*, s.v. "Voyager Program," accessed April 28, 2010. https://en.wikipedia.org/wiki/Voyager_program.
6. "Stephen Hawking: Alien Life Is out There, Scientist Warns." *The Telegraph,* April 25, 2010. http://www.telegraph.co.uk/news/science/space/7631252/Stephen-Hawking-alien-life-is-out-there-scientist-warns.html.
7. Chao Bian. "Half Steak." [In Chinese.] *Readers*, No. 5, 2012.

CHAPTER 15
1. Stone, Madeline and Jillian D'Onfro. "The Inspiring Life Story of Alibaba Founder Jack Ma, Now the Richest Man in China." *Business Insider*, October 2, 2014. http://www.businessinsider.com/the-inspiring-life-story-of-alibaba-founder-jack-ma-2014-10.
2. *Wikipedia*, s.v. "Vehicular communication systems," accessed December 23, 2014. http://en.wikipedia.org/wiki/Vehicular_communication_systems.
3. US Department of Transportation. "Connected Vehicles: Vehicle-to-Vehicle (V2V) Communications for Safety." Intelligent Transportation Systems, accessed January 17, 2015. http://www.its.dot.gov/factsheets/pdf/JPO-029%20V2V%20SAFETY%20V5.1%20F.pdf.
4. "Best Inventions of 2006: Amazing Embrace." *Time*, accessed September 1, 2008. http://www.time.com/time/specials/packages/article/0,28804,1939342_1939424_1939709,00.html.
5. "Two Ways to Play Limbo Unique." Limbo, accessed January 11, 2008. http://www.limbo.com/sap/howtolimbo?rp=unique&aid=163612.
6. *Wikipedia*, s.v. "Jacob W. Davis," accessed December 20, 2014. http://en.wikipedia.org/wiki/Jacob_W._Davis.
7. *Wikipedia*, s.v. "Levi Strauss," accessed December 20, 2014. http://en.wikipedia.org/wiki/Levi_Strauss.
8. Levi Strauss Co. "The Invention of the Blue Jean." LeviStrauss.com, accessed December 20, 2014. http://www.levistrauss.com/our-story.
9. Port, Otis. "Super-Radar, Done Dirt Cheap." *Business Week,* October 19, 2003. http://www.businessweek.com/stories/2003-10-19/super-radar-done-dirt-cheap.

CHAPTER 16
1. *Wikipedia*, s.v. "Registered Traveler," accessed August 9, 2009. http://en.wikipedia.org/wiki/Registered_Traveler.
2. "Good Cop Pull over Prank." YouTube video, 4:45. Posted by Break, April 2, 2014. https://www.youtube.com/watch?v=ZJ91qt7-brU.
3. Summers, Keyonna. "Teens Must Post Apology on YouTube." *USA Today*, June 9, 2008.
4. *Wikipedia*, s.v. "Battle of Red Cliffs," accessed February 13, 2014. http://en.wikipedia.org/wiki/Battle_of_Red_Cliffs.

CHAPTER 17
1. Bennett, John and Marry Bennett, eds. *The Boys' and Girls' Companion for Leisure Hours*. London: Houlston & Wright, 1857, vol. 2, 92.

2. Annan, Kofi. "Black Dots and Earmuffs." Highlights Kids, accessed September 5, 2016. https://www.highlightskids.com/audio-story/black-dots-and-earmuffs.
3. Haas, Birgit and Daniel Tost. "Paul Krugman: What's Going on in China Right Now Scares Me." *Business Insider,* February 25, 2016. http://www.businessinsider.com/paul-krugman-interview-china-greece-brexit-2016-2.

CHAPTER 18
1. "Utilizing RF Pattern Matching to Measure Mobile Movement." PolarisWireless.com, accessed October 30, 2012. http://www.polariswireless.com/rfpm.
2. *Wikipedia*, s.v. "Homeless World Cup," accessed March 3, 2015. http://en.wikipedia.org/wiki/Homeless_World_Cup.
3. Change Makers. "Mel Young." Ashoka Changemakers, accessed March 3, 2015. http://www.changemakers.com/users/mel-young.
4. Yu Zemin. "A Wage Earner's Dynasty." [In Chinese.] *Readers*, No. 3, 2007.
5. *Wikipedia*, s.v. "Paper Towel," accessed March 5, 2015. http://en.wikipedia.org/wiki/Paper_towel.
6. "Paper Towels." The Great Idea Finder,." accessed March 5, 2015. http://www.ideafinder.com/history/inventions/papertowel.htm.
7. Martin, Emmie. "A Major Airline Says There's Something It Values More Than Its Customers, and There's a Good Reason Why." *Business Insider,* July 29, 2015. http://www.businessinsider.com/southwest-airlines-puts-employees-first-2015-7.

CHAPTER 19
1. *Wikipedia*, s.v. "Antoine-Augustin Parmentier," accessed April 8, 2015, http://en.wikipedia.org/wiki/Antoine-Augustin_Parmentier.
2. "Yan Zi's Admonishment." [In Chinese.] Baidu.com, accessed January 3, 2017. http://baike.baidu.com/view/1491085.htm.
3. Feng Menglong. *A Collection of Wisdom (I).* Harbin: Northern Literature and Art Publishing House, 2013, 5.
4. Sebenius, James K. "Six Habits of Merely Effective Negotiators," in *Winning Negotiations.* Boston: Harvard Business Review Press, 2011, 144.
5. Armstrong, Larry. "An Idea that Really Clicked." *BusinessWeek*, January 21, 2008.

CHAPTER 20
1. Schulz, Sandra. "The Real Story Behind North Korean Jeans," trans. Christopher Sultan. Spiegal, January 8, 2010. http://www.spiegel.de/international/business/0,1518,670826,00.html.
2. Davidson, Paul. "How a Boss Saved Jobs: She Laid Herself Off." *USA Today*, November 26, 2010.
3. *Wikipedia*, s.v. "Siege of Weinsberg," accessed December 10, 2016. https://en.wikipedia.org/wiki/Siege_of_Weinsberg.

CHAPTER 21
1. Kaihla, Paul. "Best-Kept Secrets of the World's Best Companies," in *Secrets of Greatness.* New York: Fortune Books, 2006, 63.
2. Yizhe. "Love Is the Patron Saint of Peace." [In Chinese.] *Readers*, No. 23, 2008.
3. Kaihla, Paul. "Best-Kept Secrets of the World's Best Companies," in *Secrets of Greatness.* New York: Fortune Books, 2006, 78.

4. "A Monk Who Carried a Lady Across a River." Baidu.com, December 27, 2008. https://zhidao.baidu.com/question/80376483.html.

CHAPTER 22
1. Stanglin, Doug. "MIT Students Spend Only $150 to Snap Photos from Near-Space." *USA Today*, September 22, 2009. http://content.usatoday.com/communities/ondeadline/post/2009/09/68499536/1.
2. "The Amazing Monkey Waiters that Serve Tables in a Japanese Restaurant." *Daily Mail*, October 7, 2008. http://www.dailymail.co.uk/news/article-1071289/Pictured-The-amazing-monkey-waiters-serve-tables-Japanese-restaurant.html.
3. "Disaster Recovery/Redundancy," accessed January 26, 2008 http://www.sparkplug.net/solutions/business/applications.html.
4. Kamaras, Jacob. "'Just Do Your Job': Trainer of IDF Paramedics on Life-Saving Improvisation." Jewish News Service, November 10, 2013. http://www.jns.org/latest-articles/2013/11/10/just-do-your-job-trainer-of-idf-paramedics-on-life-saving-improvisation#.V59lCU3Vzwo.
5. Clinton, Hillary Rodham. *Hard Choices*. New York: Simon & Schuster, 2014.
6. "Best Inventions of 2007: Without a Trace." *Time*, accessed May 25, 2015. http://content.time.com/time/specials/2007/article/0,28804,1677329_1678027_1677985,00.html.
7. Shi Xuanwen. "Moving a Library." [In Chinese.] *Readers*, No. 23, 2005.
8. Zhang Xiaoping. "Fire the Dog!" [In Chinese.] *Global People*, No. 20, 2013.

CHAPTER 23
1. "Italy Village Gets 'Sun Mirror'." BBC, December 18, 2006. http://news.bbc.co.uk/2/hi/europe/6189371.stm.
2. "Trunk-Cam Reveals Jungle Secrets." BBC, March 25, 2008. http://news.bbc.co.uk/2/hi/science/nature/7312511.stm.
3. Aitken, Jonathan. *Margaret Thatcher: Power and Personality*. New York: Bloomsburg, 2013.
4. Wu Xin. "Helping People and Sense of Superiority." [In Chinese.] *Readers*, No. 15, 2002.

CHAPTER 24
1. *Wikipedia*, s.v. "The World Without Us," accessed September 28, 2016. https://en.wikipedia.org/wiki/The_World_Without_Us.
2. "Conjuring Performed by Chen Peisi and Zhu Shimao." [In Chinese.] YouTube video, 15:28. Posted by Comic a Basket of Basics [In Chinese], February 5, 2014. https://www.youtube.com/watch?v=8nPkVvs30qk.
3. Disney's Melinda: First Lady of Magic (website), accessed October 8, 2011. http://littleegyptmagic.com/melinda.htm.
4. [Not-So-Amazing Spiderman] "Explore Funny Commercial Ads, Ads Funny, and More!" Posted on Pinterest, accessed February 1, 2014. https://www.pinterest.com/pin/367395282072114398.
5. The Write Corner. "Writer Anecdotes – Mark Twain." *The Write Corner* (blog), October 5, 2009. http://thewritecorner.wordpress.com/2009/10/05/writer-anecdotes-mark-twain.

CHAPTER 25
1. Fucini, Joseph J. and Suzy Fucini. *Entrepreneurs, the Men and Women Behind Famous Brand Names and How They Made It.* Boston: G. K. Hall & Co., 1985, 60.
2. Groom, Nelson. "Bridge Too Far? Makers of 300m High Glass Skywalk Invite Journalist to Repeatedly Slam It with a Sledgehammer to Prove Its Safety." *Daily Mail,* June 12, 2016. http://www.dailymail.co.uk/news/article-3636768/Man-slams-430m-high-glass-bridge-iun-Zhangziazie-sledgehammer-test-safety.html.
3. Michaelis, Vicki. "Rio Wins 2016 Olympic Games in Landslide over Madrid." *USA Today,* October 2, 2009. http://usatoday30.usatoday.com/sports/olympics/2009-10-02-rio-2016-olympics_N.htm.
4. Preston, Benjamin. "Smart Explains How They Determined the Weight of Emu Poop." Jalopnik.com, June 22, 2012. http://jalopnik.com/5920599/smart-explains-how-they-determined-the-weight-of-emu-poop.
5. Places in France. "Tour d'Argent and Canard au Sang Duck Cuisine." PlacesinFrance.com, accessed October 9, 2016. http://www.placesinfrance.com/tour_d_argent_duck_cuisine.html.
6. Mosher, Dave. "'Lucky Camera' Rivals Hubble's Clarity." Space, September 5, 2007. http://www.space.com/4307-lucky-camera-rivals-hubble-clarity.html.
7. "Best Inventions of 2007: I Can See Clearly Now." *Time,* accessed August 4, 2010. http://content.time.com/time/specials/2007/article/0,28804,1677329_1678408_1678414,00.html.

CHAPTER 26
1. Neild, Barry. "The T-Shirt that Can Speak in Any Language." CNN, April 19, 2016. http://www.cnn.com/2016/04/19/travel/iconspeak-t-shirt-speaks-any-language.
2. Qian Bingge and Mao Yu. "Become Skeleton After 'Drugging' for Eight Years." *People's Daily,* June 22, 2007.
3. "The Invention of the Price Tag." *Explorations in American History* (blog), November 12, 2012. https://timespelunking.wordpress.com/2012/11/12/the-invention-of-the-price-tag.
4. van Dyk, Deirdre. "The 50 Best Inventions of 2010: Power-Aware Cord." *Time,* November 11, 2010. http://content.time.com/time/specials/packages/article/0,28804,2029497_2030623_2029820,00.html.
5. Tedlow, Richard S. "Fortune Classic: The Education of Andy Grove." *Fortune,* March 30, 2016. http://fortune.com/2016/03/21/andy-grove-fortune-classic.
6. Levenstein, Steve. "Band-Aid Solutions: Japanese Pattern Design Bandages Make the Cut." Inventor Spot, accessed December 15, 2011. http://inventorspot.com/articles/sore_winners_japanese_pattern_design_bandages_make_cut_44032.

CHAPTER 27
1. Hess, Robert B. "Cocktail Origins." *Drink Boy* (blog), September 30, 1998. http://www.drinkboy.com/Articles/Article.aspx?itemid=5.
2. McAlone, Nathan. "Netflix CEO Reed Hastings Learned an Important Lesson When He Caught His Former Boss Washing His Dirty Coffee Mugs." *Business Insider,* June 16, 2015. http://www.businessinsider.com/netflix-ceo-reed-hastings-former-ceo-washed-his-dirty-coffee-mugs-2015-6.
3. Zhao Zhangyun. "A Lady Having a Colorful Life." [In Chinese.] *Readers,* No. 4, 1985.

4. *Wikipedia*, s.v. "Warschauer Kniefall," accessed January 15, 2014. http://en.wikipedia. org/wiki/Warschauer_Kniefall.
5. Stolberg, Sheryl Gay. "Long Before His Candidacy, John Kasich Made It to the White House." *The New York Times*, July 20, 2015. http://www.ny-times.com/politics/first-draft/2015/07/20/long-before-his-candidacy-joh n-kasich-made-it-to-the-white-house/?_r=0.
6. Claro, Joe, ed. *Jokes and Anecdotes*. New York: Random House, 1996, 154.
7. Bonisteel, Sara. "A Look Inside the World's Only Toilet House." Fox News, November 09, 2007. http://www.foxnews.com/story/0,2933,310077,00.html.

CHAPTER 28
1. *Wikipedia*, s.v. "Andy Riley," accessed April 11, 2015. http://en.wikipedia.org/wiki/ Andy_Riley.
2. Chen Meichun. "Find a Person Who Understands Death." [In Chinese.] *Readers*, No. 4, 2011.
3. *Wikipedia*, s.v. "Egg of Columbus," accessed July 12, 2014. http://en.wikipedia.org/ wiki/Egg_of_Columbus.
4. *Wikipedia*, s.v. "Gordian Knot," accessed November 25, 2012. http://en.wikipedia. org/wiki/Gordian_Knot.
5. Allsop, Erin. "Love Stories of the Waldorf Astoria Hotel." Blog of Waldorf Astoria, January 17, 2014. http://www.waldorfnewyork.com/blog/love-stories-of-the-waldor f-astoria-hotel.
6. *Wikipedia*, s.v. "Deng Xiaoping," accessed July 13, 2014. http://en.wikipedia.org/ wiki/Deng_Xiaoping.
7. "The Nobel Prize in Chemistry 2000." NobelPrize.org, October 10, 2000. http://www. nobelprize.org/nobel_prizes/chemistry/laureates/2000/popular.html.

CHAPTER 29
1. "The 50 Best Inventions of 2009: Teleportation." *Time*, November 12, 2009. http://www. time.com/time/specials/packages/article/0,28804,1934027_1934003_1933950,00. html.
2. *Wikipedia*, s.v. "Transporter (Star Trek)," accessed February 26, 2015. http://en.wiki-pedia.org/wiki/Transporter_(Star_Trek).
3. *Wikipedia*, s.v. "3D Printing," accessed February 26, 2015. http://en.wikipedia.org/ wiki/3D_printing.
4. *Wikipedia*, s.v. "Mars to Stay," accessed March 15, 2015. http://en.wikipedia.org/wiki/ Mars_to_Stay.
5. *Wikipedia*, s.v. "Dennis Tito," accessed January 14, 2017. https://en.wikipedia.org/ wiki/Dennis_Tito.
6. *Wikipedia*, s.v. "Virgin Galactic," accessed January 14, 2017, https://en.wikipedia. org/wiki/Virgin_Galactic.
7. Schneider, Mike. "Businesses Target People Seeking the Final Frontier." *USA Today*, February 21, 2006.
8. Howard, Brian Clark. "Why Did L.A. Drop 96 Million 'Shade Balls' into Its Water?" *National Geographic*, August 12, 2015. http://news.nationalgeographic.com/2015/0 8/150812-shade-balls-los-angeles-California-drought-water-environment.
9. "A Prompt Decision." Baidu.com, accessed October 28, 2016. http://baike.baidu.com/ view/1583256.htm#1.

CHAPTER 30
1. *Wikipedia*, s.v. "Sima Guang," accessed August 29, 2009. http://en.wikipedia.org/wiki/Sima_Guang.
2. Fadiman, Clifton and Andre Bernard, eds. *Bartlett's Book of Anecdotes*. Boston: Little, Brown, 2000, 125.
3. Tianye, ed. *Matsushita Kounosuke's 23 Rules*. [In Chinese.] Beijing: Industry and Commerce Press of China, 2001, 193.

Printed in the United States
By Bookmasters